"Rich, deep, and faithful—*God in the Whirlwind* invites us to come before the very heart of God. No theologian understands the modern world better than David Wells, yet no theologian uses the modern world more powerfully to wrench us back to truths that are foundational and never to be superseded by the latest anything. To be read slowly and with prayer."

Os Guinness, cofounder, The Trinity Forum; author, *The Call*

"In this important book, David Wells begins the process of bringing his influential critique of late modern culture and the church down into practice. Here we have a 'practical theology' for conducting the church's life based on the reality of a God of 'Holy-love.' This particular way of understanding and preaching the doctrine of God, Wells believes, protects the church from either being co-opted by the culture or becoming a ghettoized subculture. Decades of teaching theology is boiled down here into accessible, practical chapters. I'm glad to recommend this volume."

Timothy J. Keller, Pastor, Redeemer Presbyterian Church, New York City; author, *The Reason for God*

"Almost fifteen years ago, I enrolled at Gordon-Conwell Theological Seminary, in large part so I could learn from David Wells. His books opened my eyes to a host of ecclesiastical problems and to a lost world of glorious truth. As a student, I continued to learn from his deft analysis and careful theological critique. Now it's my pleasure to commend this terrifically unique book, a fitting capstone to all that he has been building in the last two decades. Part biblical theology, part systematic theology, and part cultural reconnaissance, this is a powerful work that my generation—really any generation—cannot afford to ignore. After years of pointing out the shallowness of evangelicalism, this is Wells's masterful summary of what should be our depth, our ballast, our center. What the world needs, and what the church needs, is a fresh encounter with the holy-love of God. This book will help you start down that path."

Kevin DeYoung, Senior Pastor, University Reformed Church, East Lansing, Michigan

"A timely and necessary antidote to the spirit of the age which is manifested in the prevailing man-centeredness of contemporary evangelicalism. Wells calls for the recalibration of our lives by a clear understanding of and a devout musing on the holy love of God. This book provides a fitting finale to the story line that began with *No Place for Truth*. Stott taught us how to *preach* between two worlds, and Wells teaches us to *live* there, at the intersection of faith (Christ) and culture."

Alistair Begg, Senior Pastor, Parkside Church, Cleveland, Ohio

"Drinking from the fire hydrant that is David Wells's writing is worth the rush. The water is not only bracing but sweet. *God in the Whirlwind*, his latest, is such a torrent, first showing how we postmoderns have put ourselves at the center of the universe—and the center doesn't hold. We have more of everything and less satisfaction with it. But Wells takes us to a place where God is at the center of the universe, where God's 'holy-love,' the unique union of God's holiness and his love, defines better what we need and provides more abundantly for it. Comprehending the 'holy-love' of God and its culmination in the life of Jesus Christ reinvigorates our walk with God, our worship, our service, and our work in a fallen world. Wells shows the way, and it's a whirlwind indeed."

Mindy Belz, Editor, *World* magazine

GOD IN THE WHIRLWIND

GOD IN THE WHIRLWIND

How the Holy-love of God

Reorients Our World

DAVID F. WELLS

:: CROSSWAY

WHEATON, ILLINOIS

God in the Whirlwind: How the Holy-love of God Reorients Our World

Copyright © 2014 by David F. Wells

Published by Crossway
   1300 Crescent Street
   Wheaton, Illinois 60187

Cover design: Dual Identity, inc.

First printing 2014

Printed in the United States of America

Scripture quotations are from the ESV® Bible (*The Holy Bible, English Standard Version*®), copyright © 2001 by Crossway. 2011 Text Edition. Used by permission. All rights reserved.

All emphases in Scripture quotations have been added by the author.

Hardcover ISBN: 978-1-4335-3131-6
ePub ISBN: 978-1-4335-3134-7
PDF ISBN: 978-1-4335-3132-3
Mobipocket ISBN: 978-1-4335-3133-0

Library of Congress Cataloging-in-Publication Data

Wells, David F.
 God in the whirlwind : how the holy-love of God reorients our world / David F. Wells.
  pages cm
 Includes bibliographical references and index.
 ISBN 978-1-4335-3131-6 (hc)
 1. God (Christianity)—Love. 2. Christianity and culture. I. Title.
BT140.W45 2013
231'.6—dc23
                      2013024165

Crossway is a publishing ministry of Good News Publishers.

LB		25	24	23	22	21	20	19	18	17	16	15	14
15	14	13	12	11	10	9	8	7	6	5	4	3	2	1

To Jane
Wonderful friend, wife, mother, and grandmother
And to our family whom we love
Jonathan and JoAnna, David and Lynne
McKenna, Caitlin, Caleb, Megan, Reagan, and Allison

Contents

Preface

Two decades ago, thanks to a remarkably generous grant from the Pew Charitable Trusts, I began what would turn out to be five interconnected volumes. These were all in answer to the question originally posed by Pew: What is it that accounts for the loss of the church's theological character? The answer to this question was to come from the three recipients of this grant. My role was to take the cultural component in this issue. I fulfilled my responsibilities to Pew when, in 1993, *No Place for Truth: Or Whatever Happened to Evangelical Theology?* was published. But once I had started down this road, I found it impossible to turn aside into other interests since I knew that I would be leaving the job unfinished. So it was that three more volumes, essentially in the same project, followed: *God in the Wasteland: The Reality of Truth in a World of Fading Dreams* (1994); *Losing Our Virtue: Why the Church Must Recover Its Moral Vision* (1998); and *Above All Earthly Pow'rs: Christ in a Postmodern World* (2004). I concluded this project with a summary volume designed to make the substance of these books more accessible: *The Courage to Be Protestant: Truth-lovers, Marketers, and Emergents in the Postmodern World* (2008).

These volumes were a sustained cultural analysis, and some critics have complained that they contain no answers to the church's current parlous state. The criticism has some merit. In my mind, I assumed an answer to the dilemmas unearthed and was not always as explicit in setting this out as I should have been.

Anyone looking back on these volumes, I think, will be able to see, albeit only in sketchy description, what had been on my mind. This book seeks to fill out that description.

The more I have been engaged with what has happened in Western culture, the clearer has become my understanding of what has been principally lost in the evangelical church. It is our understanding of God's character but an understanding in which that character has "weight." We now need to return, as God's people have done so often in the past, to find again what has been lost.

Faith lives along this line between Christ and culture. It is a line filled with dangers and hidden land mines. It is one where seductive and alluring voices are heard. It is also here, though, if sight is clear, that our faith gains its sinews and strength by engaging with this world. At least it has been so for me.

And now, in this volume, I have shifted my focus. No longer am I so preoccupied with the culture part of the equation. Now I am looking out on life from the other side of things, what is symbolized by "Christ" in the Christ-and-culture juxtaposition of things. This volume reflects on what we have so often lost in our work of framing Christ-and-culture. It is the holy-love of God.

This theme cuts right through all our Christian doctrines. It is woven through the whole fabric of Christian thinking which grows out of these doctrines. In consequence, it has generated an enormous literature across the centuries that now separate us from the time of the apostles. In the bibliography, I have selected just a few of these volumes, especially those that are more recent. I have done so with the aim of providing a few pointers for those who wish to read further, and in more detail, on the main subjects in this book. Some of the books listed address cultural issues, most focus on the biblical ideas, and a few reflect current controversies.

I am most grateful for kind friends who read portions of this book when it was still in manuscript form. They are Greg Beale, Tom Petter, James Singleton, and Ken Swetland. Stephen Witmer not only read a chapter but then circulated another to a circle of pastors who met with me for a fine, vigorous discussion. They are: Paul Buckley, Andy Rice, Brandon Levering, Mike Rattin, Tim Andrews, and, of course, Stephen Witmer. Naturally, whatever mistakes and infelicities of thought remain are my sole responsibility.

CHAPTER 1

God Our Vision, Culture Our Context

Be thou my vision, O Lord of my heart,
Naught be all else to me, save that thou art;
Thou my best thought, by day or by night,
Waking or sleeping, thy presence my light.

ELEANOR H. HULL

In this book, we are on a journey. Our destination is a well-known place. It is the character of God. We are taking a journey into "the Father's heart," as A. W. Tozer put it. It is here that we find our home, our resting place, our joy, our hope, and our strength.

The goal of Christ's redemption was, after all, that we might know God, love him, serve him, enjoy him, and glorify him forever. This is, indeed, our chief end. It was for this end that Christ came, was incarnate, died in our place, and was raised for our justification. It was that we might know God. Once, we were part of that world which "did not know God" (1 Cor. 1:21). But now we "have come to know God" (Gal. 4:9). We "know him who is from the beginning" (1 John 2:13) because we know "the love of Christ," and the aim of redemption is that we "may be filled with all the fullness of God" (Eph. 3:19). And this knowledge of God, this experience of his goodness, is what our experience in life has sometimes diminished. That is why it must constantly be renewed.

This is our goal in life, that we might be God-centered in our thoughts and God-fearing in our hearts, as J. I. Packer put it. We are to be God-honoring in all that we do. And how is that going to happen if we never consider, or consider only fleetingly, or irregularly, the end toward which we travel, and the one who also walks with us through life on the way to this end?

The greatest in God's kingdom, down the ages, have always found a dwelling place here. Here they have found their sustenance, their delight, and their solace. "How lovely is your dwelling place, O LORD of hosts!" (Ps. 84:1), cried the psalmist. "My soul will be satisfied as with fat and rich food . . . when I remember you upon my bed" (Ps. 63:5–6). Knowing God is itself what deepened David's thirst to know him even more. And it has ever been so.

Knowing God fills us with a hunger for more of what we already know. "As a deer pants for flowing streams, so pants my soul for you, O God" (Ps. 42:1). David knew God at this time, but his desire for God drew him back to the great and glorious center of all reality for even more. That is, and always has been, the cry of those who know God well. And connected with this thirst for God is a deep delight in him. It is a delight we see in many of the psalms, a delight robust and virile, as C. S. Lewis said, and one which we today sometimes have to regard with "innocent envy." So, how might we know what the psalmists knew? How might we, too, learn to delight in God?

In this book, I will not be able to consider all of God's attributes. In an earlier generation, Stephen Charnock did this in his classic, *The Existence and Attributes of God*, but it fills more than 1,100 pages! Here, I must limit myself and so will be thinking only of God's character. This, as I will explain, I am summing up as his "holy-love." That is our main destination. As we think of this place, we will also think about the consequences of all of this for living in the twenty-first century.

At the very beginning, though, I want to highlight two challenges we will encounter. I am going to return to the first of these in several of the chapters that follow. The second I will mention here, and then, from here on, we will simply have to be aware of it. We have to think about these challenges in this book because we have already encountered both in our lives more times than we can even number. We are so familiar with them that we might not fully realize how important they are.

The first of these challenges may strike you as strange. I am going to identify what is the most important cultural challenge we will encounter as we try to enter into a deeper knowledge of God. It may strike you as strange that I want to raise this with you at the outset. Are we not starting at the wrong place? Do we not agree that if we want to know the character of God then all we need to do is to open our Bibles? After all, biblical truth is the foundation of our knowledge of God. It is Scripture alone that is God-breathed and, therefore, it is the source of our knowledge of God. Is this not entirely sufficient, then, for all we need to know about God and his character?

The answer, of course, is that Scripture is indeed sufficient. However, there is a *proviso* here. Scripture will prove sufficient if we are able to receive from it all that God has put into it. That, though, is not as simple as it sounds. The reason lies in what Paul says elsewhere. We are to "be transformed by the renewal" of our minds—which is surely what happens when we take hold of the truth God has given us in his Word—but also, he says, we are not to be "conformed to this world" (Rom. 12:2). The shaping of our life is to come from Scripture and *not* from culture. We are to be those in whom truth is the internal driver and worldly horizons and habits are not. It is always *sola Scriptura* and it should never be *sola cultura*, as Os Guinness puts it. This is a two-sided practice: "Yes" to biblical truth and "No" to cultural norms if they damage our walk with God and rob us of what he has for us in his Word. Being transformed also means being unconformed.

Why is this? The answer is that our experience of our culture may have affected how we see things. Given the intense exposure we have to our modernized world, we need to be alert to the way it can shape our perspective and understanding. Along the way, we will pick up on this, but shortly I want to explain what I believe is its central challenge.

The second challenge I am going to mention you may have experienced even in the short time since opening this book! It is the extraordinary bombardment on our mind that goes on every day from a thousand different sources that leave us distracted, with our minds going simultaneously in multiple directions. How, then, can we receive from Scripture the truth God has for us if we cannot focus long enough, linger long enough, to receive that truth? Every age has its own challenges. This is one of ours. It is the affliction of distraction.

The Center of Reality

The first challenge, then, has to do with our culture. How is it that our culture may get in our way of knowing God as he has revealed himself to be?

Let me begin with a baseline truth of Scripture. It is that God stands before us. He summons us to come out of ourselves and to know him. This is the most profound truth that we ever encounter—or should I say, the most profound truth by which we are encountered?—and it is key to many other truths. And yet our culture is pushing us into exactly the opposite pattern. Our culture says that we must go *into* ourselves to know God. This is the cultural question that we must begin to understand, because otherwise it will shape how we read Scripture, how we see God, how we approach him, and what we want from him. So, here goes!

I should say right away that real faith, faith of a biblical kind, has always had a subjective side to it. That is not in question. When we hear the gospel, it is *we* who must respond. It is *we* who must repent and believe. And it is the Holy Spirit who works within us supernaturally to regenerate us, to give new life where there was only death, new appetites for God and his truth where before there were none, joining us to the death of Christ so that we might have the status of sons. And not only the status but also the *experience* of being God's children. We have received, Paul declares, "the Spirit of adoption as sons" whereby "we cry 'Abba! Father!' The Spirit himself bears witness with our spirit that we are children of God . . ." (Rom. 8:15–16). All of this, of course, is internal. It takes place in the depths of our soul and it encompasses all that we are. And in no way are these truths being doubted when I say that God stands before us and summons us to come out of ourselves and know him. But what does it mean to say that God stands before us, that he is, in this sense, objective to us?

Let me begin at some distance from Christian faith and slowly work toward the center, where we want to be. Along the way, we will be thinking about how our experience in this pressure-filled, affluent, globalized culture shapes our understanding of who God is and what we expect from him.

God Is Out There, Somewhere

That God is before us will seem like an unexceptional statement. When some people hear those words they may only think that God exists and that he is in our world. In the West, the number of those who believe in God's existence has usually been in the 90–97 percent range. In 2013, though, only 80 percent of Americans put themselves in this category in a Pew study. Nevertheless, when those who subscribe to the "New Atheism" mock this belief in God's existence—a "delusion," as Richard Dawkins calls it; an "anachronism," Steven Pinker declares; and just a set of "fantasies," says Sam Harris—they find themselves outside the mainstream in all our Western cultures. Furthermore, about 80 percent of people in the West also consider themselves to be "spiritual." Remarkably, this is true even in Europe, where the processes of secularization have run very deeply for a very long time.

But the real question to ask about belief in God's existence is this: what "weight" does that belief have? The U.S. Congress had the words "In God We Trust" placed on our paper currency in 1956, but it is also clear that this belief, for many, is a bit skinny and peripheral to how they actually live. They believe in God's existence but it is a belief without much cash value. To say that God is "before" them, therefore, would be somewhat meaningless. It does not necessarily have the weight to define how they think about life and how they live. Indeed, one of the defining marks of our time, at least here in the West, is the practical atheism that is true of so many people. They say that God is there but then they live as if he were not.

How a person thinks about God, Paul Froese and Christopher Bader show in their *America's Four Gods: What We Say about God—and What That Says about Us*, is shaped by their answers to two other questions. First, does God ever intervene in life? Second, does God ever make moral judgments about what we do and say?

If the answer to both of these questions is "yes," then saying that God is before us will mean something entirely different from what it would mean if the answer to these questions is "no." If we think that God has a hands-off approach to life, how we think of being in his presence will be one thing; if we think he has a hands-on approach, it will be something quite different. Should we think of him, then, as a landlord who keeps the building in repair but does not interfere in the lives of those who live there? Should we think of him more as a cheerleader who shouts encouragement from the sidelines but is not himself in the game? Or a therapist who always maintains an arms-length relationship with the patient so that the analysis is not skewed but who knows that, in the end, it is the patient who must right his or her own ship? Should we think of God as being nonjudgmental, one who keeps his moral thoughts to himself? This is the direction in which our culture is pushing us: God does not interfere. He is a God of love and he is not judgmental.

The other angle here is how much God cares about our weaknesses and failures. Indeed, how much does he know? And what weight does he give to different failures?

Ours is a day in which information about the world—about its wars, tragedies, suffering, and hatreds—is instantaneous and simultaneous. We are becoming knowledgeable, through TV and the Internet, of everything of significance that happens. And a whole lot of what is entirely insignificant, too! This raises in our minds some interesting questions. Given the awful cruelties that go on in the world, does God really care about our own private, comparatively small peccadilloes? Does he get bent out of shape by a little moment of deceit here or there when we are simply trying to avoid embarrassment? Is it so terrible to tell a lie if there is no malice? How about a sexual weakness that we cannot resist? Or a little self-promotion that drifts loose of the facts? Does he obsess over these private failures? Does he really care? Or is he large and generous and does he overlook what we are powerless to change? Is he not more preoccupied with cheering us on than with condemning us? This, too, is where our culture wants to take us.

We hear this cultural way of thinking even being echoed in the church. Joel Osteen, pastor of America's largest church audience—not to mention his worldwide following of 200 million—takes us down this road every week. In his (saccharin-like) view, God is our greatest booster who, sadly, is frustrated that he cannot shower on us more health, wealth, happiness, and self-fulfillment. The reason is simply that we have not stretched out our hands to take these things. God really, really wants us to have them. If we do not have them, well, the fault is ours.

Actually, Osteen's message is not much different from the way that a majority of American teenagers think about God today. In his *Soul Searching*, Christian Smith has given us the fruit of a large study he conducted on our teenagers. It was released in 2005.

What is really striking in this study is Smith's findings of the view of God that is dominant among a majority of these teenagers. He calls it "Moralistic Therapeutic Deism." The dominant view, even among evangelical teenagers, is that God made everything and established a moral order, but he does not intervene. Actually, for most he is not even Trinitarian, and the incarnation and resurrection of Christ play little part in church teenage thinking—even in evangelical teenage thinking. They see God as not demanding much from them because he is chiefly engaged in solving their problems and making them feel good. Religion is about experiencing happiness, contentedness, having God solve one's problems and provide stuff like homes, the Internet, iPods, iPads, and iPhones.

This is a widespread view of God within modern culture, not only among adolescents but among many adults as well. It is the view of God most common in Western contexts. These are the contexts of brilliantly spectacular technology, the abundance churned out by capitalism, the enormous range of opportunities that we have, the unending choices in everything from toothpaste to travel, and the fact that we are now knowledgeable of the entire world into which we are wired. All of these factors interconnect in our experience and do strange things to the way we think. Most importantly, they have obviously done strange things to how we think about God.

Indeed, Ross Douthat, in his *Bad Religion*, speaks of this as a pervasive "heresy" that has now swept America. He is quite correct, though most people would not think of heresy in this way. However, what so many Americans think about God is a distortion of what is true. And as a distortion it is a substitute for the real thing. And that is why it is heretical. So, why are people thinking like this? Let me take a stab at answering what is, no doubt, a highly complex question.

A Paradox

This context, this highly modernized world, has produced what David Myers calls the "American Paradox." Actually, this paradox is not uniquely American. It is found throughout the West, and increasingly it is being seen outside the West. In prosperous parts of Asia, for example, the same thing is becoming evident. And this paradox leads naturally into the predominant view of God. So, what is the paradox?

It is that we have never had so much and yet we have never had so little. Never have we had more choices, more easily accessible education, more freedoms, more affluence, more sophisticated appliances, better cars, better houses, more comfort, or better health care. This is the one side of the paradox.

The other side, though, is that by every measure, depression has never been more prevalent, anxiety higher, or confusion more widespread. We are not holding our marriages together very well, our children are more demoralized than ever, our teens are committing suicide at the highest rate ever, we are incarcerating more and more people, and cohabitation has never been more widespread. In fact, in 2012 in America, 53 percent of children were born out of wedlock. This new norm is a sure predictor of coming poverty for so many of those children.

This paradox is not entirely new. When Alexis de Tocqueville, the Frenchman, visited America in the 1830s, he noticed that although quite a few people had become well-to-do, there was also among them a "strange melancholy." They had attained an equality with each other at a political level. However, on the social front, almost everyone knew someone who had more than they had! Political equality did not produce equal outcomes in terms of wealth and possessions.

That, at least, is how Tocqueville explained the "melancholy" that he saw. Whether this was the real explanation is not really important. What is important is that abundance is not necessarily an unblemished, unqualified blessing. We should, of course, have known that, because that is what Jesus had said a long time ago! However, today, this cultural paradox is exceedingly aggravated, and we are in quite a different place culturally than the America that Tocqueville saw almost two centuries ago.

Many therapists are now finding that this paradox has worked itself into the lives of those who come to see them. Among those are many who are younger. They often report that though they grew up in good homes, had all they wanted, went on to college, (perhaps) entered the workplace, they are nevertheless baffled by the emptiness they feel. Their self-esteem is high but their self is empty. They grew up being told they could be anything that they wanted to be, but they do not know what they want to be. They are unhappy, but there seems to be no cause for their unhappiness. They are more connected to more people through the Internet, and yet they have never felt more lonely. They want to be accepted, and yet they often feel alienated. Never have we had so much; never have we had so little. That is our paradox.

This two-sided experience is probably the best explanation for how so many people, teenagers and adults alike, are now thinking about God and what they want from him. On the one hand, the experience of abundance, of seemingly unlimited options, of opportunity, of ever-rising levels of affluence, almost inevitably produces an attitude of *entitlement*. Each successive generation, until recently, has assumed that it will do better then the previous generation. Each has started where the previous one left off. And this expectation has not been unrealistic. That is how things have worked out. It is not difficult to see how this sense of entitlement naturally carries over into our attitude toward God and his dealings with us. It is what leads us to think of him as a cheerleader who only wants our success. He is a booster, an inspiring coach, a source of endless prosperity for us. He would never interfere with us in our pursuit of the good life (by which we mean the pursuit of the good things in life). We see him as a never-ending fountain of these blessings. He is our Concierge.

Purveyors of the health-and-wealth gospel, a "gospel" that is being exported from the West to the underdeveloped parts of the world, seem quite oblivious to the fact that their take on Christian faith is rooted in this kind of experience. Had they not enjoyed Western medical expertise and Western affluence, it is rather doubtful that they would have thought that Christianity is all about being healthy and wealthy. At least, in the church's long, winding journey through history, we have never heard anything exactly like this before. What appears to be happening is that these purveyors of this "gospel" have assumed certain goals in life—to have the desired wealth and sufficient health to enjoy it. Faith then entitles them to get these things from God. And where this kind of Christianity has been exported—for example, to many countries in Africa—this is the faith that is being advertised. This is so quite literally. When leaving the airport in Johannesburg, South Africa, a few years ago, I noticed a billboard with a simple question. It asked, "Do you want to get rich?" Below that question was a telephone number. That, I was told, belonged to a health-and-wealth ministry.

In many African cities, in fact, there are "miracle centers" where the afflicted pay a price and go in to get their miracle. At least they are assured that a miracle can be had. The temple money-changers so angered Jesus that he physically tossed them out of the building, but we take their modernized progeny in the health-and-wealth movement in our stride. They just blend into our consuming societies and our expectations that God is there at our beck and call. They are simply part of the vast, sprawling evangelical empire.

While it is the case that we moderns have had this experience of plenty, it is also the case—and this is the other side of the paradox—that our experience of plenty is accompanied by the experience of emptiness and loss. We carry within us many deficits—a sense of life's harshness, frustrations at work, bruised and broken relationships, shattered families, an inability to sustain enduring friendships, lack of a sense of belonging in this world, and a sense that it is vacant and hostile. So we look to God for some internal balm, some relief from these wounds.

We become inclined to think of God as our Therapist. It is comfort, healing, and inspiration that we want most deeply, so that is what we seek from him. That, too, is what we want most from our church experience. We want it to be comforting, uplifting, inspiring, and easy on the mind. We do not want Sunday (or, perhaps, Saturday evening) to be another workday, another burden, something that requires effort and concentration. We already have enough burdens and struggles, enough things to concentrate on, in our workweek. On the weekend, we want relief.

It is not difficult to see, then, how this two-sided experience, this paradox, has shaped our understanding of God. It leaves us with a yearning for a God who will come close, who will walk softly, who will touch gently, who will come to uplift, assure, comfort, and guide. We want our God to be accepting and nonjudgmental.

It also leaves us with the expectation that somehow this God of plenty will dispense his largesse in generous dollops to us. Maybe even through a lottery win. Perhaps we could win Powerball, or maybe some sweepstakes prize. That is the kind of God we want. This is what we expect him to be like.

God Disappears Within

This attitude, as I have been arguing, probably grows out of our experience. But our experience rests on nothing less than a shifting of the tectonic plates beneath our Western societies. It is the end product of at least two closely related mega-changes that have been underway in our culture since at least the 1960s. They are, first, that in our minds we have exited the older moral world in which God was transcendent and holy, and we have entered a new psychological world in which he is only immanent and only loving. This is the framework in which we now understand everything. And this means that the changes in our way of seeing things that are rooted in our experience will now be confirmed in our cultural context.

Second, we are now thinking of ourselves in terms, not of human nature, but of the self. And the self is simply an internal core of intuitions. It is the place where our own unique biography, gender, ethnicity, and life-experience all come together in a single center of self-consciousness. And every self is unique because no one has exactly the same set of personal factors. It is no surprise that we are now inclined to see life, to understand what is true, to think of right and wrong, in uniquely individual ways. We each have our own perspective on life and its meaning, and each perspective is as valid as any other. And none of it is framed by absolute moral norms. This is where the overwhelming majority of Americans live.

These changes I tried to describe in my *Losing Our Virtue: Why the Church Must Recover Its Moral Vision*. Although the lost moral world and the emergence of the new self can be described separately, they actually happened together and each fueled the other. Let me pursue this briefly.

In the 1960s, when these cultural changes were afoot, they seemed quite radical. This was at the heart of the insurgent New Left. The influential books from this time, such as Theodore Roszak's *The Making of a Counter Culture* and Charles Reich's *The Greening of America*, were an attack on Enlightenment rationality—as if, as the Enlightenment supposed, our reason is entirely unbiased! But the other side of that message was an unrelenting preoccupation with the self, with its intuitions and states, and this, of course, went hand-in-hand with the way culture was working on people. What had begun in the radical New Left in time morphed into the commonplace assumptions of the postmodern world. This radicalism became mainstream. And out of this has come what Philip Rieff has called "psychological man." This is the person who is stripped of all reference points outside of him or herself. There is no moral world, no ultimate rights and wrongs, and no one to whom he or she is accountable. This person's own interior reality is all that counts, and it is untouched by any obligation to community, or understanding from the past, or even by the intrusions of God from the outside. The basis on which lives are being built is that there is nothing outside the self on which they can be built. And this self wants only to be pleased. It sees no reason to be saved. This is therapeutic deism, whose morals are self-focused and self-generated.

In the aftermath of the 1960s, the words that came into vogue to describe all of this were individualism, narcissism, the "Me Generation," and the Age of Aquarius. It was the time of Transcendental Meditation and *Jesus Christ Superstar*. It would provide the grist for books such as Tom Wolfe's brilliantly acidic novel, *The Bonfire of the Vanities*. This novel depicts New York in the 1980s through the lives of four tawdry characters who have no higher good than their own self-interest and really no self other than what they project in their appearance. They are vain and empty. They are nothing but a collection of poses and self-projections. It would be paralleled later by Oliver Stone's 1987 movie *Wall Street*. This movie followed the lives of some Wall Street traders who were driven solely by greed and who inhabited a totally amoral world.

In time, the new therapeutic preoccupations of the Me Generation would, of course, seep into the church, although in less glaring and more sanitized versions. Looking back on this time, Wade Clark Roof said that one of the defining marks of the Boomer generation was its distinction between the inward and outward aspects of religion, that is, between what he called spirit and institution. The institutional aspect of Christian faith, the church, came to be viewed with skepticism. Credence was given instead to what is internal. Not to church doctrine, which others had formulated. Not to church authority. Indeed, not to any external authority at all. Rather, it is in private intuitions that God is found. Boomers were "believers" in their own private worlds and "disbelievers" in what the church does and says.

Here, in fact, were the seeds that by the end of the 1990s had produced throughout the West millions of people who were spiritual but not religious. In both America and Europe, around 80 percent said they were spiritual. And while this included a number who were also religious, there were many of the spiritual who were decidedly hostile to all religions. They were opposed to doctrines they were expected to believe, rules they had to follow, and churches they were expected to attend. They resisted each of these. They would not be encumbered by religious or social expectations that others imposed on them. The impulses that began in the 1960s had by the '90s become dominant. And, of course, TV and the Internet fed this disposition. There are a surprising number who get their spiritual uplift week by week only from the comfort of their own living rooms or from their computers. They never go to church. Well, they "go" to church but do so in their own way.

When Roof did his analysis, he described this as a generational habit. This, he said, is how Boomers are. The truth is, though, that this outlook is not lodged in a single generation. Those that followed the Boomers—the Gen Xers and then the Millennials—had exactly the same habits. This is what Smith's study on teenagers also picked up. No, this is not a generational matter. It was, and is, a *cultural* matter. This is what is happening to people who are living amid a highly modernized society. They are in the midst of the "American Paradox," and they are part and parcel of both its postmodern mood and its solutions.

This was the soil on which Oprah built her TV empire. The followers who watched her show week by week were as conventional as apple pie in their own minds. The Pied Piper whom they followed, though, really is not. She heralded an age when God is found in the self, when salvation is only about therapy, happiness is just around the corner, and consumption is everyone's right. And the nice thing about Oprah is that she herself is not perfection on toast. She is so very human. Her follies and shortcomings are all on display in moments of painful honesty. It was as if she was in her own private confessional—though confessing to herself—but the whole world was privileged to listen in.

The cultural attitudes that Oprah mined, of course, affected much more than just personal satisfaction or even religion. In his *Twilight of Authority*, Robert Nisbet wrote of how those attitudes were undermining the entire political process as well. Across the board, he said, given our self-preoccupation, our total self-focus, there is a retreat from what is important to the community to what is important only to the individual, from the weighty to the ephemeral, from others to ourselves. And our national conversation about these things is as far removed as it could be from the days when people had the nation's good in their minds. Perhaps the epitome of this were the seven multi-hour Lincoln-Douglas debates of 1858, reported nationally by newsprint, when serious issues were seriously debated at great length.

Now, our national issues are debated on TV. When a nation becomes absorbed in trivia, Neil Postman said (in *Amusing Ourselves to Death*), when life is reduced to nothing but entertainment, and the public discussion of our nation's well-being is carried out in the baby talk of small TV sound bites, then we are getting the first whiffs of cultural death. No longer is there a way to talk about what is good for society, and no longer is there an appetite to talk about any good other than that of private self-interest.

There come those times in a nation's life, Os Guinness has written, when its people rise up against the founding principles of their own nation. This is one of those times in America. It is far more dangerous than any terrorist attack. It is, in fact, "a free people's suicide," as he puts it in the title of his book. Why? Because what holds the republic together has never been simply the Constitution and our laws. The law is an exceedingly blunt instrument when it comes to controlling human behavior. There are many things that are unethical that are not illegal. Most lying, for example, is not illegal but it is always unethical. Our criminal and civil laws can control only so much of our behavior. It is virtue that does the rest. And that is precisely what is being eroded in this self-oriented, self-consumed culture.

Here is the acid that is eating away at the nation's foundations, de-grading objective values, uprooting older customs, and leaving people with no clear sense of purpose and, indeed, no purpose at all other than their own self-interest. Under the postmodern sun, everyone has a right to their own version of reality. When this comes about, any culture loses its ability to renew its own life. The culture of the past is then converted into superficial formulae that float around the air waves and are passed, person to person, on the Internet. It is served up again as *kitsch*, and everyone pretends this is the same, deep old thing it once was. It is not. When this happens, we are in the "twilight of American culture," as Morris Berman argues.

Things Get Blurry

This disposition was articulated by Jean-Francois Lyotard in his *The Postmodern Condition*. With all of its French prolixity, its strangeness, it seemed like a misfit in America as books go. But we had already advanced down this road ourselves, maybe not with the same French *hauteur* but nevertheless toward the same conclusions. Writer after writer, and movie after movie in the 1990s, assumed that there is no independent reality, no reality "out there." What we have, each one of us, is a private framework of understanding, and there are no "facts" to lean on. Facts exist only when we come to understand them within our own private worlds. Thomas Kuhn, who had written about sci-entific theory-making, was now widely invoked to explain much of what was happening in culture. Everyone began to speak of "paradigm shifts" as easily as they did of "burgers and fries."

So it was that the boundaries between things began to get a bit sketchy, then to disappear. America was ready for this. As James Living-stone remarks, Americans needed no prodding from "tenured radicals" to go down this road. There are a number of these fallen boundaries of which we should be aware.

The distinction between soul and body was a boundary that disappeared increasingly after the 1960s as our culture began its self-transformation. All that we are, it came to be assumed and then asserted, is animal. All that we are is just our body.

The problem is, though, in this new world we struggle to find personal reality. We do not always know how to express our individuality. We yearn for something that will set us apart from everyone else. A little external decoration, like being pierced and tattooed, helps! Actually, it was not just tattoos. It was everything that went along with being *cool*. Everything that made one stand out as a one-of-a-kind body, as different, and in that difference, as mysterious, and in that mystery as something that was, well, oh-so-desirable. Now *that* is what life is about!

But if the distinction between ourselves and animals has gone by the wayside, then this opens up a new discussion about rights. That is what happened next. With earnest countenances, there were those who assured us that animals are no different from humans and should be accorded the same rights. It has even been proposed that animals deserve to have lawyers to help them secure their rights—though, if I may say so, no animal deserves some of our lawyers!

This disappearance of boundaries happened not only in relation to the body. It is gender, too. The manipulation of gender, its bending, remains on the edges of society, among the other exotica. But homosexuality is an entirely different matter. Homosexuality has gained significant cultural acceptance, and that acceptance is now right in the mainstream. Indeed, it was right in the center of President Obama's inaugural address in 2013.

That there is this widespread support for homosexuality is itself significant. But of far greater significance is the fact that it is only one part of a profound, multipronged effort to redefine the family. We are in the midst of a massive social experiment. We are redefining the most basic building block of any society. The Marxists tried to redesign the class system of their day. That attempt now lies in ruins. Today, many Western societies are attempting, in an experiment equally bold, to rewrite their societies' ground rules about families. One suspects, though, that the outcome will not be very different. When these social experiments collapse, they bring behind them immense confusion, disorder, and suffering.

But this is not the only change we are seeing. Once we began to think of ourselves as not other than animal, it no longer seemed clear to us that we were actually that different from being mere computers. We are just our DNA working itself out through various internal mechanisms. That was a vein mined in some of our movies, like *Blade Runner*, from an earlier time, and *The Matrix* more recently.

There is a chicken-and-egg dilemma here. Which came first? Did we first break down these boundaries and then find that the older boundary between ourselves and God had also gone? Or did that boundary go first and, once it had disappeared, all of life had to be reimagined? However it happened, the external God has now disappeared and has been replaced by the internal God. Transcendence has been swallowed up by immanence. God is to be found only within the self. And once that happened, the boundary between right and wrong—at least as we had thought about these things—went down like a row of falling skittles. Evil and redemption came to be seen as the two sides of the same coin, not the two alternatives in life.

The truth is that all of life is being reconceived and reimagined. However, this attempted rebuilding of ourselves and our society on different foundations is leading us, if I may be so bold, into a dead end. The truth is that we are not doing very well. When God—the external God—dies, then the self immediately moves in to fill the vacuum. But then something strange happens. The self also dies. And with it goes meaning and reality. When these things go, anything is possible. Huxley's dystopian novel, *Brave New World*, does not seem so far off into the future after all.

We know ourselves now to be on a fast-moving train hurtling down the tracks, and it is absurd to think that by leaning over the side and digging our heels into the ground we could have the slightest effect on the train's velocity. People sense this. Many do. There is panic in the culture because we know our era is ending. Our horror movies are not just stories. They are a kind of mirror of ourselves. They surface the inchoate sense that we have, the sense of dread, the sense that all is not right in our world, that out there is a lurking menace whom we cannot see. We intuitively feel that a terrifying calamity looms over us, but we just do not quite understand what this is or even where it is.

Here We Are

The American church is on the forefront of encountering this modernized world. How it should manage this engagement, though, has become its most perplexing dilemma. And it is also its most urgent challenge. Clearly, it has often been tempted to adapt Christian faith to this context, rather than to confront the context where that is required. Instead of becoming an alternative view of life, Christian faith has often become an echo, in many ways, of what is happening in this kind of modernized culture.

Jesus would be surprised to see how easy the kingdom of God has become as we have made ourselves relevant to the culture.

There are, in fact, gut-wrenching changes taking place in our Western societies. Our world is being shaken to its very foundations. Instead of offering great thoughts about God, the meaning of reality, and the gospel, there are evangelical churches that are offering only little therapeutic nostrums that are sweet but mostly worthless. One even wonders whether some current churchgoers might even be resistant were they to encounter a Christianity that is deep, costly, and demanding.

That is why we must come back to our first principles. And the most basic of these is the fact that God is there and that he is objective to us. He is not there to conform to us; we must conform to him. He summons us from outside of ourselves to know him. We do not go inside of ourselves to find him. We are summoned to know him only on his terms. He is not known on our terms. This summons is heard in and through his Word. It is not heard through our intuitions.

These are our most basic principles because they deal with our most basic issues and our most basic calling. That calling is to know God as he has made himself known and in the ways that he has prescribed. We are to hear this call within the framework he has established. He is not there at our convenience, or simply for our healing, or simply as the Divine Teller handing out stuff from his big bank. No, we are here for his service. We are here to know him as he is and not as we want him to be. The local church is the place where we should be learning about this, and God's Word is the means by which we can do so.

But I must go further. It is not enough to know that God has given us truth that corresponds to what is there, that corresponds to him who is there. Additionally, this is the Word that God himself uses to address us personally. In doing so, he makes us knowers of himself. He comes from outside our circumstances. He is not limited by our subjectivity. He is free to break in upon us, making us his own, and incorporate us into his great redemptive plans which have been unfolding across the centuries. The Holy Spirit re-speaks Scripture's truth to us today and opens our minds and hearts to receive it. Thus we are given, not just *a* view of God and of ourselves, but *the* view. And not just the right and true view. We are given God himself, who comes to us through his Word by the work of the Holy Spirit. It is *God* who makes us knowers of himself.

God as Holy-love

God, then, is objective to us in the sense that we stand before him. We are accountable before him and accountable within the world of his holiness. We know him savingly only because he has drawn us into a knowledge of himself. "In this is love," John writes, "not that we have loved God but that he loved us and sent his Son to be the propitiation for our sins" (1 John 4:10). We "love because he first loved us" (1 John 4:19). The way love is defined, and what gives it its body of meaning, is the sacrificial, substitutionary death of Christ. That is what supremely defines God's love, and this will be taken up in the chapters that follow.

John's sentence defining love would have been completed quite differently in the West today. In this is love, many would say, that God is there for us when we need him. He is there for what we need from him. He is love in that he gives inward comfort and makes us feel better about ourselves. He is love in that he makes us happy, that he gives us a sense of fulfillment, that he gives us stuff, that he heals us, that he does everything to encourage us each and every day. That is the prevailing view of God today, and when Osteen reiterates all of this he shows how perfect is his cultural touch. The Bible's view, by contrast, is quite different because its world is moral. Ours today is deeply, relentlessly, and only therapeutic. The Bible's world is defined by God's character of holiness. Ours today is not. It is psychological.

This is the difference between the God who is objective to us and the God who is subjective in the sense that he has disappeared into the self. It is a difference essential for us to grasp as we begin our study.

When postmoderns think about life in a psychological framework, they do so from a center in the self. It is the self that determines what salvation means and what life means. When we think about life within the moral framework that Scripture gives us, then we are thinking of it with God at its center. It is he in his holiness who defines the salvation we need and he in his love who provides what we need, in Christ. In a postmodern view, we are at life's center; in a biblical view, we are not. It is God who is life's center. If we do not understand these differences, we will be at sea when we start to think about how God has actually revealed himself.

This interplay between love and holiness is, as we shall see and as we already know, very hard to hold together simultaneously. In fact, there are many who think it quite improper to do so. In the West, we greatly approve of the thought that God is love but we reject the thought of his holiness. This, some say, is part of the primitive past from which we have evolved. We have come of age and can no longer believe in harsh myths like divine judgment. By contrast, there are other cultures, especially where radicalized Islam is present, that despise the thought that God is love and think of him as only holy. Love is seen as part of soft, Western sentimentality. This means that their societies have only harsh laws coupled with all of the mechanisms of revenge and retaliation for wrongs done. There is no forgiveness.

Christianity, though, uniquely combines love and holiness because in God's character they are, and always have been, combined. However, I am thinking of God's love and his holiness here as comprising the many aspects of his character of which Scripture speaks. I therefore am going to be speaking of God's *holy-love*. This term is not entirely satisfactory. It may even suggest precisely what I am arguing against, that love is basic and holiness is secondary and is what qualifies that love. But that is not what I mean. The problem is that if I cannot use the shorthand of *holy-love*, I am stuck with something that is unworkably cumbersome. It would be something like "God's holiness-and-God's-love-in their-union-with-each-other." If I were to use this long description as many times as I use *holy-love* in the pages that follow, readers would quickly find it annoying! So, I am staying with *holy-love*.

Today, our constant temptation, aided and abetted as it is by our culture, is to shatter the hyphen. We want God's love without his holiness. We want this because we live in our own private, therapeutic worlds that have no absolute moral norms. God's holiness, therefore, becomes a jarring and unwanted intrusion. His love without his holiness, however, is one of those things in life that we simply cannot have. And, indeed, it will become one of our greatest joys to be able to understand how God is *both* holy and loving.

The Center of Our Attention

Pings and Jingles

But before we start our journey into the character of God, let me briefly take up the second challenge which I mentioned at the beginning of this chapter. It is distraction.

When Maggie Jackson writes a book called *Distracted: The Erosion of Attention and the Coming Dark Age*, and Susan Cain writes one called *Quiet: The Power of Introverts in a World That Can't Stop Talking*, and John Freeman writes *The Tyranny of E-mail*, it is clear that Houston has a problem! And this is just the tip of the iceberg. There is now a considerable literature pondering all of this—how tense, unfocused, confused, endangered, and distracted we have become amid our brave new world. Indeed, as 2013 began, George Barna published quite an extensive study on what temptations people admitted to experiencing. It may be, of course, that people were reluctant to admit to finding some of the more unsavory sins tempting. However, what they did own up to were procrastinating (60 percent), worrying (60 percent), and eating too much (55 percent). These topped the list, and they are all typically Western issues. But next came a newer temptation. Spending too much time on the various forms of media came in at 44 percent.

Technology expands human powers. It has mightily expanded our knowledge of life, of our world, of what is happening. It greatly increases the access we have to others . . . and that they have to us. Jackson speaks of the "snowstorms of information" we encounter each day from the 50 million websites we can visit, the 75 million blogs, the millions of books to which we have access, and the TV that we watch. Our life is now punctuated by incessant computer pings, cell phone jingles, and beeps of one kind or another. We are acutely aware that we are living life on multiple fronts simultaneously. We have to do this or we will be left behind, so to speak. In the workplace, one-third say that they are unable to think about their work as they skip from task to task. Attention shifts, on average, every three minutes. Actually, the problem is also compounded by the fact that people keep interrupting themselves! It is a world of virtual meetings and romances, of texts, of bullet-points, of instant decision making, and lost rules. Jackson thinks of this as a kind of cultural ADD. She is right. But it is also the acute onset of high modernity.

But there is something important here for us to understand. It is that we must come to our triune God *through* this world and, therefore, in our minds, we must deal with this world. There is no direct flight to God! A direct flight is what monks and mystics across the ages have always thought they could find. Monks in their aching solitude or mystics in their emancipation from their own rationality have always thought that they could take leave of this world. They imagined that they could find a place where, or a way in which, they would be undistracted. Then they would come to know God directly, face-to-face, and intimately, in an unmediated way for the mystics, and without interruption for the monks. They would be in this place free from the conflicts and confusions of life.

Jerome, one of the fathers in the early church, was one of these for a while. He set off to live in the desert as a monk in order to carry out his solitary pursuit of God. Alone, he thought, he would be free from all of the complications, temptations, and distractions of life. Picture me, he says to his reader, alone in the desert, the "companion of scorpions," his body stiff and cold in the night air. But even though his body was chilly, his mind was "hot with desire" and filled with visions of the dancing girls of Rome.

Jerome had stumbled onto a truth. It is that we are never free of ourselves. And in ourselves we carry the sights, sounds, and struggles of the world we have known and, perhaps, tried to leave behind. For us today, that means this highly pressurized world of constant overstimulation, constant demands, and unceasing distraction. Brief retreats are helpful, but our lives cannot be on an unending retreat. It is in *this* world, not somewhere else, that we must learn to be God-centered in our thoughts and God-honoring in our lives. We must learn to walk with God *through* our world with all of its anxieties and temptations. In his time, John Bunyan said this in his classic, *Pilgrim's Progress*. It is a book about the many different situations in life, with their own challenges and temptations, through which Christian made his way en route to the Celestial City. That was a biblical insight. It is in our world, with all of its complexities, that we must live before the face of God.

I am confident that we can do this. After all, were we unable to live out a biblically faithful life, then God's redemption would be limited and it would fail to accomplish its end. Does that sound plausible? Indeed not!

Focus

What, then, is the alternative to distraction? It is the self-discipline to focus. This means finding the determination to leave aside all of the other interests, the urgent demands, all of the clutter that competes for our attention while we do this. Attention and focus are the fuels that actually enable us to get things done, as Jackson observes. Withdrawal and ordering are the two keys to attention—being able to withdraw from the alternatives, at least for periods of time, and focus the mind on something that we have isolated. And here, our focus is the truth God has given us of himself, his greatness as seen particularly in his character and redemptive work.

How are we going to be able to do this? If we are convinced that we need, above all, to know God, to know who he is in his character, that will trump every competing interest. But we have to be utterly convinced. Being halfhearted and divided in our focus will not get us where we want to be. As Jonathan Edwards observed a long time ago, we act on our strongest motive. If our strongest motive, our deepest desire, is to know God, it will generate the discipline that we need to pursue this, because we will want to know God more than anything else. If this is not our strongest motive, we will find ourselves with multiple, alternative, and competing foci. These will inevitably distract us. If we are not self-directed, we will be tumbled along by our culture. And that is when we will lose our ability to reflect on the deeper issues of life. Without this ability to stop, to focus, to linger, to reflect, to analyze, and to evaluate, we begin to lose touch with the God who has called us to know him.

This lack of attention, from one angle, is the result of having to answer too many e-mails, too many phone calls, wanting to visit too many blog sites, having to choose between too many products, needing to keep up too many relationships (perhaps many of them virtual) and to do too many other things. However, from another angle, all of this speaks to what we *really* want. Would we prefer the illusion of a relationship via the virtual world, or do we want the real thing, which is face-to-face and flesh-and-blood? Would we prefer merely to have the pose of being Christian, living only with our appearances, or do we want the real thing, God himself?

God, however, cannot be downloaded as can the reams of information we have at our fingertips from the Internet. Acquiring information is one thing. Understanding it is another. Learning to become wise by incorporating that information into a framework of understanding, and doing so before God, is yet something else. This, like many other things of value in life, takes time. There are no shortcuts here. Instantaneous knowledge from the Internet is one thing. Learning to know God is something quite different. The knowledge of God is, in fact, a lifetime pursuit, not an instantaneous download. God has made himself known in Scripture, but we need to learn how to walk with him through life in the light of what we know of him. This journey never ends until, like Christian in *Pilgrim's Progress*, we finally cross the great river and are welcomed to the shores of eternity and the presence of God. Can we, then, set aside the impatience that the Internet tends to breed, and the habits of being distracted which our highly compacted modern lives create, in order to focus on what really matters?

I am confident that we can. We can all find a way to tame what distracts us from our pursuit of God. We can all teach ourselves to focus.

We can all untangle ourselves from our appetite for instant results and immediate gratification. The most worthwhile things in life often come to flower only over long periods of time. We can teach ourselves to see this and change our frame of reference. Redirecting our minds in this way and learning to focus is a wondrously liberating thing. It allows us to untether ourselves from everything that wants to consume our attention, our energy, and even our soul. It frees us from the tyranny of the urgent. When we are thus untethered, we are free to be where we want to be. Where we want to be is before God. "I have set the LORD always before me," said David, and his conclusion was that "because he is at my right hand, I shall not be shaken" (Ps. 16:8). Even the modernized world will not shake us if we really want to walk with God!

My theme, then, is the holy-love of God. Because that is so, our redemption is the place where we must start, because it is here that we begin to see God disclosing his character to us. We need to see how God's saving designs unfold as we move from the Old Testament toward and into the New Testament. Two chapters will be spent on this. We need to understand clearly the similarities and differences between Abraham's knowledge of God from the Old Testament and ours today as reflected in the New Testament. In both, there is God's promise of justification. That is the similarity. So, what are the differences?

This will be followed by two chapters that look at God's character, the one on his love and the other on his holiness. We will then be in a position, in chapter 5, to consider the atonement. That promise of acceptance with God first made to Abraham could not be realized without Christ's work on the cross. Here, as in a crucible, we will be able to see how the love of God, his grace, provided what his holiness demanded. In each of the chapters that follow the chapter on Christ's work on the cross—chapters on sanctification, worship, and service—I will be showing how at their very center is God's holy-love. My focus throughout will be to offer a biblical theology of God's character, but I will be doing so, all the time, with an awareness of the culture in which we live, at least those of us who live in the modernized West. This is a wonderful journey that Scripture sets before us.

Come, then, let us take our first steps down this road!

CHAPTER 2

The Gospel across Time

In Christ alone is all our trust
For full and free salvation.
With His own blood He ransomed us
From ev'ry tribe and nation.
For us He lived and died.
Now, at the Father's side,
Full knowing all our needs,
Our High Priest intercedes.
He lives to make us holy.

GARY A. PARRETT

Where We Start

It might seem that the best way to begin a study of God's character, his holy-love, is to open a concordance and look up all the instances of holiness and all those of love and see if a synthesis is possible. This would yield much that would be helpful.

But there is a better way. It is to begin at the beginning and see how God revealed his character across time. In doing so, we find that as God's redemptive history moved toward its goal, it provided what are the contours of our subject. It was moving toward Christ, in whom it culminated. From that time on, the Holy Spirit's work became that of applying to sinners the benefits of Christ's work on the cross. This progressive unfolding of the purposes of God is, at the same time, the unfolding of the character of God. We see more and more clearly what God's redemptive plan was, as we move from Abraham toward Christ, and we also see the principles in that plan as it unfolded. That should be no surprise. It is the same triune God at work in this plan. It is the God who James says is one "with whom there is no variation or shadow due to change" (James 1:17). And redemption means the same thing whether a person was born millennia before Christ or is yet unborn. It is redemption from sin, and that, in the nature of the case, can only be by grace.

We therefore need to try to understand—and this is where we are going to start—what in this history changes and what does not change. What are the continuities and what are the discontinuities? And what, across the long stretches of time that make up the Old Testament, do we learn about God's character?

Adam, we know, was created to be God-centered in his thoughts, God-fearing in his heart, and God-honoring in all that he did. But of course he fell, and his vision of God was lost, as was his understanding of his place in God's world. It is this vision, this goal, that is being restored by Christ in those who are his. And for us today, being God-centered as we were intended to be means we must first become Christ-centered. Indeed, we cannot be God-centered unless we are first Christ-centered, because we must first be redeemed. Being God-centered has to be premised upon that redemptive work, that forgiveness, that inward regeneration without which we can neither be subject to God nor believe his Word. It is here, within this long history that led up to Christ and here, within this nexus of ideas, that we find the disclosure of God's holy-love. So, our task in this book is to explore this history and unpack these ideas.

In this and the next chapter, then, we are going to explore this link between God-centeredness and Christ-centeredness. And we will do so by looking at some of the ways in which the Old Testament revelation unfolded as it moved toward Christ. We need to see this because this is where God's holy-love comes into view, and that is what we are pursuing in this book. Supremely, as we will see, it is in the Father's giving of the Son, and in Christ's self-giving on the cross, that we have the greatest, and final, revelation of what this holy-love means.

A Dilemma

However, the moment we see this we stumble upon a dilemma. If Christ is thus so important to the unfolding of God's redemptive purposes, then how could David, who had not heard the gospel of Christ, have come to the deep knowledge of God that he did? Indeed, it almost seems at times as if David had a deeper and truer knowledge of God without the gospel than we sometimes have with it. Could this be so?

If we are perplexed about this question, we are in good company. So, too, were the apostles, at least initially. They struggled to understand God's ways as they traveled in their minds from the Old Testament and into their own time with their experience of Christ. They had known him. They had followed him. They had heard his teaching and seen his miracles. They had seen him crucified and then, astonishingly, resurrected. They therefore were asking themselves how their knowledge of God through Christ related to what those in the Old Testament had known. And that is our question, too.

That Abraham became the pivot in how the apostles sorted this out is clear from the fact that Peter, Paul, James, and the anonymous writer to the Hebrews all referred back to him (Acts 3:25; Rom. 4:2; 9:7; Gal. 3:6–9; James 2:21–23; Heb. 2:16; 6:13; 7:1–10; 11:17). They were all working out what it means to know God through Christ, given the fact that the promise of justification was first made to Abraham (Gen. 15:6). So, how did that promise relate to what Christ had done? Theirs was not a narrow consideration of how one text relates to another but, rather, of whether there are connecting principles along the line of this redemptive story that are like the ligaments that hold our bodies together. If there are these connections, what are they?

These ligaments, in fact, lie in three things that have not changed across the centuries that divide us from Abraham. They are, first, that the *cause* of our acceptance before God has not changed. For Abraham as for us today, it is grace. Nor yet, second, does the *instrument* of our acceptance change. For Abraham it was faith and for us it is faith, too. And now for the less obvious part to the answer: Third, the *ground* of our acceptance is also unchanged. It is *Christ*. That is certainly and obviously so today but I will argue it was so for Abraham, too. Everyone who is justified—or who in previous ages was justified—is made acceptable by God through Christ's death on the cross. There, sin was credited to him, innocent though he was, and there his righteousness was credited to believers, sinful though they are. Thus it is that those from the Old Testament period were, and we today are, justified.

If all of this is true, then we are in continuity with those who lived during the Old Testament period who were part of the "remnant, chosen by grace" (Rom. 11:5). They were descended from Abraham ethnically. However, the promise of justification was not just for Abraham. It was for us, too. We who are Gentiles are also "children of Abraham" (Rom. 9:7–8). It is "those of faith who are the sons of Abraham" (Gal. 3:7). Abraham was at the head of this deep and long stream of justification that has coursed through history, making its way through the ancient people of God and now flowing on down the centuries, spilling out into all of the countries of our world and now showing up in every culture.

Grace

When the apostles went back to first principles, they began with grace. The only explanation of Abraham's standing before God, of his call to know God, was an unearned, undeserved, inexplicable grace.

Abraham

When we first meet Abraham, he stands out as quite admirable despite the fact that he was living in an unusually corrupt pagan culture. Here, one would think, might be someone whose righteousness, whose immediate obedience to the call of God, would naturally commend him to God. But that turns out not to be the case. Had Abraham's "works"—the actions and words that flowed from his character—been the basis of his acceptance before God, they would have been seen as his "due," just as a wage is owed and then paid after the work is done. That, though, is precisely what Paul counters. Justification before God is no one's "due." It is not and cannot be earned. It is, and only ever can be, a "gift" (Rom. 4:4).

As Paul teaches, this theme continues from Abraham's time to ours. It is true that John does appear to set up an antithesis between the Old and New Testament in this regard when he said, "the law was given through Moses; grace and truth came through Jesus Christ" (John 1:17). This could not mean, though, that in the Old Testament people knew only the law whereas in the New Testament God's ways have suddenly turned toward grace. Nothing could be further from the truth. It was grace at the beginning, and it is grace now. The difference is that in the Old Testament, God's loving-kindness was invisible. In the incarnation, though, his grace and truth were made *visible* in the person of Christ. What changes is not the presence of grace in this river of redemption, or its nature, or its necessity, but only its revelation. The language of grace becomes the language *par excellence* of the New Testament epistles because the apostles could look back on Christ in whom that grace had been exhibited. He was "full of grace and truth" (John 1:14).

It is striking how Paul, in speaking of Abraham's justification, moved seamlessly from saying that for Abraham it was not by "works" to saying that for those in Paul's day it was not by the "works of the law" (Gal. 2:16; 3:2, 5, 10). In fact, he used these assertions as substitutes for each other. For example, when speaking of justification, he said in Romans 3:28 that it is not by the "works of the law" but in Romans 4:6 he said simply that it is not by "works." On the face of it, these would seem to be equivalent statements in which Paul was showing how the principle of "works" was being encountered in his own time as "the works of the law." What may seem to be simple, though, has turned into a highly controverted matter in the learned academy today.

The traditional view is that when Paul spoke of "the works of the law" he was thinking about people commending themselves to God on the grounds of their obedience to what the law prescribed. He had in mind that kind of Jewish legalism that began with the Mosaic law. From this there had blossomed hundreds of other rules and sub-laws. And there were Jews who imagined that by earnest observation of all of these requirements people could build up enough moral standing before God to warrant being justified at the end of time. That was why Paul and Peter had such a sharp falling out. Peter, who knew that circumcision was not a ground of our acceptance before God, nevertheless was demanding that Gentiles honor it (Gal. 2:11–21). He was violating the very principle—grace in its opposition to works as a basis of acceptance—that was at the heart of gospel. No wonder Paul "opposed him to his face, because he stood condemned" (Gal. 2:11).

A Different View

Today, though, a counterargument has arisen. It is that the "works of the law" refers, not to this kind of legalism, but to matters that were distinctive to Jewish national identity—and that is a little different. This included male circumcision, food laws, temple worship, keeping the Sabbath, and all the other obligations that devolved upon them as being Jews. In this reconstruction, Paul's contention, in effect, was that Jews had become racists, that they would not allow salvation outside of their ethnic boundaries unless, as in the case of "God-fearers" and proselytes, those people became one of them.

There is no doubt that Jews did think this way, but the question is whether this kind of ethnic exclusivity was what Paul had in mind when he spoke about the "works of the law." Did Paul really argue that it was their sense of Jewish identity that stood in the way of their believing the gospel, or was it their confidence in their moralism? Was it sin that stood in the way of Jews being accepted by God, or was it their exaggerated, harmful, ethnic self-consciousness? If we go with this new understanding of Paul, it leads to an entirely different gospel message.

However, this new perspective on Paul, though it has generated an enormous literature, is actually irrelevant. Consider what Paul argued in Galatians. There, he distinguished between the covenant made with Abraham and the one that came "430 years afterward" (Gal. 3:17) which was made with Moses. However the Mosaic covenant might have played out over the years, however it was used to fortify Jewish national identity in the Second Temple period, has nothing to do with the promise made to Abraham. And it is to Abraham that we must go. The covenant made with Abraham was one of grace; that made with Moses, which involved the keeping of the law, was one of works. The Mosaic covenant brought condemnation, not justification, because it was all about law keeping. The problem is that "all who rely on works of the law are under a curse" because "no one is justified before God by the law" (Gal. 3:10–11). The law which came with the Mosaic covenant was not, therefore, an alternative to the promise of justification that had been made to Abraham. Paul said that the covenant made with Moses did not "annul" and make "void" (Gal. 3:17) the covenant made with Abraham. And, in fact, even in its inception, glorious as that was, what had been established under Moses was already "being brought to an end," Paul said (2 Cor. 3:7, 11).

The covenant made with Moses was a *provisional* step until the coming of Christ. It was necessary to the identity of the Jewish people. But that is exactly why it had to be provisional. How could God create a multinational people—those from "every tribe and language and people and nation" (Rev. 5:9)—for Abraham if they all had to become part of the Jewish nation and be subject to all of its dietary and ceremonial laws? The fact is that when the promise was made to Abraham, God pointed far down the road of time to the ingathering of people into saving faith from around the world. That was the promise. It was that "I have made you the father of many nations" (Rom. 4:17), as Paul recalled.

The moral aspect of the law could, of course, continue since that reflected the character of God, his holiness, but the rest of the Mosaic requirements would have to pass away if the promise made to Abraham was to be realized. And so it happened. It was in Christ that these promises were realized, and because of Christ, they now are to be preached to Jew and Gentile alike.

Paul therefore insisted that the Gentiles, to whom he was writing in his letter to the Galatians, were not to be encumbered by the same demands and rituals—the "works of the law"—as the Jews had been. As a matter of fact, these expressions of Jewishness had never been the Galatians' to start with, and so when he told them to set aside the "works of the law," he could not have been thinking about Jewish identity.

The truth is that the impediment to being in Christ, for Paul, is not ethnic consciousness per se, nor yet pride in Jewish rituals. It is what lay behind these things. It is *sin*. And sin creates in each person, Jew and Gentile alike, their own captivity to its impulses.

The Reformation

Many years after Paul, in the sixteenth-century Reformation, justification was being re-debated. This first principle of grace—that grace excludes works—had to be retrieved again. The way the Reformers secured the graciousness of grace was by joining to it the word *alone*. We are justified by grace *alone*. Their argument was that whatever is added to grace as a basis of our acceptance before God in fact detracts from it. Whatever is intruded into salvation as a ground of acceptance, be it moral earnestness, complying with religious rituals, or church obedience, diminishes the unmerited nature of God's saving favor. This was, in fact, the very argument on which Paul had stood his ground against the first-century Judaizers. And that was also why the Reformers rejected the Catholic understanding, which saw a life of obedience in the church as completing what grace had started in baptism. If our justification is in any degree earned then it is, to that degree, owed. Something that is owed is something that we have a right to receive. We are entitled to it. We can stretch out our hands for the reward that is properly ours. But that is exactly what Paul opposed.

It has been tempting to some to think that the Reformers skewed biblical teaching by making justification central and saying, as Luther did, that it is by this belief that the church stands or falls. Could we not major in one of the other metaphors for salvation that the New Testament offers? Is not reconciliation just as important? Or redemption? Or release from the captivity of dark powers? Are these not alternatives that we might choose among, instead of justification?

To move down this road is not helpful because these various metaphors are never offered to us as alternatives in Scripture. They are but the different facets of the same diamond. The work of Christ is many-sided, and we do have to have all the sides to see the work in its totality. This will be taken up in a later chapter.

However, at this point it needs to be said that among these various word-pictures and images, justification does hold a central place. The whole weight of the Old Testament rests on this idea of sacrifice, of sins being transferred to another, and all of this taking place within the understanding of the Abrahamic covenant, so the context is legal. It is no leap in logic, therefore, to say that the courtroom context of justification—with the law, a judge, a charge, a verdict, and a sentence—is precisely what connects with the overwhelming context of Old Testament revelation. New Testament justification through

Christ's substitutionary death is the end to which all of that pointed. This is what Abraham glimpsed. It is what we will take up again in a later chapter.

Abraham's acceptance had to be by faith, not faithfulness, precisely because his standing was only by grace and not on the ground of "works." It was never because of his faithfulness. In this, we have the foundations laid for the great things to come. The "Scripture, foreseeing that God would justify the Gentiles by faith, preached the gospel beforehand to Abraham" (Gal. 3:8). And what was declared to him was not "for his sake alone, but for ours also" (Rom. 4:23–24). This gospel was, and is, a message of grace that stands in defiance of every natural self-justifying instinct we have. It stands for all ages, places, peoples, and cultures. It stands because behind it is the unchanging God of eternity, who cannot lie. We who count solely on his grace "have strong encouragement to hold fast to the hope set before us" (Heb. 6:18).

Faith

The second theme that remains unchanged as we move from the Old Testament to the New Testament is faith. Faith is clearly not our faithfulness, since our acceptance is not of works. Rather, faith is the empty hand that reaches out to receive the gift that only God can give. In biblical terms, faith requires both belief in the promise made and commitment to the Promise Maker. It is never a blind leap, as if we were launching ourselves over a precipice and then hoping, against all precedent, that somehow we will not hit the earth below. Nor yet is it merely superficial assent, like someone saying that they believe the weather might change in a day or two. It is, as Packer says, both *credence* and *commitment*, and not the one without the other. This is what we see in Abraham's case, and this becomes the paradigm for New Testament believing (Gen. 15:6; Rom. 4:3; Gal. 3:6–9; Heb. 11:17–19).

The very first unmistakable reference to faith in the Bible was in connection with this promise to Abraham. He was promised an heir, from that heir a seed, a land, and that he would be a blessing to all nations. "And he *believed* the LORD, and he counted it to him as righteousness" (Gen. 15:6). So, why is this moment so foundational, so prototypical? There are two reasons.

Belief

First, Abraham took God at his word, which becomes the key to all of God's subsequent dealings with fallen sinners. Abraham believed that what had been said would come about. At this point in his life, he had had some experience with God. He had been called long before to leave Haran, and he had done so. He gave up his place and his people. His destination at the time of his call, though, was unknown. He "went out, not knowing where he was going" (Heb. 11:8). He had to discover that along the way as God directed him. In this he was taking his first steps in faith. But now he had arrived at this climactic moment when God gave him this promise of an heir, an innumerable seed, and a land.

The most striking thing about Abraham's faith at this moment is this: he knew himself to be utterly incapable of bringing about any of these things himself. Only *God* could do this. And Abraham was counting on this. Consider the elements in the promise made to him.

Clearly, an heir was entirely beyond the bounds of possibility for him. Abraham was, at this point, an old man, and his body was "as good as dead" (Rom. 4:19). Sarah was "past the age" of being able to conceive (Heb. 11:11). Abraham therefore initially stumbled over this promise. It seemed impossible (Gen. 17:17). And there were ramifications to this. Without an heir, how could he have a "seed"? How could his "offspring" be as numerous as the stars? (Gen. 15:5). This, he came to see, was a promise that only *God* could bring about, and that is exactly what happened.

So, too, with the other parts of the promise. The land of Canaan was swarming with hostile tribes, and Abraham never did take possession of it. Indeed, he was quite incapable of doing so, and he stumbled initially over this promise as well (Gen. 15:8). And, as we know from later history, the conquest of these peoples did entail a fierce and protracted struggle. This promise had to be held in faith. Abraham, against everything that he saw, against all the odds, against the impossibility of it all, believed that the time would come when God would deliver on what he had said.

So too for the other blessing that God had promised. It was staggering in its proportions. As Paul put it later, "in you shall all the nations be blessed" (Gal. 3:8; cf. Gen. 12:2–3; Gen. 15:5; 18:18; 22:17–18). Far beyond an heir was this extended blessing into a multinational people as numerous as the stars in the sky. What, one wonders, went through Abraham's mind when he heard that promise? Whatever he thought, he also knew that this was far, far beyond the bounds of human possibility. All he could do was to entrust himself to the Promise Maker that he would bring about what was promised.

Commitment

Here, then, are the two sides to faith. Credence—believing the promises—and commitment to the One making the promises. Abraham would not have entrusted himself, indeed would not have believed what he had been told, had he not been fully persuaded of the utter sufficiency and trustworthiness of God (cf. Heb. 11:11). To say, then, that Abraham was a man of faith was to say that he was God-centered. It was to say that he saw God as the God of the impossible. As improbable as God's promises seemed at times, he was, nevertheless, a Promise Maker who was utterly reliable and able to bring about what he had promised. Abraham walked in the assurance that, to him and to his offspring, God would always be "their God" (Gen. 17:8) and he would be unrelentingly faithful.

Christ

The third element in common as we move from the Old Testament to the New Testament, at least in terms of knowing God, is that Christ is the ground of our acceptance. This was true of Abraham as it is for us today. However, this truth had to be *inferred* by those in the Old Testament period. For us today, it is truth that is historically grounded. We now look back on the cross. Its truth is something that we no longer need to infer but, rather, we joyfully and confidently *declare*. So, how do we connect what we know for certain today with what those in the Old Testament did not know as clearly?

Alone the Way

Let us begin by noticing that, on their face, the New Testament statements about the uniqueness of Christ as our means of access to the Father are unqualified. They are statements of principle. They are not limited to any specific time. That, at least, is the way they read because they have no addendum. "I am the way, and the truth, and the life," said Jesus, and "no one comes to the Father except through me" (John 14:6). He did not limit this statement to those who would come after him. Had Jesus said that this was a truth for those coming after him, he would have suggested that before the incarnation people came to the Father by a different route. But he did not. Christ, then, was the access to the Father for those who were justified who came *before* him, such as Abraham and David, as well as for those who came after him. So the single point to note here is that Jesus declared himself to be, not *a* way to this end, but the *exclusive* way. Nowhere else, and in no one else, can this access to God be found.

The same is true of Peter's bold declaration about Christ before the high-priestly family of his day. "And there is salvation in no one else," he declared, "for there is no other name under heaven given among men by which we must be saved" (Acts 4:12). This is the conclusion to his brave address. There is no mistaking his meaning. If the messianic rule had begun (Acts 4:11), if the age to come was dawning, it had come and was dawning only in Christ. There is no messianic rule inaugurated elsewhere, and there is no salvation outside of this rule. There is, therefore, no access to God but through Christ, no authority outside of him to whom appeal can be made, no one else "under heaven" to whom anyone can go. And this access, this "name," has not been chosen by us but it has been "given" by God. It has been given by revelation. No one discovers it on their own. No one finds it in the religions or spiritualities, or in themselves. We have it because of the supernatural disclosure of the saving will of God that reached its climax in Christ. It was to him that the Scriptures pointed. It is only through Christ that people "must be saved." We must see that Christ is the only way, because that is what he is. There "is one God, and there is one mediator between God and men, the man Christ Jesus, who gave himself as a ransom for all" (1 Tim. 2:5–6).

But does this apply backwards as well as forward? Did those who were justified in the Old Testament, such as David and Abraham, find their acceptance through Christ or in some other way? Let us think about this.

If their justification was not because of their "works," then its basis had to be in some source other than themselves. This much is clear. So, where might we find this source?

In the Old Testament system of sacrifices? It is certainly true that God himself had made provision for sinners to approach him in this way. All of these sacrifices came to a climax on the Day of Atonement. This was the day when "all the iniquities of the people of Israel" could be confessed, and when people would be cleansed from "all" of their sins (Lev. 16:21, 30).

There were three important lessons that went along with this. First, sin could not be forgiven without the payment of a price. That is what was declared in the death of the animals sacrificed. Sinners who had by their sin forfeited their lives were spared that forfeit by God's own provision. And the death of the animals was a reminder of the seriousness with which God treated this matter.

Second, sin was forgiven because of a substitute. These animals had their lives taken in place of those whose sins needed atonement.

Third, there was a necessary element of appropriation by those who thus sought forgiveness. Those who were present were there not simply to watch a ceremony but to have their sins forgiven. Those who came on this day were to "do no work," were to be "clean," were to respect the day as a Sabbath, and were to "afflict" themselves (Lev. 16:29–31). The gravity of their offenses against God was to be understood. They were to repent and accept his means of forgiveness.

As God's revelation unfolded through the Old Testament, much greater clarity emerged on the substitute in sacrifice toward which the sacrificial system was pointing. We see this, for example, in the passages that foretell the coming suffering servant (e.g., Isa. 52:13–53:12). We see that this messianic servant will offer himself in penal substitution for his people. Indeed, he does so in a way that brings to completion what the Day of Atonement pointed toward.

After the incarnation, it was easy to see that Christ was that final substitute. He did pay the great price in our place. We are to embrace this divine provision of forgiveness by faith. But our question remains: what was the ground of acceptance by God of those who came *before* Christ?

Clearly, it was not the sacrificial system. It could not have been in

Abraham's case because he predated it. No, this sacrificial system was a *pro tem*, provisional, didactic solution until Christ came (Gal. 3:24–25).

This, of course, was the argument of Hebrews. The Old Testament sacrifices were not themselves efficacious. They could not be, because they "cannot perfect the conscience of the worshiper" (Heb. 9:9). These sacrifices had to be repeated endlessly year after year (Heb. 10:1, 11). Why? Because "it is impossible for the blood of bulls and goats to take away sins" (Heb. 10:4). Why? Because these were animal sacrifices, and the very fact that they were repeated showed that none of them, nor all of them together, could ever be ultimately efficacious. They were only provisional.

But "when Christ had offered for all time a single sacrifice for sins, he sat down at the right hand of God" (Heb. 10:12). The entire system, at that moment, came to a conclusion. Christ's sacrificial work was complete, and his redemptive reign in his people and in the universe began.

Eternal Perspective

Is it unreasonable to suppose, then, that in the mind of God, the justification afforded Abraham was granted in advance based on the final, substitutionary work of Christ toward which all of the Old Testament sacrifices pointed? These were like today's promissory notes, which do not themselves have value but whose value lies in the later payment that they guarantee. In pointing toward Calvary, in prefiguring what Christ would do, these sacrifices gave enough ground to trust in the graciousness and pardon of God, but that pardon could never be finally grounded in any of these sacrifices themselves. Even for those in the Old Testament period, it could be grounded only in Christ, whom the Father knew was coming in "the fullness of time" (Gal. 4:4). "Christ," Peter says, "was foreknown before the foundation of the world but was made manifest in the last times . . ." (1 Pet. 1:20). Based on what the Father determined from all eternity with respect to Christ, he was able to justify those who came to him in faith before Christ had come. He did so, though, based on Christ's finished work that was yet in the future. God had an "eternal purpose that he has realized in Christ Jesus our Lord" (Eph. 3:11).

It is this eternal perspective that Scripture gives us after Christ's incarnation that now throws light back onto Abraham. Indeed, had it not been for Paul, we might not have seen the full significance of part of God's promise to Abraham. Abraham was promised a "seed." This unexpected gift from God had been mentioned before the climactic moment of Abraham's justification.

Earlier, God had said that Abraham's "offspring" would enter the land (Gen. 12:7; 13:15). They would become exceedingly numerous (Gen. 13:16; 22:17), yet they would be strangers and "sojourners" in this land (Gen. 15:13; 17:8). However, God would be with them and bless them (Gen. 26:3–4).

Much later, when Paul came to look back on this narrative, he made a striking argument. Although this seed was made up of many people, what Abraham had been promised was not the plural, "offsprings." Paul clearly knew the Genesis narrative and knew of God's intended blessing that Abraham's offspring would be as numerous as the stars. But he nevertheless made the point that the promise was about a *singular* offspring: "to one, 'And to your offspring,' who is Christ" (Gal. 3:16).

This has mightily perplexed commentators, not a few of whom have wondered if Paul had become a bit muddled! This, though, is not primarily a linguistic argument but a *theological* one. Perhaps that is why Paul seems so obscure to us today!

Early on, Abraham was made to see that the stream of redemptive history was not coextensive with all of his many descendants, his "seeds." Rather, it was to flow down only one side of his progeny. It was to flow, not through Ishmael, who would nevertheless become a great people, but through Isaac (Gen. 17:20–21; Rom. 9:7). It was to run, not through Esau, but through Jacob. This was the stream of God's electing grace which was to pass on down the ages, cutting right through the people of Israel and then on into our world today. It links all of those who, like Abraham, have been justified. These are Abraham's "seed." They find their unity and existence in Christ. In him was realized all that had been promised to Abraham.

Abraham, mysteriously, knew this in faith. And many, many years later, Jesus said that "your father Abraham rejoiced that he would see my day. He saw it and was glad" (John 8:56). This is not the only glimmer we have of the preincarnate Christ among his Old Testament people.

Jude, referring to the exodus, said that it was Jesus who "saved a people out of the land of Egypt" and afterward "destroyed those who did not believe" (Jude 5). Furthermore, as they embarked on their wandering, God's people were sustained by Christ. They "drank from the spiritual Rock that followed them, and the Rock was Christ" (1 Cor. 10:4).

God at Work

"Regeneration" is specifically New Testament language. Yet it is hard to see how Abraham, David, and the rest of the people of God who were justified could have been so without also being regenerated. How were they able to receive God's promises and walk in faith if they did not have a spiritual nature imparted to them by the Holy Spirit? Indeed, Paul hints at this. When recounting the struggle between the progeny of Hagar and those of Sarah, he says of the former that they were born of the "flesh" but of Isaac he says that he "was born according to the Spirit" (Gal. 4:29; cf. 4:23). As we move forward into the New Testament, this aspect of the Spirit's work is given greater clarity. What now becomes possible for us to know, in a way not possible in the Old Testament, is that this regenerating work is directly connected to Christ's work on the cross and his resurrection. This is resurrection life in the "age to come," which is gloriously intruding into our fallen world already by the Holy Spirit's agency.

My conclusion, therefore, is that the cause of our acceptance with God is grace. This is unchanged as we move from the Old Testament into the New, and now down to our own time. Equally unchanged is the instrument of our justification. It is faith. And, finally, unchanged too is the ground of our acceptance. For those justified in the Old Testament, as for us today, it is Christ. It is Christ in his substitutionary death on the cross. This was the case for Abraham. He had to look forward in anticipation to that death. It is so for us today who now look back on it with thanksgiving.

If this is all true, is there no difference between those who were justified in the Old Testament and those who are justified today? As this stream of redemptive history moved forward, through Christ, and into the present, has anything changed? These questions will be taken up in the next chapter.

CHAPTER 3

So Much More

Christ, our Lord to heav'n ascending
With the Father there to reign.
Leaving earth, the Spirit sending
Till the Day He comes again

JULIE TENNENT

There is only one kind of salvation in the Bible because there is only one Mediator between God and sinners. That is the theme we were pursuing in the previous chapter. However, were we to leave the matter there, we would not have accounted for some differences. These differences arise from the historical development, the unfolding of God's redemptive purposes, as we move from the Old Testament into the New Testament. We need to see clearly both the enduring principles—what we considered in the previous chapter—and the way in which these are filled out with the passing of time. That is what we must now consider.

What Changes?

There are two important differences when we compare justification in the Old Testament with justification in the New Testament. These differences set off believers today from Abraham. And it is these differences that allow for a deeper knowledge of God as contrasted with what those in the Old Testament period could know. First, Abraham had to look forward in faith to the moment when God would act in Christ. We now look back. For us, the knowledge of Christ's substitutionary death is an *explicit* part of our knowledge of God, but for Abraham, because Christ had not yet come, it could only be future-oriented and *implicit*. It is true that Abraham was to be given an extraordinary lesson in substitution through the required offering of his own son, Isaac (Gen. 22:1–14), but this was only a foreshadowing of what was to come. Isaac was not Christ.

Second, although the Holy Spirit was active throughout the Old Testament period, he was not active overtly in relation to *Christ* except by way of prophecy. After the resurrection and ascension of Christ, though, the work of the Spirit and that of the Son could be correlated, and they were. The Holy Spirit's work now is to apply what Christ secured on the cross. It is, therefore, to point us to Christ, always and everywhere. The Spirit points us to this objective revelation of God, this appearance of God in human flesh, this incarnation of his holy-love, this conquest on the cross by his holiness because of his love.

Now, the Holy Spirit's work is to point men and women to Christ, the unique Son of God, and to convict the world of sin, righteousness, and judgment (John 16:8–11). This is explicitly the only way of salvation. Those who imagine that the Holy Spirit ever validates religious seeking apart from Christ, or gives religious fulfillment apart from him, or invests other religions with saving meaning, or inspires revolutionary political movements, have made a serious misjudgment. It has been tempting for those embarrassed by the gospel's uniqueness to propose many ways around it. And some have seen Christ as being "anonymously" present in other religions. Some have even seen him "anonymously" present to those of no religion. But the very fact that Christ is said to be anonymous is itself an argument for the fallaciousness of this view. The Holy Spirit witnesses only to the known, historically revealed Christ, not to a phantom of our imagination. The work of the Spirit is conjoined to the work of Christ on the cross, and that cross happened in space and time.

We should not pass by this point too quickly. Christianity is not simply about Christ. It is about *this* Christ. Christian truth formed around this Christ will not blend itself into other ways of believing or being religious. Its gospel is as unique as the Christ whose gospel it is.

To affirm this truth today invites charges of intolerance and bigotry. It runs counter to our whole modern mentality which tells us that there are many roads to God, that private choices should not be imposed on others, that each choice is as valid as any other. Christ and his gospel, therefore, need not be understood in the same way by everyone. Indeed, they really should not be spoken about openly in the public square at all. Perhaps this can be whispered behind closed doors, it is thought, but it should not be talked about out in the open, not in the marketplace, not in the neighborhood, not in the newspapers, or in any other places where this kind of talk might be overheard. Today, we think that each person must find his or her own way of being spiritual, something that is comfortable to that person; each spirituality is particular to each person.

That was exactly what the early church encountered. It is exactly what the early church rejected, and had it not had the courage to do so, the gospel would have been entirely lost.

Toward Christ

Unlike all of those who preceded Christ, we are now able to look back on the incarnation, on Christ's life, death, and resurrection. We now know what they could only anticipate in faith. However, although Christ is unique as God-incarnate, and unlike anyone else, he is not disconnected from what preceded him in the Old Testament revelation.

That was his message to two dispirited and confused disciples shortly after his resurrection. They were on their way to the small village of Emmaus. They were perplexed by the recent events that had led up to the crucifixion. They did not know that it was the resurrected Jesus who had suddenly joined them on their walk. "O foolish ones, and slow of heart to believe all that the prophets have spoken!" was his rebuke after listening to their conversation. "And beginning with Moses and all the Prophets, he interpreted to them in all the Scriptures the things concerning himself" (Luke 24:25, 27).

Quite a few books would have become unnecessary if we had a record of that lecture! But what we do know is that Jesus elaborated on how Old Testament themes converged on himself. He was their end and completion. What we do not know is how exactly he developed these themes and which ones he chose.

I am going to select just three possibilities here: Adam, the exodus, and David. There are a number of additional themes, all of them important, which lead from the one Testament and into the other, but they cannot be in our focus here.

Adam, the exodus, and David are each types of Christ and his work, though obviously in different ways. In Scripture, a type is an event or person, within the flow of redemptive history, that foreshadows what comes later. The event is repeated later, or the person "reappears," thus establishing a parallel between the first act of God and what comes later. But when the later reenactment comes in Christ, it is so much greater and grander than what came earlier and what merely pointed toward him. Those were anticipations; he is the realization of what was anticipated.

However, we need to be careful about this matter. There has been a lot of fanciful writing about Old Testament types, as if by seeing some parallel with something that happened later in the New Testament we are, for that reason alone, better off. The key interpretive point here is that the New Testament itself must affirm this type and apply it to Christ.

Types in the Old Testament were possible for a simple reason: God's acts are always consistent with one another. How he acted redemptively in the Old Testament therefore foreshadows what he would do in Christ. The New Testament then takes up this parallel and shows us how the earlier act presaged the later and greater one.

In Christ, then, the exodus was reenacted in a glorious way, David's throne was restored in an altogether grander way, and Christ reversed what Adam did and then did what Adam failed to do. These three themes in the Old Testament will show us what advantages there are to those who can now "receive what was promised" (Heb. 11:39).

Adam

First up, then, is Adam. There are three theological connections between Christ and Adam. One has to do with Christ's life, one with his death, and the other with his rule. The first and third of these have been largely overlooked, while most attention has been fixed on the second.

The first connection between Adam and Christ has to do with

Christ's life. This is not developed quite so explicitly in the New Testament as is the parallel to Adam in Christ's death. Indeed, the idea of a connection of Christ to Adam in his life is today heavily under assault in the learned academy. It has to do with the so-called "covenant of works" in the garden of Eden. Whether we wish to call it that or not is unimportant. The important point is to see how Scripture develops the parallel between Adam and Christ. And this is key to our understanding of what was going on in Christ's life and to how we are enabled to live as his disciples.

Here it is. Adam was born sinless. As sinless, he had a natural disposition to love God and to honor him in all that he did. There was, though, a prohibition that God had set before him (Gen. 2:17). This prohibition tested Adam's obedience. Had he passed that test, his sinlessness would have moved toward maturity. This, of course, did not happen.

Temptation arrived. It came first to Eve. She was seduced into having misgivings about God's goodness: "Did God actually say . . . ?" (Gen. 3:1) was her way into this doubt. Surely, this could not be the case? Would God really impose such an unreasonable limitation on you if he had your best interests at heart? Once this seed of doubt had taken root, then the Tempter brazenly built on it by promoting disbelief about God's word: "You will not surely die . . ." (Gen. 3:4; cf. Gen. 2:16–17). No, there is no reason to believe that! Then, when Eve began to falter, the Tempter was able to deliver his final, lethal blow. God, he said, was hiding something from Eve that was really good for her. He was withholding it, the insinuation was. This was being done out of . . . what? Spitefulness? God did not have her best interests at heart. This "tree of knowledge," illegitimately forbidden to her, would make her "wise," giving her a God-like relation to good and evil (Gen. 3:5–6). Why would God withhold something so good from her? Eve fell, deceived by Satan's "cunning" (2 Cor. 11:3). She then drew Adam into her fall, and with him the whole human race. Adam, who had been put into the garden to learn how to walk with God, in full obedience, never learned that lesson. His sinlessness never blossomed into mature completion. Instead, he sinned. His development toward a full-orbed, obedient, tested godliness was halted abruptly. He and Eve, in consequence, were ejected from God's presence.

Here, though, is the striking comparison. Christ, like Adam, was also born sinless. But unlike Adam, he learned to walk before his Father in joy and complete obedience. He was assaulted by the Tempter but never once yielded. In triumphing, he brought to completion what Adam had failed to do. He "learned obedience through what he suffered." In so doing, he became "perfect" (Heb. 5:8–9) or fully complete. We therefore see in Christ all that Adam was supposed to be but never became. Christ picked up the thread of humanity which Adam had dropped and brought it to full completion. We see in Christ, in his humanity, not only what Adam should have been but also what we should be. Here is total righteousness worked out in the hot furnace of evil opposition. In "every respect" Christ was "tempted as we are, yet without sin" (Heb. 4:15). Our humanity was not draped as a cloak over the second person of the Godhead. Rather, the second person of the Godhead lived within our humanity, making it entirely his own. Christ was the great insider to the human experience. In him was exemplified all that the law ever required. That is why Paul, praying for the Philippian believers, asked that they might be "filled with the fruit of righteousness that comes through Jesus Christ" (Phil. 1:11). Because of his life and death, Christ is able to help "the offspring of Abraham" (Heb. 2:16) and bring "many sons to glory" (Heb. 2:10).

The second and most familiar connection between Adam and Christ has to do with the atonement (Rom. 5:12–21). Adam was a "type of the one who was to come" (Rom. 5:14), Paul said. Adam was the representative head of the whole human race just as Christ is of the redeemed part of humanity, those who are Abraham's seed. The parallel between Adam and Christ is not in the numbers each represented but in the *way* in which they represented those people. Just as Adam acted on behalf of those whom he represented, so Christ acted on behalf of those whom he represented on the cross. Where the analogy diverges, of course, is that Adam sinned and in that sinning brought death, condemnation, and death. By contrast, because of "the free gift by the grace of that one man Jesus Christ" (Rom. 5:15) there has come righteousness, justification, and eternal life.

This parallel is so well known, and has been written about so extensively, that there is no need to pursue it further at this point. It is enough that we remind ourselves of this connection and how we cannot understand the redemption that Christ has brought unless we see it in this context.

There is a third connection between Adam and Christ, but this, like the first, has often passed unnoticed. It has to do with the cultural mandate. To Adam was given a blessing and to him was given the earth to use: "Be fruitful and multiply and fill the earth and subdue it, and have dominion . . . over every living thing that moves on the earth" (Gen. 1:28). The earth was Adam's to enjoy richly. And being sinless, he would also have enjoyed it morally.

In what sense can this mandate be called "cultural"? The mandate clearly was not for a bare domination of nature such as we see all too often in industrialized nations, where the profit motive trumps all other considerations. This was not bare rule by force but rule that reflected who God is. It was, then, work that rested on moral principles.

Despite the fall, this mandate was not rescinded. Indeed, it was reinstituted for Noah after the flood (Gen. 9:1, 7), was reiterated to Abraham, Isaac, and Jacob (Gen. 28:3–4), is echoed by the psalmist (Ps. 8:6–8), and is then taken up by the writer to the Hebrews (Heb. 2:6–9). What is interesting about Hebrews is that the writer worked out the cultural mandate in relation to Christ. His thought is extraordinary.

Hebrews begins by reiterating the greatness of our human creation—we were made "for a little while lower than the angels" (Heb. 2:7)—and then moves to the cultural mandate that is still in effect. Everything, the writer said, was put "in subjection under his feet" (Heb. 2:8). We have a position of high rank in creation. And with that rank goes a kind of delegated sovereignty over creation. It is intended by God to be exercised in accordance with his will and under his hand.

That we have exercised our sovereignty over the creation is obvious. We have conquered distance by trains, autos, and planes. We are transcending space. We are knowledgeable of all of the great events and tragedies taking place in our world on a daily basis through TV and the Internet. We have cracked DNA, conquered some diseases, and we can hold many others at bay. We have filled our lives with abundance, at least where our world has become modernized, especially in the West and parts of Asia.

And yet, there is something wrong with this picture. Despite having "everything in subjection" to us (Heb. 2:8) by God's creation mandate, "we do not yet see everything in subjection to him," that is, to us humans (Heb. 2:8). This is the paradox in our existence.

The exalted role given to us in creation by God has turned into a frustrating defeat. It has gone dreadfully awry. Instead of using the creation as God's gift to us, we use it as a substitute for him (Rom. 1:18–25). We use its resources for our own selfish purposes, for the "good life," a life of comfort, ease, abundance, and all too often, waste. We have, in the West, produced unprecedented affluence, but we have also become the victims of what we have produced. What we have to do to get our hands on this abundance fills us with anxiety, unfulfilled yearning, conflicts, an inability for repose, ceaseless distraction, a sense of confusion, and relentless striving.

We also find that creation itself is disordered (Rom. 8:20–23). Blight and disease afflict our crops. Earthquakes, famines, tsunamis, droughts, and floods all destroy and kill. There are predators and deadly snakes (cf. Isa. 11:6–9). Nature is, indeed, "red in tooth and claw."

And while we have dominated creation, annihilated space, and ransacked the world for its resources, we have also filled the earth with our fumes and poisons. Instead of being kings who control everything, we find that much of the domain we were given is quite beyond our control. Sometimes it is hostile to us. No, at present "we do not yet see everything in subjection" to us (Heb. 2:8). Most of all, we do not see human drives, ambitions, loves, passions, and hopes brought into subjection. What we see are men and women who are, in fact, powerless to be other than what they have become.

However, we do "see" Jesus (Heb. 2:9). What has sent shudders through creation and what disorients life is not a decree from God. Nor yet is it his revocation of the cultural mandate. It is sin. And what will restore life, and creation itself, and restore our place in creation, is redemption from that sin.

We therefore look to Jesus, who is "crowned with glory and honor" (Heb. 2:9). He was so crowned before his incarnation and is now crowned subsequent to his resurrection and ascension (Phil. 2:5–11). And yet despite who he was, he had to pass through a valley "of the suffering of death, so that by the grace of God he might taste death for everyone" (Heb. 2:9).

This is a death that has both personal and cosmic significance. We know that Christ conquered all of the powers arrayed against him when, on the cross, he "disarmed the rulers and authorities and put them to open shame, by triumphing over them" (Col. 2:15). And yet there is a paradox here, too. He has the power "to subject all things to himself" (Phil. 3:21), for his conquest is total and irreversible. But not all things have been subjected to him yet. Evil still runs rampant in the world. Creation is still bespoiled. And human life is still brought low through all of its fallen impulses. So we wait in hope for that time when all will be placed under the feet of Christ. And part of that conquest has to do with our place in the creation.

We now look forward to the time when the cultural mandate will be worked out, in the presence of God, as it should have been in Genesis 2. Then, it will be without sin and without all of the anguish and paradoxes that we know in our world today. Christ's reign will take the redeemed to heaven, indeed, to a new garden where we will also find the "tree of life" (Rev. 22:2). In this new garden, this renewed Eden, the cultural mandate will be reenacted in an entirely new way. There, "night will be no more" and, instead, "the Lord God will be their light" (Rev. 22:5). The entire cosmos will have been swept clean by Christ. Evil will have been put forever on the scaffold, and what is true and right will be forever on the throne. There, everything will finally be in subjection, not to us but to our triune God through Christ, and we will enter into this subjugation. We will enter into this victory in a final and completed way. We will live forever in this cleansed place doing what Adam, in the end, was unable to do. We will live as those who are wholly God-centered, thinking our thoughts after him with hearts that are undivided, wholly redeemed, and wholly serving the one by whom we have been redeemed. This was prefigured in Christ's life on earth, and it will become true of all who belong to him, the Lamb, in heaven. As this vision opens before our eyes, like those in all ages, we say: "Come, Lord Jesus!" (Rev. 22:20).

Those who came before Christ anticipated the day when sin would be atoned for finally and completely in a substitutionary death of the suffering Savior. We now look back on that. They could not see what a perfect life lived before the face of God would look like. We can. And they could not see into the future. They could not see how God's redemptive purposes would envelop the whole cosmos and restore what had been lost by way of sin. Today, we have glimpses of this. Because we are further along the road of redemption, we have the means for a deeper knowledge of God than was possible before. To us has been given a new covenant, a more glorious covenant, one written on "tablets of human hearts" (2 Cor. 3:3). As deep and great as was David's knowledge of God, ours should be more complete and even more glorious. We have greater, more explicit grounds, to which the Holy Spirit constantly points, to love God and serve him with all of our heart. This is what has changed.

The Exodus

The exodus was also a type of Christ's redemption. The Old Testament believers looked back to this event with a sense of wonder for all that it told them about the power of God. As time passed, they also began to look forward in hope to its reenactment on an even greater and grander scale in the future. This is the hope that led right to Christ.

An essential part of their understanding was that because of his character, God is utterly predictable, unlike the pagan gods, who were not. God will always act in ways that are consistent with one another. That was why Israel's history played so large a role in its faith. They looked back on what God had done in the past, in their national life, and were encouraged or warned because what God had done before, he would do again. It was why remembering was so important. In these moments, pious Israelites would return in their minds to the great moments in redemptive history when God had acted in exceptional, awesome, saving power. They would recall those moments of deliverance, reciting the narratives and reappropriating their meaning (e.g., Ps. 77:14–20; 78:12–55; Acts 7:17–36). And this habit, of course, carries into the New Testament in many ways, too. Perhaps the most obvious is the Lord's Supper: "Do this in remembrance of me" (Luke 22:19).

The converse of this pattern was also true. When Israel forgot these moments of deliverance, when they lived as if these events had never happened, when this redemptive narrative faded from their minds, then they ceased to be God-centered. They ceased to be God's people in their minds and in their ways, those who were living in the light of who God was and who he had called them to be.

In the dark days of Judges, for example, God sent a prophet to remind his people of these truths: "Thus says the LORD, the God of Israel: I led you up from Egypt and brought you out of the house of slavery. And I delivered you from the hand of the Egyptians. . . . And I said to you, 'I am the LORD your God; you shall not fear the gods of the Amorites. . . .' But you have not obeyed my voice" (Judg. 6:8–10). Samuel said something similar. After their great deliverance, they "forgot the LORD their God" (1 Sam. 12:9). And Nehemiah recounted the same story of deliverance at the exodus, the same disobedience, but then he laid out the grounds of hope. "You," he said, "are a God ready to forgive, gracious and merciful, slow to anger and abounding in steadfast love" (Neh. 9:17).

But words of grace were often lost in the clamor of life. Jeremiah was living in just such a time. God said that "my people have forgotten me days without number" (Jer. 2:32). A little later the prophet said that God's people "have perverted their way; they have forgotten the LORD their God" (Jer. 3:21). Later still, God said through Jeremiah that these people would be scattered because they "have forgotten me and trusted in lies" (Jer. 13:25). And again, "my people forget my name by their dreams that they tell one another" (Jer. 23:27). Finally, the prophet declared that these people were like lost sheep who "have forgotten their fold" (Jer. 50:6). This kind of forgetfulness was always a precursor of calamity.

It was not unknown for a nation taken into captivity to rise up and free itself. It was, though, entirely unknown for a nation to be freed by *God* in order that it might walk before him in covenant. That was unique, and it was to be remembered by Israel because it spoke to who Israel was and to the kind of God who had delivered them. And it spoke to the importance of the covenant whose promises had been put in jeopardy by the captivity.

After the Israelites' exile, hope began to be rekindled that God would once again deliver them. No doubt, they were thinking most immediately of their captivity. But Hosea, Jeremiah, Ezekiel, and especially Isaiah (Hos. 2:14–23; Jer. 23:7–8; Ezek. 20:34–36; Isa. 52:3–12) all saw the day coming when God would lead his people into a fresh wilderness to learn once again of his provisions and graciousness. However, there would be a difference. Now, the first hints appeared that the "Egypt" they would be leaving behind was, in fact, sin. Hosea spoke of their bondage, not in political terms but, rather, as being spiritual (Hos. 7:16; 9:3; 11:5; cf. Ezek. 19:4).

Are we surprised, then, to read that the remnants of this hope were still alive in the New Testament period? Anna saw Christ and rejoiced, for she was one of those looking for the "redemption of Jerusalem" (Luke 2:38). It is not clear exactly what she was hoping for. However, Matthew saw in Hosea's words, "out of Egypt I called my son," a parallel to the early life of Christ (Matt. 2:15). Christ was recapitulating in himself Israel's history, becoming all that they had never been. He was the true Israel. But there is more. There were those who still remembered God's promise that he would one day raise up a prophet like Moses (Deut. 18:18–19). When they witnessed Jesus's acts and heard his words, they asked, "Are you the Prophet?" (John 1:21; see also John 6:14; 7:40). Yes, indeed! But "worthy of more glory than Moses" (Heb. 3:3), as much more as the builder is worthy of, than the house that he built. And under this great new Moses, deliverance was wrought. He was not only the Moses-like leader but—and here is the twist—he was also the Passover lamb: "For Christ, our Passover lamb, has been sacrificed" (1 Cor. 5:7).

Jesus, then, was true Israel; he was a new but far greater Moses; and he was the Passover lamb and the final sacrifice for sin. He was all of that in one person. And from him arises a deliverance far, far greater than the original deliverance from Egypt. It is not a political liberation but a liberation from the guilt and the bonds of sin. God's supernatural deliverance is "already" being experienced, for we are justified and have been reconciled to God, but it has "not yet" run its full course. It will not have done so until that moment when all sin has been finally and decisively removed from the cosmos. "When all things are subjected to him, then the Son himself will also be subjected to him who put all things in subjection under him, that God may be all in all" (1 Cor. 15:28).

The exodus narrative in the Old Testament has been seized upon by the liberation theologians as a justification for their theology. This was a theology of the 1970s and '80s, more Catholic in its beginnings than Protestant, and more South American than North American. But it spread fast, and certainly in the 1980s and even '90s it had captured the Western academic imagination. It is heard in some churches today, though the echoes are now getting fainter.

What these theologians wanted varies. The movement began as a response to the poverty caused by the perceived injustices of capitalism. In this form, liberation was seen as God's rescue of the poor, but this liberation was understood within a Marxist analysis of their society. It was the liberation of the poor from the oppressive class system. When it moved to North America, liberation was understood as God's actions in society on behalf of blacks in their struggle against white racist society. Still others saw God acting on behalf of women in the context of male prejudice and dominance. In Asia, the same kinds of ideas were popularized for the developing world in Kosuke Koyama's *Water Buffalo Theology*. In each of these situations, it was assumed that the exodus provides a way of seeing what God is "doing" in societies today. And the Christian hope, it was said, is that we can expect to see new forms of liberation today that follow the same pattern as we see in the liberation of the Jews from Egypt.

But no liberation theologian should have walked down this road, however just their grievances might have been. God's deliverance at the exodus does not give us a paradigm of what he is "doing" in the world today. Our world history, and the particular history in each of its countries, is not the redemptive history that reveals the character and saving actions of God. The way the exodus event is interpreted in Scripture is that it was a foretaste, not of an earthly triumph, but of Christ's work on the cross. The issue of social injustice is to be confronted on an entirely different basis.

These are the themes that threaded their way through Israel's history. They came together in Christ and reached their climax in him. They are there in his history. They are there in a final and objective way. They are there unmistakably. This is what has changed in the knowledge of God. These themes are now, in their completion, for all time, set forth in Christ. They are there in his history. They are there in a final and objective way. They are there unmistakably. That is what has changed.

David

David was promised that his throne was being established "forever" (2 Sam. 7:13). This throne would never be vacated. However, so many who came after David were not worthy of it. They acted in faithless and destructive ways. And so a yearning began to grow that one day God would once again act and bring back another David, but one even greater than great David himself. Through Jeremiah God promised to "raise up for David a righteous Branch" (Jer. 23:5). But Isaiah's prophecy is even more dramatic. A child will be born, he said, "and the government shall be upon his shoulder" (Isa. 9:6). What kind of government will this be, we might well ask, and what kind of child is this going to be? The child, we are told, will sit "on the throne of David" (Isa. 9:7). But he will be called "Wonderful Counselor, Mighty God, Everlasting Father, Prince of Peace. Of the increase of his government and of peace there will be no end . . ." (Isa. 9:6–7).

In the later chapters of Isaiah, this hope was given greater specificity (especially in Isa. 52:13–53:12). The servant is sometimes spoken of in Isaiah as the nation: "But you, Israel, my servant . . ." (Isa. 41:8). However, in the later chapters of the prophet, it becomes clear that this servant cannot be other than divine. Not only is he righteous in contrast to the people, who are blind and deaf, but he does what no mere human being can do. These are the "new things" that he will declare.

This servant is like David a warrior-king, but at the same time, he is a servant-king. He will make war, not on earthly foes, but on sin. He "has borne our griefs and carried our sorrows" (Isa. 53:4). He was "stricken," and "crushed," and wounded for so doing (Isa. 53:4–5). Why? Because "the LORD has laid on him the iniquity of us all" (Isa. 53:6; see also 1 Pet. 2:22–25). But like a triumphant king he will now hand out the victor's spoils. What are these spoils? They are God's righteousness (Isa. 53:11–12). Because this servant-king has completely fulfilled the requirements of the Mosaic law, unlike Israel, and because he has the full favor and blessing of God, he is able to declare those who are sinners as righteous. He gives them what they could not gain for themselves by giving to them what he himself has attained. That is the kind of government he will usher in. Indeed, this is the government which Christ has inaugurated, for he is this servant to whom Isaiah pointed so long before (Luke 22:37; Acts 8:32–35).

When Christ came, therefore, his kingdom was as different from David's as the new exodus from sin was from the old exodus from Egypt. Those who thought about this kingdom in terms of political power and the conquest of old enemies were in for a sharp disappointment. It was not to be like that at all. Before Pilate Jesus said, "My kingdom is not of this world. If my kingdom were of this world, my servants would have been fighting, that I might not be delivered over to the Jews" (John 18:36). It was not a political realm Jesus had come to establish. It was, rather, the inauguration of God's rule, a rule, according to Jesus's many kingdom statements in the Gospels, with two points of focus: salvation and judgment.

This kingdom was the entrance into time and space, in a way quite impossible before the incarnation, of the messianic rule. It had been impossible before because without the King there could be no kingdom. This is the realm in which we find salvation, not political triumph, and from which there comes the final conquest of all evil. From first to last, this age, this kingdom, is *God's*. It is his to give and to take away; it is ours only to enter and to receive. And we cannot enter it on our own terms, or buy it as we might a product in the mall. No, the kingdom is where and how God rules, and this rule is exercised only in and through Christ. It is *his* kingdom. This is the kingdom that, in its post-resurrection phase, Paul speaks about so triumphantly. Christ is now seated at God's right hand. His conquest is complete. He is "far above all rule and authority and power and dominion, and above every name that is named, not only in this age but also in the one to come" (Eph. 1:21).

The hope that first breathed in the Old Testament, faint and indistinct as it was, has now reached its fullness and completion. What was hoped for has now come. It is that Christ has reversed what Adam did and has completed what Adam left undone. And Christ will lead those who are justified into the presence of God, bringing the final moment of healing to the wound in reality. For in Christ there has come a new liberation, not from military might but from the foes of darkness that blight human life and bring guilt and death. He has also picked up the fallen reign of David, not simply ruling one people but now ruling peoples from every place and culture on earth. And not only these peoples, but he now rules over every power and authority in the universe. All that was hoped for has come. It is exhibited before us. It is there for all time and eternity. That is what has changed.

The Work of the Holy Spirit

The second and final matter that changes in the New Testament relative to our knowledge of God is this: the work of the Holy Spirit is now directly coordinated with Christ and his work. This clearly could not have been the case in the Old Testament because the incarnation and resurrection had not happened.

That the Holy Spirit was present in the Old Testament period is clear. He was there at the beginning of creation, breathing order into the ancient formless void (Gen. 1:2), and the work that was thus begun was and is being continued (Ps. 104:29–30). He equipped people for particular tasks and leadership. And he was the one through whom God's word came to the prophets (e.g., 2 Sam. 23:2). More specifically, it was the Holy Spirit "in" the prophets who "predicted the sufferings of Christ and the subsequent glories" (1 Pet. 1:11) that were yet to come.

However, when we come into the New Testament, the work of the Holy Spirit is put into a narrower frame. The larger vista of creation and history fades from view. These aspects of the Holy Spirit's work have not been retracted. Rather, the attention after the incarnation is focused completely on the Holy Spirit's work in relation to Christ.

Clearly, there was a historical sequence of events that had to take place. John explained at one point that the Spirit was to be given to believers but that "as yet the Spirit had not been given, because Jesus was not yet glorified" (John 7:39). The disciples had to "wait" for this moment (Acts 1:4). The point is that, once the moment arrived, it would be the Spirit's work to apply what Christ had wrought on the cross. He would do so by advocating to sinners the truth of Christ, opening hearts to believe on him (Acts 16:14), granting repentance and faith (Eph. 2:8–10), indwelling believers, and leading them to glory.

This work of the Holy Spirit had been long promised but could not be realized until Christ had come and ascended. This ministry is the means by which "the blessing of Abraham might come to the Gentiles," but this blessing comes only "in Christ Jesus" (Gal. 3:14). This is how God has gathered a people, vast and ethnically diverse, who are Abraham's progeny because they, like him, know what it is to be justified by grace through faith (Rev. 5:9–10).

This coordination of the Spirit's work with Christ's is evident in many ways. We were washed, sanctified, and justified, Paul says, "in the name of the Lord Jesus Christ and by the Spirit of our God" (1 Cor. 6:11). Elsewhere he said that "the Spirit of God dwells in you" (Rom. 8:9) and then in the same breath spoke of Christ "in you" (Rom. 8:10). The Holy Spirit "helps us in our weakness" (Rom. 8:26), while of Christ it is said that we do not have a high priest "who is unable to sympathize with our weaknesses" (Heb. 4:15). The Holy Spirit "intercedes for us with groanings too deep for words" (Rom. 8:26), Paul tells us, and then immediately he speaks of Christ, at the right hand of the Father, who "is interceding for us" (Rom. 8:34). In all of this we have a beautiful picture of the complete, unbroken coordination that there is between the Son and the Holy Spirit.

The triune God accompanies his struggling people. As we walk through life, the Son intercedes for us by pleading the merits of his work. The Spirit intercedes for us by presenting those prayers that are in accordance with the Father's will to the Father. Throughout the New Testament, in fact, we see this close correlation between Son and Spirit as together they work to bring God's people to their appointed end in glory. Are we in any way surprised, then, to read that the Holy Spirit is now not only the "Spirit of God" (Rom. 8:9) but also "the Spirit of Christ" (Rom. 8:9; 1 Pet. 1:11), "the Spirit of his Son" (Gal. 4:6), and "the Spirit of Jesus Christ" (Phil. 1:19)?

Bottom Line

As we look back, then, we can see that our knowledge of God is exactly like that of Old Testament believers in three important ways.

We know God by grace alone, through faith alone, because of Christ alone. In two important ways, though, we stand on higher ground than they did.

First, all that the Old Testament believers hoped for, which at that point was not realized, came to a final fulfillment in the person of Christ. We see in him all that they yearned for, and we see in him all that we should be. Second, the Holy Spirit's work is now to point us to Christ, to join us to him, to deepen our life in him, to make him our sovereign Lord, to fill our hearts with gratitude for what he has done, and to lift up our eyes to see all that is yet to come.

Indeed, this is what is unique about Christian faith in contrast to all other religions and spiritualities. Faith is not simply faith in God. It is not about connecting to a power greater than ourselves in the world or, for that matter, in ourselves. It is not about our private choice to be spiritual. No, it is instead all about receiving God's promises of redemption, about receiving them at the only place and in the only way that we can receive them. It is about coming through Christ to receive what the Father has for us in him. And when we take hold of Christ, and of the promises made to us and received in him, we have the most important thing that God wants us to have. "For all the promises of God find their Yes in him. That is why it is through him that we utter our Amen to God for his glory" (2 Cor. 1:20).

The fact that Christ was *God* incarnate, that in him "the whole fullness of deity" dwelled (Col. 2:9), means it is here that we see most luminously what we cannot see elsewhere—because there has been no other incarnation. Here we see the character of God most fully. Here we find how all of the lines of Old Testament teaching about God have run their course because they have converged upon Christ. They have ended on and in him. In him, we are face-to-face with God, albeit veiled, and in him we see personalized, and finalized, the disclosure of what holiness and love are really like.

More than that, at the cross we see the mysterious interactions between Father and Son that happened when our sin was taken into the holy being of God. We hear the cry of dereliction, "My God, my God, why have you forsaken me?" (Matt. 27:46). We are seeing and hearing what is in the very depths of God's being as the demands of love encounter the demands of holiness. Christ, in his life as in his death, has given us the white-hot center of the whole disclosure God has made of himself. To lose this center, to allow it to pass from the center of our focus, is to miss exactly what we should be seeing.

In a strange way, though, we are also walking the same kind of road along which Abraham walked. For him, there was the staggering promise of an heir, a seed being a blessing to all nations, and the land. Not one of these promises was within Abraham's grasp to bring about. Indeed, that was the whole point. He was simply called upon to believe not only that all of these promises were within God's power but that God would keep his word to bring them about.

For us, now, it is the promise of final deliverance from sin and the promise of a world cleansed of all evil that we are called to believe. It is the promise of being forever in the presence of God in worship, joy, and service. These, too, are far, far beyond our capacity to realize ourselves. We are but pilgrims and aliens who journey toward this end and who, in ourselves, are incapable of bringing ourselves there by so much as a single step. We are simply those who are on their way because, by God's grace, we have been started on the way. However, although we have entered the "age to come," we are still anchored in "this age" by our own internal inclinations and habits. Though we have been redeemed in full at the cross, we know ourselves not yet to be fully redeemed from sin. And so, like Abraham, we have these great promises of the joy and deliverance to come. And like him we have to hold these in faith. We believe the promises—credence—because we are utterly persuaded of their truthfulness. We believe them because we are utterly persuaded of the greatness and trustworthiness of their Promise Maker—commitment.

CHAPTER 4

The Love of God

Love divine, all loves excelling,
Joy of heav'n to earth come down,
Fix in us thy humble dwelling,
All thy faithful mercies crown.
Jesus, thou art all compassion,
Pure, unbounded love thou art;
Visit us with thy salvation;
Enter ev'ry trembling heart.

CHARLES WESLEY

Nothing seems quite so self-evident to us today as the love of God. Those who may know little else about the Bible will, nevertheless, know of its declaration that "God is love" (1 John 4:8, 16; 2 Cor. 13:11). And love is what we most like about God. Even if we have experienced too little of it in life, we know what we want. And what we want, we are told, is in God in abundance. He is the source of love. In 2008, George Barna found that 75 percent of Americans want, as one of their life's goals, to have a close relationship with this God. And the dominant image they have of him is that he is love.

Have we realized, though, that this is a curiously modern way of thinking? It is true, of course, that we have been created by God as relational beings. We are made to know, to give, and to receive love. Nevertheless, the way in which we are now thinking about love in our society owes less to creation and much more to our empty, bruised spirits. The benefits of our highly modernized world all come with costs, and those costs we must pay internally. And we are. It is not unnatural, then, that we so easily take on the pervasive habits of psychologizing that have become normal in all of our Western cultures. In the West, we live in societies that look inward, as I have argued. The fact that our societies are so deeply subjective is very important for us to understand.

In other ages, unlike our own time, the love of God has been anything but self-evident. The harshness of life, its brevity, its seemingly random catastrophes, its hollowness, its moments of malignancy, and its violence have all seemed to point in another direction. Perhaps to a God of indifference or, worse yet, a God who is hostile to human life. Perhaps he is so remote as to be untouched by it. In the first century, it was the cross that dispelled thoughts like these. It was to the cross that the early church fathers returned again and again as they confronted their pagan world. How could anyone think that God is hostile to human life, or indifferent to it, or removed from it, if he gave his own Son? That was their argument.

Of course it is not wrong to think that God is love! There is everything right about it, because that is what Scripture declares. The question, though, is whether we are thinking about this truth in a biblical framework or not, and whether we are drawing the right conclusions from it or not.

In this chapter, we are beginning to look at what our hybrid term, God's *holy-love*, stands for. However, I am reversing the order here. We will look at his love first and then, in the following chapter, his holiness. Why reverse them?

My reason is more a concession to how we typically think than anything else. In the prior chapter, we were looking at the ways in which the Old Testament revelation came to a focus and conclusion in Christ. Christ's incarnation, and his self-giving on the cross, were expressions of God's love and grace: "For God so loved the world, that he gave his only Son . . ." (John 3:16); it is "the goodness and loving kindness of God our Savior," Paul says, that has "appeared" (Titus 3:4).

What is perhaps not so obvious is that God in eternity determined, in his holiness, to cleanse the world of the evil that would invade it. Because Christ is the means to doing this, we might say with good reason that the incarnation came about as much because of God's holiness as because of his love. But Scripture says less about this angle than about the love that explains why there was an incarnation. And so this theme is what I want to continue in this chapter.

And I have an ambitious agenda. First, I want to explore a little further why it is we assume that we know automatically what God's love is. Second, I am proposing that we can understand all of God's character under the language of his holy-love. Third, we need to see more specifically how this love was revealed to us. Finally, we will see how the Bible transitions into the language of grace when it describes the action of God's love on sin.

Up the Down Staircase

Yes We Can!

Why do we assume that we intuitively know what God's love is? This is not a problem for which we need Einstein. The answer is rather simple. But let me see if we are all on the same page.

Here is the straightforward answer to why we think as we do. We assume we know what God's love is because it connects with our experience in a way that many of his other attributes do not. And why is this? The answer, obviously, is that there is no parallel in our experience to many of God's other attributes such as his eternality, omnipresence, omniscience, or omnipotence. But there is to his love.

With respect to his eternality, for example, we know ourselves, by contrast, to be mortal. We flourish for a moment, "like a flower of the field," and then the wind arises and "its place knows it no more" (Ps. 103:15–16). We are, as James puts it, "a mist that appears for a little time and then vanishes" (James 4:14). Such is our lot. We live under the shadow of our impending death, hanging each year and each moment as by a thread. God, by contrast, is eternal, and his "years have no end" (Ps. 102:27). There can never be any psychological parallel to this in our experience.

Similarly, we are limited by space but God is not. We are always in only one place at any one time. Not so with God. He is not limited and, in fact, is everywhere simultaneously. We can hardly even conceive of this. "Such knowledge is too wonderful for me," said the psalmist, "it is high; I cannot attain it" (Ps. 139:6). In this matter, God is totally and completely different from what we are.

With respect to what we know, much is incomplete. We also discover sometimes that what we thought was true is not. But God knows everything, and he knows it exhaustively, perfectly, and simultaneously. "Even before a word is on my tongue," said the psalmist, "behold, O LORD, you know it altogether" (Ps. 139:4). By contrast, we have no such experience of omniscience. We are aware that what we know is often provisional until we know better. Our knowledge is also sequential. We are always waiting for events to unfold. How very different is God in what he knows!

And while in this life we might be given power of one kind or another, our power, even in the greatest of earthly circumstances, is but a shadow of what we see in God. His power is without limit; ours never is. After laying out the magnitude of God's power in bringing about the creation, Isaiah then posed this question from God: "To whom then will you compare me, that I should be like him? says the Holy One" (Isa. 40:25). It was a rhetorical question. There is no one to whom we can compare him. God stands utterly alone in his power. There are no effective obstacles to the realization of his will. Indeed, not even death can stand in his way. We see his "great might" at work when he raised Christ "from the dead and seated him at his right hand in the heavenly places, far above all rule and authority and power and dominion . . ." (Eph. 1:19–21). The gospel is "the power of God for salvation . . ." (Rom. 1:16), for through it, and on the grounds of our trust in Christ, we are raised "up with him" and he has "seated us with him in the heavenly places . . ." (Eph. 2:6). All of this is utterly beyond our mere human capabilities.

These attributes of God—eternality, omnipresence, omniscience, and omnipotence—are entirely without parallel in our personal experience. We know nothing like these attributes in ourselves. However, God's love is in a different category. With this we can connect, because here he seems to be much more *like* us. And we do think that we know what love is like, because we have experienced love in our lives. We write about it, sing about it, celebrate it, and yearn for still more of it. So it is that we come to think that if God is so much greater than we are, then part of his greatness is to have so much more love than we have. He has so much more to give than we do. And we have so much more to receive from him than we have received. That is what we assume. And we assume, therefore, that we know what it means to say that "God is love."

If this is the way we have approached this matter, we could not be more wrong if we tried! Everything about our presumption is wrong. The way we are thinking is wrong, our framework of understanding is wrong, and our conclusions are wrong. We are going up the down staircase. We are beginning, not with who God has revealed himself to be, but with our intuitions as to who we think he is. We are making projections from our own selves—our often very needy and bruised selves—and framing God in their light.

That people do this is not novel, of course. Long ago, Augustine spoke of those whose understanding of God was cast in the light of "the nature and affections of the human soul." Nothing seems to have changed in this habit. The only thing that has changed is our external cultural context. This is the context that has deeply psychologized all of our understanding. The way this works out here is that we now think of God's love in terms of inward, therapeutic benefits which, God being God, he will hand out to us.

May I spend a little more time on these issues before we get to the heart of the matter? I want to do so because it is often in our approach to this great subject of God's love that we lose our way.

Up and Down

The most important point to grasp here is this: God's kind of love comes from *above*, not from below. It is the opposite of what we assume. It is contrary to the way our culture inclines us to think. In fact, it goes against our deepest instincts. It is politically incorrect, too.

God's love *descends* to us. His is the initiative from first to last. When he took action on our sin, it was his love that offered up his Son to be the Mediator between himself and sinners. It was his love that sent the Holy Spirit to open sinners' eyes to understand the meaning of that gift. We could not make our way back to him, so he made his way to us; we could not make our way up to him, so he made his way down to us.

Those who begin *below,* as so many do today, assume that God's love is whispered first in their inner senses, that it is part of their nature, that it is part of creation. And they assume that it becomes real to them when they experience its therapeutic benefits. As such, this love is within easy reach. Indeed, hearing that comforting voice within is even easier than entering a twelve-step program. All that is needed is that we listen. God waits on us to admit him so that he can make his love real. That is how so many people think.

And this is how much religion outside of Christian faith has thought about God's love, too. In fact, Anders Nygren, in his *Agape and Eros,* made the argument that there really are two families of religion in life. His book was not at all a narrow study on these two Greek words for two different types of love—*agape* and *eros.* He was using these words as symbols for two types of religion. His book has been much criticized, but his central point is hard to resist. What sets apart these two families of religion is that one begins *above* and the other begins *below.* One begins with God and the other begins with self. One is self-centered and the other is God-centered. One is self-made religion and the other is initiated and carried through by God in Christ.

The one begins in the human yearning for God, for the fulfillment of this yearning. But it is not merely yearning. It is *need.* In this understanding, God becomes valuable to us to the extent to which our inward needs are met. It is our need that defines God's usefulness to us, what we want from him, and even who he is.

Certainly, in our context today of a high-pressured, chaotic, and fast-moving world in which we easily get devoured, the soul is constantly being jarred. Need, deep psychological and emotional need, is ever present. In our engagement with this modernized world, we are often left empty, dissatisfied, and pained. We begin to yearn for something kinder, larger, more accepting than what we have experienced in life. We want something much more. And God looms before us as the way to find that. This search becomes a journey, and the journey becomes a ladder. One end rests in the self and the other, the far end, enters the heart of God. And we make our way upwards from one end to the other, climbing out of our need and into his satisfaction of it.

It is true, of course, that I am putting this a little too simply. There

is not a single ladder as I have suggested. Some make their way upwards by meditation, some by self-affliction, some by disengagement
from the world, and some by plumbing the inward depths at the bottom of which is the divine, as in New Age. But one way or another,
we begin the ascent into God and his love.

It Has Always Been So

These are really modern versions of the two approaches to understanding acceptance with God that have been around for a long time. In fact,
they are succinctly set before us in Jesus's parable of the Pharisee and
the tax collector (Luke 18:9–14). In this story, the two men arrived at
the same destination. They both came to the temple. They both came
to worship. And they both prayed. So, they had much in common at
the beginning. However, their respective prayers came from two very
different places, for these two people lived out their lives in very different ways. Actually, though they were in the same temple, they lived
in entirely different worlds.

The tax collector, no doubt, was a collaborator. Tax collectors
worked for the occupying power of Rome and were deeply resented
by the Jews. Not only were they on the wrong side of the power equation, but all tax collectors lived with the unsavory reputation of lining
their own pockets while collecting taxes for the Romans.

The Pharisee, by contrast, was respected, upstanding, and what we
might call a solid citizen. He was morally upright and had an influential social position as a religious leader in Jewish society. And religion
was no mere plaything for him. He was punctilious and devout. We
may look askance at the way he paraded his own virtue. He proudly
contrasted himself with "this tax collector" because, as he said, "I fast
twice a week; I give tithes of all that I get" (Luke 18:11–12). Parading
virtue like this always smacks of something else. But no doubt he was
telling the truth. He counted it so important to find acceptance with
God that he curbed his own desires, and he assumed as a self-evident
truth that God would recognize this and reward him.

It is really what is hidden in this story, however, that has the sting.
We are not Pharisees, but what this particular Pharisee had is still commonplace today. It is pride. And with this pride comes self-sufficiency

and self-blindness. These are what, in the Pharisee's case, led to this display of self-congratulation. But this pride is always beneath the surface. It is concealed. It is what, in his case, lay behind the self-assured attitude. And what lay there was an inner self-sufficiency. It had a self-authenticating but self-deluding power to it. We see this plainly. The Pharisee in the parable did not. He was oblivious to how ridiculous he really was.

The tax collector, by contrast, had no social cover when he was in the temple and no self-delusion about his own wretchedness. He was face-to-face with himself as he stood before God. He stood there naked. The Pharisee, who stood tall and erect, was blind to what was inside him. He looked God in the eye as he prayed, quite unaware of what he had become. The tax collector assumed no such familiarity—might we even say, equality?—with God. He had no such self-assurance. He stood "far off." He was bent over. He "would not even lift up his eyes to heaven, but beat his breast, saying, 'God, be merciful to me, a sinner!'" (Luke 18:13).

What separates these two families of religion is apparent right here. It is that in the one, a sense of undoing before God, of inner wretchedness because of sin, brings with it the recognition that now an avalanche has fallen. Now there is an insuperable barrier that blocks our way back into God's presence.

In the other, there is no such sense. Instead there is the confidence that there is an ascent that can be made, a hill that can be climbed, and then acceptance with God can be expected. That acceptance awaits the climber, for God surely is obliged to reward the effort.

It is from these two starting points, illustrated by these two figures, that all the other religious divergences arise. In the one conception, the movement is upwards. In the other, it has to be downwards. In the one, we find in ourselves the resources to make the journey to God. In the other, there is no journey except God provide its means and take us by the hand to its end. The one, then, is all about self-assertion albeit clothed and hidden in noble religious language. The other is about grace, and that grace can work only as the self is not simply mortified, or disciplined, but dies. In one, there is self-seeking; in the other, there is self-abnegation. One wants; the other stands empty-handed because it knows it has no claim on God's attention, patience, or goodness. In the one, the self grasps what it wants. The other knows that it can grasp nothing and must, instead, be grasped by the divine *agape*-love.

The one who sees that having God is an advantage to be seized has made a calculation. There is a profit-and-loss mentality at work. The other, though, knows that the self must be laid down at God's feet. There are no grounds for bargaining and no incentive to do so. The dead, as it were, cannot make deals. The upward journey happens in the one because it seems worthwhile to make that journey. The self is in it for what can be gotten out of it. But in the other, it is not at all about grasping what is of value but the reverse: it is God in his love who has bestowed value on the lost sinner, on the one who will not even raise his or her eyes to heaven but instead says, "God, be merciful to me, a sinner!"

This is where we must start. We must start with God himself if we are to learn about the nature of his love. We must start above, not below. We must start with who he is and not with our sense as to who he is or what we want. We must do so because God is known only to the extent to which, and in the ways that, he has made himself known to us. So, we must await his summons. Not only so, but we come as offenders, law-violators, the guilty. We must come to him in the only way that will suffice. That is, we come through the person and because of the work of Christ.

God's Holy-love

There are different ways of organizing what God has disclosed of himself and of his character. In this book, I have decided to think of this as his "holy-love." And there is a hyphen between these two words!

There are two reasons for this hyphenation. First and most obviously, it is that alongside the declaration that "God is love" we need to set the parallel and accompanying biblical truth of his holiness. "God is light" (1 John 1:5) and he is "a consuming fire" (Heb. 12:29). He is love, light, and fire simultaneously. He is the source of all that is utterly good, and such is his holy nature that he will, in judgment, consume all that has reared itself against him and against what is good. He both judges and is loving simultaneously.

Second, the hyphen between these two sides of God's character is our reminder to ourselves that actually there is only one character in God. There are not two sides to it. He is simultaneously loving and holy in such a way that we never encounter his love without his holiness or his holiness without his love. Indeed, his love is an expression of his holiness, and we never know his love except in the context of what is eternally right. This duality is reflected in Paul's observation on Israel's history: "Note then the kindness and the severity of God," he exclaims. There is "severity toward those who have fallen" through unbelief, but there is "God's kindness" toward those who continue in trust (Rom. 11:22). Kindness and severity. In short, God's holy-love.

Indeed, we see this two-sidedness in the very passage in which God is declared to be love. No sooner did John make this declaration than he immediately defined what love in God is like. It was this love that "sent his Son to be the propitiation for our sins" (1 John 4:10). It is not love in general, not just good will, not simply a general benevolence, not an undiscriminating affection, not romantic love, but love whose heart is sacrificial, self-emptying, and whose connections are with what is moral. That is why John immediately spoke of propitiation. It was this love that found the way to the turning away of God's wrath from those whose sins deserved his judgment. His love and his holiness are a part of each other and were both present in Christ's atoning work.

It is easy to affirm both, but holding them together, and seeing his love in its constant relation to his holiness, has proved much more difficult. In the life of the church they have often drifted apart. In the liberalism that has so devastated the mainline denominations in recent decades, for example, God's love has been universalized and then unhitched from his holiness. The result is a Christianity that is benign, culturally at home, racy, politically correct, and endlessly tolerant. It wants to be on the cutting edge of culture, but it is there only because it has a yearning to catch each new breeze that blows. It loses depth as it loses its hold on biblical truth. It prizes love—but it is love of a cultural kind—and it prizes holiness—but it is holiness only of a political kind. And it ends up with neither in any biblical sense.

Indeed, it would be true to say that the impact of modernized culture on Christian faith is frequently to push it in this liberal direction. It is, therefore, not only the classical liberals in the mainline denominations who have fallen prey to this pressure. So, too, have others, including some evangelicals.

But these are not the only examples of the difficulty we have in holding on to both truths. On the other end of the spectrum, among those most rigorous biblically, are some who are also quite prone to legalism. Legalism is the sin of the overly conscientious, and, it often turns out, it is the sin of those unable to fully accept God's grace. They evolve rules upon rules to preserve themselves from failure. These are self-made rules, not the moral teachings of Scripture. Having so many gives a sense of security. But the outcome to it all is usually little different from what the legalists think. God's love gets eclipsed in practice by his holiness, and then his holiness gets reduced to the accountant's old ledger book. People's failures are scored, judgment rendered, and self-assurance gained. But even while this may have the appearance of moral rectitude, unfortunately it so often parts company with mercy, kindness, and forbearance.

In twentieth-century liberalism, then, we ended up with love that was separated from divine holiness. In legalism, wherever it is found, we end up with "holiness" that has parted company with love.

Much of what we know of God's character, I believe, can be arranged under this language of his holy-love, and I think it helpful to do so. Under the rubric of holiness, we might include his righteousness, goodness, justice, jealousy, and wrath. Under his love, we include his mercy, compassion, kindness, and patience. And yet this duality in the character of God is only in the language we use—holy-love. The truth is that his love comes as part of his holiness and his holiness likewise permeates all that he is, including his love. Every act of mercy, then, is at the same time an act of righteousness; every act of wrath has, at the same time, gone hand in hand with patience; every act of kindness, every act of goodness, is a reminder that the universe in which we live is one where evil and chaos also rear their heads and that therefore these acts of goodness are harbingers of the day (yet to come) when truth will be put forever on the throne and evil forever on the scaffold. All of this was there when God made himself known to Moses at the giving of the law. God revealed himself as "merciful and gracious, slow to anger, and abounding in steadfast love and faithfulness, keeping steadfast love for thousands, forgiving iniquity and transgression and sin." And then, as it were, in the same breath, God said he would "by no means clear the guilty." He would, in fact, visit the sins of the fathers on the third and fourth generations (Ex. 34:6–8).

Love and holiness belong together and work together. Love is characteristic of every aspect of God's being as well as every action that issues from it. This is equally true of his holiness. When he created, what came forth was good, and, at the same time, he created in love. God's holiness and his love are always and everywhere inseparable because they equally belong in the same utterly perfect and glorious character.

In our time, as we have already seen, all religion which is from "below" dissolves the hyphen in God's holy-love. It thinks of the love of God apart from its connections to his holiness. When that happens it always leads us far from the Bible's own way of thinking, because we always end up with divine love that has severed any connections with atonement. It is love that asks for no atonement and needs no atonement. This is quite different from the nature of the actual love that fills and defines God's being.

When the Bible speaks about God's love toward sinners, it so often turns to the language of grace. Grace is God's undeserved love in its action on our sin. And sin, if it is to be forgiven, is where the holiness of God must necessarily be encountered and its demands resolved. And God's holiness can be encountered safely only within Christ, which is where, at one and the same time, we also come face-to-face with the love of God. The hyphen linking his holiness and his love cannot be dissolved without undoing the revelation God has made of himself to us in Scripture.

We now need, therefore, to think about this love of God, this love in God. Love was there before the creation, and it defined the nature and relations of the three members of the Trinity. It is from "above" that this love descends. It descended and was personalized in Christ. So it is that we will move easily and naturally from thinking of God's love to thinking about God's love as the grace that meets us in Christ and of which we stand in daily need as sinners.

Love Revealed

Since God is love, and always has been, it would be natural to think that nothing could be added to the revelation he has given us of himself in the Old Testament. After all, what more can be said than that God loves his people? It might seem natural to think this way, but it is also quite mistaken.

From the Old Testament

That God, from the very beginning, disclosed himself as the God of mercy and of infinite loving-kindness is obvious. This was a constant theme in the story of God's Old Testament people even as it remains a constant theme among God's people today.

At the beginning of their long sojourn, God's Old Testament people learned that he had chosen them simply and only because he had "set his love" on them (Deut. 7:7; cf. Deut. 10:15). It was not because they were an impressive people. They were, as a result, assured that "he will love you, bless you, and multiply you" (Deut. 7:13). His love was not predicated on anything that they had done.

God's blessing could, of course, be lost through disobedience. And it frequently was. The story of God's ancient people as they wandered through time is a sorry one. When God, as it were, turned his face from them, they lost his blessing and protection. They often were overrun by enemies as a result. But within Israel were those bound into the Abrahamic covenant by God's electing love. This could never be lost. It stands for all eternity.

We read of David's son, Solomon, that "the LORD loved him" (2 Sam. 12:24). But it was not only Solomon whom the Lord loved. The psalmist declared that "the LORD loves the righteous" (Ps. 146:8). How often God's loving-kindness was celebrated, prayed for, and yearned for in the psalms! "Wondrously show your steadfast love" (Ps. 17:7); "Oh, continue your steadfast love to those who know you" (Ps. 36:10); "your steadfast love and your faithfulness will ever preserve me!" (Ps. 40:11); "Answer me, O LORD, for your steadfast love is good" (Ps. 69:16); it is the Lord who "crowns you with steadfast love and mercy" (Ps. 103:4); "the LORD is gracious and merciful, slow to anger and abounding in steadfast love" (Ps. 145:8). In what is a frequent refrain, the prophet

Isaiah said that it was "in his love and in his pity" that the Lord re- deemed them (Isa. 63:9). And we see the enduring love of God not only affirmed in these brief statements but also shaping the entire prophecy of Hosea. God presented himself there as a betrayed husband who nevertheless still yearned for, and would not abandon, his wayward wife, Israel (Hos. 3:1; 11:8).

No one can be in doubt, then, that in the Old Testament, God is the God of steadfast love, of enduring mercy, and of infinite patience. And nothing could be more absurd than the older liberal Protestant insistence that the God of the Old Testament was the God of law and judgment while that of the New Testament is the God of love and grace. Clearly, God was the God of love, of kindness, and of mercy in the Old Testament even as he is, simultaneously, the God of judgment in the New Testament. If he were not, then the cross was a tragic mis- take—which, of course, some liberals also imagined. This proposal by the liberals to distinguish between the God of the Old Testament and the God of the New Testament was an attempt to abandon the biblical teaching on judgment and replace it with thoughts of universalism and interreligious dialogue. The Protestant world has paid a heavy price for their adventure.

The Trinity

And yet, when we come to the New Testament, something momentous does happen in the unfolding of God's inner nature. It is momentous, though, in terms of our understanding. It is not, of course, that his love changes, or deepens, or mutates. How could it? What happens is that our *understanding* of it changes, and this change happens because of the final and full disclosure to us of God's tri-unity. As the Trinity comes fully into view, a curtain is pulled aside and we are allowed to glimpse into the inner relations between Father, Son, and Holy Spirit. That puts entirely new depths into our understanding of what it means to say that God is love. "God shows his love for us," Paul declared, "in that while we were still sinners, Christ died for us" (Rom. 5:8). Christ "loved me and gave himself for me" (Gal. 2:20). Here is not only redemption: here is the white-hot center in God's final self-disclosure of his love.

There were, of course, hints in the Old Testament that God is tri-personal. The divine "us" statements at the beginning of Genesis were, from the start, considered enigmatic by the rabbis: "let *us* make man in our image" (Gen. 1:26); "man has become like one of *us* in knowing good and evil" (Gen. 3:22). So, who are the plural "us"? And who were Abraham's unusual visitors (Gen. 18:1–21)? And who was the "Angel of the LORD" who appeared from time to time in the Old Testament narratives (e.g., Gen. 16:7–11)? Clearly, he was divine.

These mysteries disappear, however, when we enter the New Testament period. It was the incarnation of the Son that precipitated the issue of the Trinity, for he is at one and the same time fully divine and yet personally distinct from the Father. And, following Christ's resurrection and ascension, the Holy Spirit, the other "Paraclete" (John 14:16; 15:26; 16:7), was given. This completed the revelation of God's tri-unity, for the Holy Spirit is both fully divine and yet personally distinct from both the Father and the Son. So, there is one God but three persons.

In light of these events, and as we look back on the Old Testament from the vantage point of the New Testament, the divine "us" passages now make sense, as do the mysterious encounters Abraham had with the supernatural beings, as do the various appearances of the Angel of the Lord. The final unveiling, by God himself, of his own tri-personal being adds depth and completion to our understanding of his love.

Christ

When the Holy Spirit descended on Jesus, those who were there heard the words, "This is my beloved Son, with whom I am well pleased" (Matt. 3:17). This was one of three occasions in the New Testament when the Father's voice was heard, the other two being the transfiguration (2 Pet. 1:17) and a moment shortly before the cross (John 12:28). That the words heard at the baptism were the public declaration of Christ's messianic status and role is clear, for Psalm 2:7, cited on this occasion, is part of a messianic psalm. And yet, there is more. Christ is also "beloved" of the Father. It is true that "beloved" can be taken to mean "only" (e.g., Gen. 22:2), but there are Old Testament echoes here (Isa. 42:1–3; cf. Matt. 12:18) that also point to the Father's love for the Son. Christ is his "beloved" Son. Later, Paul would write that

Christians have found acceptance in "the Beloved" (Eph. 1:6) and that God has transferred us out of darkness and into "the kingdom of his beloved Son" (Col. 1:13). Augustine spoke here of "the Son of his love," and that may well be a felicitous way of speaking.

Certainly Jesus, again and again, made reference to this love in his relationship with the Father. Embedded in other things that Jesus said are these affirmations: "The Father loves the Son" (John 3:35); "For this reason the Father loves me" (John 10:17); "as the Father has loved me, so have I loved you" (John 15:9); and then, in his High Priestly Prayer, Jesus said that he had declared the character of God to the disciples "that the love with which you have loved me may be in them" (John 17:26).

This love, of course, was preincarnate. The Son enjoyed it from all eternity. In his High Priestly Prayer, and in a moment of tenderness for the disciples, Jesus asked that those whom the Father had given him—the immediate disciples and beyond them those from every tribe and nation who would come to know him—would be with him in heaven and would see the glory "you have given me because you loved me before the foundation of the world" (John 17:24; cf. Rev. 5:6–14).

It is the "foundation of the world" where we need to begin thinking about this love. We must start in eternity past. It was there, before the creation of the world, that the Father chose all of those who would come to know him through Christ and "gave" them to Christ (John 17:2). This is paralleled exactly by what Paul said later. It was "before the foundation of the world" that the Father "chose us" in Christ (Eph. 1:4). These, Jesus said in his prayer, are "yours" (John 17:9). It was for these that Jesus "came down" so that none should be lost of those who had been "given" to him (John 6:38-39).

The incarnation is here described so simply. The Son "came down." It is, of course, far from simple. Elsewhere in John we read that Christ was "sent." Indeed, forty-two times we encounter either this language or this thought. "I came from God," he said, "I came not of my own accord, but he sent me" (John 8:42). The Father "consecrated" him and "sent" him into the world (John 10:36; cf. John 3:31; 12:46; 13:3; 16:27). This was the "definite plan and foreknowledge of God" in accordance with which Christ came and was "delivered up" to death, as Peter was to put it (Acts 2:23). But we should not lose sight of the profundity of the divine love that accounts for this sending and this coming down.

We are thinking here of the one who, in eternity, was in the "form" of God. He had all of the essential characteristics and defining attributes of God. He had the very "godness" of God (Phil. 2:6; cf. John 1:1). He was "the radiance of the glory of God" (Heb. 1:3), the total reality of who God is (Col. 1:15; cf. John 10:30). It was he who set aside all of this glory in order to carry out a very costly act of service. That he would strip away his bright glory to become not only incarnate but someone of little account, unrecognized for who he was, disparaged, rejected, and laughed at by those in power, a person of no status though he was the very center of the universe and its Creator, is an expression of humility so deep that words are inadequate to grasp it. Yet this is only a part of the picture.

We also see that Christ did not clutch onto his place in heaven (Phil. 2:6) but joined with the Father in the plan to redeem lost sinners. He joyfully set aside his status and "emptied himself" (Phil. 2:7). He who had been in the "form of God" took on what might be seen as its antithesis, "the form of a servant" (Phil. 2:7). This, though, is an optical illusion. God, in his essential nature and as an outcome of his love, was also by nature a servant. So Christ obscured his divine attributes, putting them into abeyance, and took on the life of an inconsequential servant. He entered our life with all of its quarrels and discord, its arrogance and deceit, all of its godlessness, its self-serving spiritualities and misleading religions. He was met, not with the worship which was his due, but by great "hostility against himself" (Heb. 12:3). He was also met by the full force of the lying, leering, murderous evil in Satan. You know "the grace of our Lord Jesus Christ," Paul says as he reflects back on all of this, that "though he was rich, . . . he became poor, so that you by his poverty might become rich" (2 Cor. 8:9).

Are we to suppose that in the far mists of eternity, when our calling and redemption were only in the mind of God, Christ was unaware of what this would entail? Was he caught by surprise after he became incarnate? Do we ever hear him reproaching the Father for not having told him what this mission of redemption would cost? Of course not! The point about Christ's love is that he *knew*. He knew from the very start. But such is this love, this self-giving, self-sacrificing, self-abasing love that he freely and joyfully gave of himself to do what had to be done, knowing all that was entailed. Indeed, there is no other motive sufficient to account for what he did than this extraordinary love. For only this kind of love would pay the cost which this kind of mission required. He saw that his own self-giving reached a greater end by becoming incarnate than by not so doing. He willingly chose not to enjoy the worship of the angels in a place of utter holiness for an uninterrupted eternity for the gain that redemption would bring.

Today, we read the Gospels from our own place in the world. Here, it is assumed, the one who orders in life is the superior. The person who orders has the authority. The one who is ordered is the inferior. It is so in the armed forces, in organizations, and in corporations. In our society, this kind of hierarchy of authority is essential to our productivity if we are to work together, for we are all inclined to pursue our own self-interest at the cost of others. The exercise of authority has the aim of reining in waywardness in order to aid the collective effort. It is therefore natural to think, even though it is mistaken, that there must be a hierarchy of importance in the Godhead. And we translate that as, perhaps, gradations of divine being as well. It might seem as if there is a greater divine being and a lesser one within the Godhead, for it is the Father who *sends* and it is the Son who is *sent*.

However, this cannot be. In biblical terms, a hierarchy of being—one more divine and the other less—would produce multiple gods and would reduce the Trinity to a committee. It is a violation of everything we know to be true about God.

The answer lies along entirely different lines. In the mind of love, with its humility and self-abnegation, the fact that the Father consistently takes the initiative and the Son accepts the Father's direction says nothing about a greater and a lesser divine status. It says everything about the love that suffuses the whole being of God. This matter of sending and of being sent never plays out as a question of status.

And the infinite kindness of the Son in being willing to be incarnate, to die, to bear the sins of sinful people, is a matter of unending joy to the Father. "For this reason the Father loves me, because I lay down my life that I may take it up again" (John 10:17). This is what love is like. It does not stand on ceremony, is not proud, does not bridle at directions from others. It is always joyful in the accomplishment of good for others, even when that becomes costly. It pays the cost. It is no wonder, then, that Paul can say that "the goodness and loving kindness of God our Savior appeared" (Titus 3:4) in Christ's incarnation and death on the cross.

The generosity of love is everywhere seen in the relation between Father, Son, and Holy Spirit. The Father, for example, gave to the Son those who would be redeemed. They are those "beloved in God the Father," who are being "kept for Jesus Christ" (Jude 1). But the Son responded by saying, "they are yours" (John 17:9). The Father has given "all things" to the Son (John 3:35; 13:3), and yet, at the end of the ages, all things will be surrendered up to the Father by the Son, "that God may be all in all" (1 Cor. 15:28). The Son glorified the Father while on earth (John 17:4–5), and yet in heaven Christ will be in the center of worship, for that is where the Father wants him to be. Is this not the heart of love? It magnifies the other, wants the other to have the glory, and wherever possible gives to the other.

Self-effacement is the other side to this kind of generosity, and we certainly see it very clearly in the work of the Holy Spirit. Indeed, it is so evident that we might even miss his presence, or at least miss much of it in the New Testament narrative. His task is to point men and women, not toward himself, but to Christ. There is complete harmony between Son and Spirit, but there is this necessary deference in the economy of salvation. The Son secures our redemption and the Spirit applies it. The Spirit came "from the Father" (John 15:26) even as Christ "came from God" (John 16:27). The Spirit is the Spirit of truth (John 14:17), while Jesus *is* the truth (John 14:6).

It is the Spirit's role, not to call attention to himself, but to point to Christ. He "will bear witness about me" (John 15:26), said Jesus. He did so by guiding the apostles into recording with complete fidelity all that had been revealed in Christ (John 16:13; cf. 1 John 2:27; 2 Tim. 3:16) so that the church would have this objective revelation in its hands and in its pulpits. In subsequent generations, after Christ had ascended, it was this truth that would be preached. And at its center is the person of Christ. It is this preached Christ who is heard in the world, and it is because of the Spirit's work that there are those who come to believe in him. The Spirit convicts the world of its unbelief (John 16:8–11) and points men and women to Christ.

The Patience of God

The love of God, that love which fills the whole being of God, in which the Son rejoiced and which produced such self-effacement in the Holy Spirit, also explains something else. It explains God's patience.

Do we not marvel at how long this narrative of redeeming love has taken to unfold? It began, as we have seen, in the eternal counsels of God. It touched earth in the promise to Abraham, who is praised as a man of faith. And so he was, but he also stumbled as he followed the divine call. And once his spiritual progeny became a people, it was to them that God gave "the covenants. . . . the law, the worship, and the promises" (Rom. 9:4–5). And yet, despite these enormous privileges, they were frequently rebellious and often faithless. When Paul recounted part of their history, he said God "put up with them in the wilderness" (Acts 13:18). He put up with them! The psalmist used even stronger language. God, he recorded, said that for "forty years I loathed that generation" (Ps. 95:10). And the conclusion to Stephen's speech, which proved fatal to him, was that the Jews throughout their history had been a "stiff-necked people, uncircumcised in heart and ears," and, he said, "you always resist the Holy Spirit" (Acts 7:51). More broadly, the same unbelief, the same idol-making propensities, had been present in all of the surrounding nations in Israel's history. God, however, never rushed to judgment. His hand was stayed. On Mars Hill, Paul declared that the "times of ignorance God overlooked," though now "he commands all people everywhere to repent" (Acts 17:30). God overlooked the ignorance!

God, in his patience, has not been quick to judge, though he could have so acted with full justification. But he waited. He waited until the plan of redemption had unfolded and in the person and work of Christ his promises of mercy could be proclaimed and accepted. He waited and then commanded repentance and belief in Christ. And still he waits.

Why, then, has God not judged the nations? Why is he, as Jesus said, "kind to the ungrateful and the evil" (Luke 6:35)? Why does he not obliterate the space in which sin and rebelliousness fester? Why does he not move quickly to terminate evil? Is it that he is unaware of what is happening in life? Does he not know what is happening in the church? Does he not know that there are places in the world today where persecution rages? Is he unaware that there are countries in which atheism has been made the official "religion"?

The apparent absence of God has, at times, spurred questions like these. God, through Isaiah, chided his own people for saying, "My way is hidden from the Lord, and my right is disregarded by my God" (Isa. 40:27). These people thought they could get away with something, falsely thinking that God was distant and ignorant. But the reverse side of this coin is seen among those who know that God is neither distant nor ignorant and yet they are at a loss to know why, then, evil still persists. Why? Is he unconcerned? No. That, of course, is fallacious. Why, then, does he not act? Why does he wait? How many people, in every age, have asked themselves these questions? I have myself, many times. So, what is the answer?

"You," the psalmist declared, "are a God merciful and gracious, slow to anger and abounding in steadfast love and faithfulness" (Ps. 86:15; Ps. 103:8; cf. Ps. 145:8). This was how God had first disclosed his character to Moses (Ex. 34:6–7). Subsequently, it became a central part of the prophets' message. It was repeated in different ways, at different times, and in many different contexts: "Return to the Lord your God, for he is gracious and merciful, slow to anger, and abounding in steadfast love" (Joel 2:13; cf. Nah. 1:3). He has "endured with much patience vessels of wrath prepared for destruction" (Rom. 9:22), Paul said.

And yet this mercy, this patience toward human wrongdoing, sometimes strains our ability to walk with God. How can God bear with what is cruel and destructive in society? Why does he tolerate what is wrong in the church, sometimes for long, long stretches of time? How can he remain so inactive, seeming to turn a blind eye to all that is wrong? How can God hold open the door for so long? Jonah resented this (Jonah 4:2). Jeremiah suffered because of it. It gave him "pain unceasing" and a wound that was "incurable" (Jer. 15:15–18). But this is what God is like!

Paul laid waste the church and saw to it that Christian believers were imprisoned or destroyed. He was there, for example, at Stephen's death. Luke tells us that "Saul approved of his execution" (Acts 8:1). And yet, God did not immediately judge him. Perhaps there were Christians at this time, when friends were falling, who asked themselves where God was in all of this. Did God not see that the church was sinking beneath these waves? But when Paul himself looked back on this time, he saw something else. He marveled at how Christ had displayed his "perfect patience" (1 Tim. 1:16). Christ did this so that others might benefit from Paul. And the fact that Christ has not yet returned is not a sign that God has forgotten, or that now he is looking the other way, or that he is indifferent. No, he is not "slow to fulfill his promise." He waits because of his great forbearance (2 Pet. 3:8–10). He waits until the bride of Christ has been completed.

Amazing Grace

The love of God in its action on sin, in the New Testament, typically is spoken of under the language of grace. This does not mean, of course, that grace is not implied in many Old Testament passages, for it surely is. We cannot miss its notes. We hear its music.

Knowing that God could not be other than faithful to himself and therefore to his covenant, David sang that "goodness and mercy shall follow me all the days of my life" (Ps. 23:6). He counted, not on his own obedience to the law for this blessing, but upon God's unmerited kindness (Rom. 4:5–8). This kindness was steadfast and immovable (Ps. 89:33). These are the truths that are at the heart of the New Testament doctrine of grace. And, as we have seen, when Paul looked back to Abraham, he saw that his standing before God, his acceptance, was to be explained by God's grace alone. Certainly, then, the reality of God's grace was present in the Old Testament although the specific language really is not.

With the incarnation of Christ, though, this changes. Now, the loving-kindness of God, his goodness that gives the unearned favor, the undeserved forgiveness of sin, is made explicit in a way that far exceeds what was known in the Old Testament. It all meets us in the person of Christ. Now, these great themes are opened to our sight in a way that they never had been before. Now we see new depths in God's mercy, because now we see its cost in a way that is far deeper.

Now we see even more clearly the peril from which we have been preserved. New aspects to his kindness open up before us because now we understand how his grace reaches us and what is entailed in his pardoning actions. Now, we understand that it was because of his grace that he pursued us so relentlessly until, when there was no place for us to run, and nowhere else for us to hide, our hearts were turned, renewed, recreated, and lifted up to know God in his forgiving love. Then it was that we saw that we had run, but that wherever we had gone he had gone before us. He had, from all eternity, overtaken us at every point and in every place. But he overtook us only at very great cost to himself as our sin was taken into his very being through Christ.

However, because the working of God is silent and unseen, we often misread what has happened, and not least with respect to our own salvation. Surely we are like Paul, who had been set apart in eternity long before he was born and then was "called" by his grace. Then, in time, Paul said, God "was pleased to reveal his Son to me" (Gal. 1:16). Is it not so with us, too?

In order to believe, though, we must repent. That is in the call of the gospel. It is God who commands repentance, and it is we who must deliver. And yet here, too, we encounter the hidden hand of God as he graciously gives to us what he commands. This is illustrated in Paul's observation concerning some who were caught in the coils of evil. Perhaps, he said, God may "grant them repentance leading to a knowledge of the truth" (2 Tim. 2:25). And we are to believe in Christ and accept his death in our place on the cross, but can we forget that it is "by grace [that] you have been saved through faith. And this is not your own doing; it is the gift of God, not a result of works, so that no one may boast" (Eph. 2:8–9)? God's call to belief, the repentance, the belief itself, the life of faith (2 Cor. 12:9) all go back to God's grace and his grace alone, from its start in eternity to where it will also end, which is in the eternal presence of God (Rom. 8:31–39). Are we surprised, then, that Paul should speak of "the riches of his grace" (Eph. 1:7) that leads to our forgiveness, that the gospel is "the gospel of the grace of God" (Acts 20:24; cf. Gal. 1:6)? So it is that we "stand" in this grace (Rom. 5:2), for this is what makes us who we are (1 Cor. 15:10).

This grace, though, is not other than his love. It is his love in its action on our sin. So it is that the language so easily switches. God "shows his love for us in that while we were still sinners, Christ died for us" (Rom. 5:8). Paul spoke of the Son of God who "loved me and gave himself for me" (Gal. 2:20). Christ "loved the church and gave himself up for her" (Eph. 5:25). We are now his "beloved" (Rom. 9:25). And nothing will ever separate us "from the love of Christ" (Rom. 8:35).

It is, though, one of the seeming anomalies of Scripture that, while this theme of God's love is sounded so resoundingly and so unmistakably, it is rare that it speaks of our reciprocal love for God. It is true, of course, that Jesus identified the "greatest" commandment as that of loving God with all of our heart and strength. The significance of this will be taken up in a later chapter. Yet this language is rare.

Far more common is the language of faith. Indeed, we cannot love God without exercising faith, because we cannot love except as we believe his promises and trust in the Promise Maker. We cannot love God from within ourselves as we love our work, our country, or our spouse. Our love for God happens only within our redemption. In this context, we meet God's grace in connection with the gospel, and that gospel truth is grasped by faith alone. And that entry into redemption is followed by a life of faith, of daily walking with God by receiving the truth of his Word, believing it, and acting on it. It is thus that we show our love for him.

This chapter is only a beginning. We will be returning to the love of God and to its union with his holiness throughout the chapters that remain. We have much yet to explore. However, at this point, we have seen enough to have our souls filled with wonder and gratitude for who God is.

This is what our best hymn writers have seen. "Depth of mercy! Can there be / Mercy still reserved for me? / Can my God his wrath forbear— / Me, the chief of sinners, spare?" So wrote Charles Wesley. And then there is John Newton's well-known hymn: "Amazing grace! how sweet the sound, / That saved a wretch like me! / I once was lost, but now am found, / Was blind but now I see." Indeed, all of our best hymn writers have been amazed, awestruck, dumbfounded by the love of God. They delight in the love of God in its action on sin, which is God's grace. And so should we.

CHAPTER 5

The Splendor
of Holiness

My God, how wonderful thou art,
Thy majesty how bright,
How beautiful thy mercy seat,
In depths of burning light!

FREDERICK FABER

It is impossible to think of the love of God apart from his holiness. The
reason is that God's character is encountered as he is, as the encounter
with the one, almighty, and all-glorious ruler of eternity. So, when it
comes to his character, it is all about the unity, the mutual interpen-
etration of his holiness and his love. "Bless the LORD, O my soul, and
all that is within me, bless his holy name!" (Ps. 103:1), exclaimed David.
But then he moved on immediately to illustrate how the holiness he
had just extolled—"his holy name"—spilled out in love: ". . . who forgives all your iniquity, . . . who redeems your life from the pit, who
crowns you with steadfast love and mercy" (Ps. 103:3–4). And so it is
throughout Scripture. This is what we are looking at from many different angles in this book.

And yet, love and holiness are not the same thing. The key is to
know where their differences lie.

The differences are not what we may think, or what our culture
inclines us to think they are. We today usually see our world through
therapeutic categories. This, I know, has been said before . . . and it will

101

be said again! The reason for repeating this is its importance. We must train ourselves to set the character of God in the framework that he gave us rather than in the framework we so often use in understanding our lives today.

In recent decades in America, we have drifted out of the moral world in which we once lived and which the biblical authors inhabit. Now, we think not of right and wrong but of inward hurts and psychological healing. We look less for redemption and more to techniques of self-management. So, we naturally associate love with open arms, warmth, listening, caring, healing, and acceptance. With holiness, we associate what is colder, more distant, more alarming, and more impersonal. We think of rules, standing before the face of justice, condemnation, and rejection. In some religions there are "holy men" who separate themselves from life and live in their own peculiar ways. We see them from time to time on TV. They reinforce what we are inclined to think about holiness anyway. It is that what is holy is alien, cold, odd, uninviting, distant, and sometimes inhumane.

We are instinctively drawn to love. We are easily repelled by holiness.

In this chapter, we'll look for some clarity on this subject. We need, first, to think more concretely, more biblically, about the meaning of holiness. Here, we will be looking at holiness in God. (In a later chapter, we will follow out the consequences of this holiness for Christian living.) Second, we will explore three of the expressions of God's holiness: his goodness, his righteousness, and his wrath.

What Holiness Means

Here I am thinking of "holiness" as the umbrella term that covers an array of God's moral perfections. For our understanding, these are distinguished in Scripture. They can be considered separately and, indeed, they often are. Across the ages, many people have treated holiness as one of these perfections, and they have seen it as distinct from God's other moral perfections. But this, I believe, is unhelpful. We need to see these perfections together and in their connections with one another. I will be arguing that these perfections make up his holiness.

Nowhere does Scripture give us a succinct definition of what holiness in God means and yet, despite this, we are not really in any doubt. God is, in David's phrase, "the Holy One of Israel" (Ps. 71:22; 78:41; 89:18). Later, we encounter a few variations on this. In Ezekiel, he is the "Holy One in Israel" (Ezek. 39:7). In Hosea, God is "the Holy One in your midst" (Hos. 11:9), and Habakkuk addresses him as "my Holy One" (Hab. 1:12). They all knew what this meant.

This name, "the Holy One of Israel," stands out, not only because it appears so often but also because it is so central. God, it is true, is known as the Mighty One of Israel. But there are no references to him as the Merciful One of Israel, the Just One of Israel, or the Patient One of Israel, true as all of these are. God is abounding in mercy, always just, and amazingly patient. But his holiness includes all of these other perfections and much more. It is a fundamental statement of who God is and what he is like. Holiness in God is everything that sets him apart from the sinful creation, and it is everything that elevates him above it in moral splendor.

We find this truth from the beginning of Scripture through the ideas of separation. It was taught step-by-step, beginning with the difference between ceremonial cleanness and uncleanness, places that assumed special sanctity because of the presence of God, and times that were set apart for special purposes. Things and times were separated *to* God and separated *from* common usage. God stands entirely apart from the sinful creation because of his moral splendor.

When Moses was keeping his father-in-law's flock, he saw a remarkable sight one day. It was a bush that was on fire but was not being consumed. As he approached to investigate this amazing thing, he was addressed directly by God: "Do not come near; take your sandals off your feet, for the place on which you are standing is holy ground." Moses "hid his face, for he was afraid to look at God" (Ex. 3:5–6). Even at this early stage, it was already evident that it is not just places and things that have been separated out from common use. Those who have been called by God's grace have been separated, too, and they must be separated to him. This basic separation to God, effected by grace, requires an ethical separation within ourselves. Those who know God must be separate from what corrupts life. But on the other side of this coin is the matching truth: those who know God have seen a glimpse of moral splendor, a glimpse of the light that endures forever, for it radiates from the very being of God.

Majestic Otherness

Isaiah's Vision

It is in Isaiah, in particular, that this truth about God's elevation over what is created and his separation from all that is fallen in creation becomes so focused. Indeed, the title "the Holy One of Israel" is used twenty-nine times in the book (e.g., Isa. 1:4; 5:19; 10:20; 43:3), suggesting the centrality to the prophet of this truth of God's character. There is little doubt that this designation was rooted in the vision of God that marked Isaiah's calling into prophetic ministry.

Isaiah was not unique in being granted a vision of God. Before Jeremiah began his ministry, he saw a vision of God (Jer. 1:4–10). So, too, did Ezekiel. His vision, with its remarkable symbolism, ended with his statement, "such was the appearance of the likeness of the glory of the LORD" (Ezek. 1:28). Daniel's vision of God came later on, when he had already begun his ministry. He was enabled to see into heaven's throne room, filled with angels (Dan. 7:9–14), from whence God's decrees come forth by which civilizations rise and fall.

Each of these prophets records how a vision of God began or sustained their ministries. Each vision accented something in God's character and, given the days in which these prophets lived, was especially important for them to understand. Jeremiah prophesied during the last five kings of Judah, until Jerusalem fell. To him was given a direct assurance of God's providence in life, an assurance he surely needed during this stormy time. Ezekiel spoke to desolate captives in a foreign land. To him was given a vision of God's omnipotence that not all of the failures of God's people could negate. This is what made Ezekiel so unsparing in what he said and so courageous in saying it. Daniel, one of Nebuchadnezzar's captives taken off to Babylon (Dan. 1:1–6), was assured of God's sovereign purposes at work in the nations and so was able to look beyond his people's disheartening circumstances and speak with hope.

But to Isaiah was given something else. It was a vision in which God's holiness was manifest. Undoubtedly, this strengthened the prophet in a time of spiritual and moral emptiness when the prosperity of the times had dulled the senses. It was a time of "wild grapes" (Isa. 5:1–4), which are not the kind one wants, and this despite everything that God had done to make Israel productive. But what was shown to Isaiah reaches far beyond his time. It comes down to our time, too. It reaches down into every generation, for God is always, invariably, and everywhere holy.

It was in the same year that King Uzziah died that Isaiah saw God. This was a time of great uncertainty. Uzziah's reign had been long and, in some ways, very successful. The land was prosperous. The sky, though, was filling up with clouds of uncertainty. Three years before, in the northern kingdom, Jeroboam II had died and anarchy was setting in. Now, the peaceful stability in the south was suddenly thrown off balance by Uzziah's death. However, what was apparently on the minds of most people was rather different from what was on God's mind. They were worried about their peace and prosperity. They clearly had grown cold to God. Is this not the correlation we see so often in life? Peace and prosperity, in a curious chemistry, produce spiritual decay. So it was then. And into this situation came a vision of God.

On this day, "I saw the Lord," Isaiah says (Isa. 6:1). What, we might ask, did the prophet actually see?

His statement seems to contradict what God said to Moses. He was told that though he could know God's grace, he could not see his face (Ex. 33:20). And then there is also John's statement that "no one has ever seen God" (John 1:18), and Paul's that "the blessed and only Sovereign, the King of kings and Lord of lords" is one whom "no one has ever seen or can see" (1 Tim. 6:15–16). God can, though, reveal himself. He can disclose what is true about himself in ways that we can comprehend. This is what he did here. He gave Isaiah a vision of himself. Isaiah was not seeing by naked sight, for he could not have endured what he saw, but God was showing him deep truths about himself.

Isaiah reports his vision of God in two parts. On the one hand, he saw how glorious and majestic God is. He was on his throne, "high and lifted up; and the train of his robe filled the temple" (Isa. 6:1). He was ruling as King and Judge. The fact that his robes flowed out and entirely filled the temple meant that there was room for no one else. This divine authority is unique. It cannot be shared with another. Isaiah was initially speechless.

On the other hand, the seraphim, the burning angelic beings, were in awe and reverent worship before God. They called out to each other, perhaps antiphonally, saying, "Holy, holy, holy is the LORD of hosts; the whole earth is full of his glory" (Isa. 6:3). It is possible that this might be a reference to the Trinity. But it is more likely that it is speaking to the fact that God's nature as holy is infinite. This would be the Hebrew way of saying that.

Here, then, are the two sides to God's own disclosure of his holiness, and they need to be held together. On the one side, there is his glory as the one who is transcendent. On the other side, there is what explains this glorious transcendence, at least in part. It is his utter moral purity. And when both sides are placed alongside each other, when we understand the one in the light of the other, we get the full picture of God's holy being. Let us consider these two aspects.

In this vision, Isaiah saw God on a high or elevated throne. This throne bespoke an authority unmatched and a sovereignty unchallenged. God is other than all that he has made and stands above everything that is created. More than that, he is in his nature the measure of all moral reality. In this sense, he stands not only over creation as its King but also over against all that is fallen in creation as its Judge. Isaiah needed to grasp this more deeply because of what lay before him.

Before him lay a mission impossible. After he was commissioned and sent on an errand into the wilderness, he asked, "How long, O Lord?" (Isa. 6:11). It was not really a question about the *length* of his prophetic ministry. It was, rather, a question about how long he would have to endure an *unsuccessful* ministry. It would be a mission in which the people to whom he went would hear but not understand, would see but never have any perception (Isa. 6:9–13). How long, indeed!

This statement about Isaiah's impending failure was certainly declaring the result of his ministry. But more to the point, it was also stating what God's *purpose* in the prophet's ministry was. His ministry was to be an expression of God's judgment. God was about to assert his holy will against this his disobedient, indifferent, and recalcitrant people. Through the prophet, the blindness and deafness of God's people was going to be exposed. "Make the heart of this people dull," God declared, "and their ears heavy, and blind their eyes." Why did God give the prophet such a dreadful commission? The answer was a little chilling: "lest they see with their eyes, and hear with their ears, and understand with their hearts, and turn and be healed" (Isa. 6:10).

Judgment was coming upon this stubborn, wayward people, and so, before Isaiah began, he was shown this sight of God elevated on a throne, sovereign over the universe. On the threshold of the appalling prospect of coming judgment, and his own ministry as a harbinger of that judgment, Isaiah was strengthened to do what was painfully difficult but which was, nevertheless, necessary. This kind of ministry, after all, is always resented. "Which of the prophets," Stephen asked much later, "did your fathers not persecute?" (Acts 7:52). God was preparing the prophet for the ordeal that awaited him.

Although this vision was given to Isaiah in his own particular circumstances and with its own specific details, it also contains a thread that runs throughout Scripture. It is the thread of God's transcendence. We hear it early on in Moses. "Who is like you, O Lord, among the gods? Who is like you," he sang, "majestic in holiness, awesome in glorious deeds, doing wonders?" (Ex. 15:11). And we hear it frequently in the Psalms. God is addressed as the "Most High," and it is not difficult to see the connection between this divine name and what Isaiah saw, which was the Lord, "high and lifted up." So David says that he will sing praise "to the name of the Lord, the Most High" (Ps. 7:17; see also Ps. 9:2; 18:13; 21:7; 47:2; 57:2). God is "exalted over all the peoples" (Ps. 99:2; 113:4; cf. Deut. 32:8; Dan. 4:17; 4:25, 32) of the earth and over all the so-called gods (Ps. 97:9). The Lord, "the Most High, is to be feared, a great king over all the earth" (Ps. 47:2).

It is not merely in earthly affairs that Scripture sees this sovereign God at work and ruling. We see it, most importantly, when he establishes his own redemptive kingdom in the face of evil (e.g., Dan. 7:21–22). This is where we are engaged, not only by his power but also by his loving-kindness. In a beautiful declaration, Isaiah later on returned to the language he had heard when he saw the Lord "high and lifted up." This God, he said, "the One who is high and lifted up, who inhabits eternity, whose name is Holy," is the one who dwells in a "high and holy place" but who also dwells with him who "is of a contrite and lowly spirit" (Isa. 57:15). There is judgment coming upon God's people, Isaiah knew, but God does not abandon sinners who come to him in humility, not trusting in their own righteousness as a ground of acceptance before him. Despite his might and glory, God "dwells" with even the most insignificant of humans if they come to him in the right way!

This vision of God ruling in his great power is, in fact, the consistent biblical vision. This is the God, Jeremiah said, whose "glorious throne" was "set on high from the beginning" (Jer. 17:12). All of this was clearly on the minds of the New Testament authors. The most cited Psalm is 110:1: "The LORD says to my Lord: Sit at my right hand, until I make your enemies your footstool." This, in fact, was recalled by Jesus before the high priest. Was he or was he not the Son of God? Jesus replied, "you will see the Son of Man seated at the right hand of Power and coming on the clouds of heaven" (Matt. 26:64). A little later, Hebrews spoke of Christ, after the resurrection, being "seated at the right hand of the throne of the Majesty in heaven" (Heb. 8:1). And, as we come to the end of the Bible, this is the enduring image that we are given. It is of a throne. And around this throne, in worship before the triune God of the universe, are those "living creatures" who never cease to say some of what Isaiah heard the seraphim saying: "Holy, holy, holy, is the Lord God Almighty, who was and is and is to come!" (Rev. 4:8). And to this ascription of praise the "living creatures" added the words, "Worthy are you, our Lord and God, to receive glory and honor and power, for you created all things, and by your will they existed and were created" (Rev. 4:11).

Today, thrones have no place in most people's lives. People may have seen a throne in a museum somewhere, but all that it once connoted has now gone, swept away before the tides of revolution and democratization. Where thrones still are occupied, such as in Britain, they are mostly of ceremonial importance.

But once it was quite different. Once, thrones radiated meaning. They symbolized the sovereign's authority and will. It was from the throne that societies were shaped, for good or ill, and declarations made. Thrones stood for power, wealth, sometimes justice, and always the entitlement to rule. This is the image that we have here in Scripture, though purged, of course, of all of its human imperfections.

This idea of God's great power, authority, and sovereign rule is also captured by spatial images. The throne in Isaiah's vision was elevated. God's "majesty is above earth and heaven" (Ps. 148:13), the psalmist declared. Later James spoke of the godly wisdom which we should seek: "the wisdom from *above*" (James 3:17). The greatness of God is captured in this simple image of his being "above."

A Lost Vision

In the 1960s and '70s, there were theologians who gained the public eye by mocking all of this. They found it impossible to believe in a God who is "up there" or "out there." They wanted to replace the image of height by one of depth. God is "in here," they argued, in the very center of our own being, indeed of all being. If they humanized God in this way, they also massively diminished him.

In Britain, this move produced, in the 1960s, the secular theology of Bishop Robinson's *Honest to God*. In the United States, it spawned the "death-of-God" theology which, in 1966, ended up being touted on the cover of *Time* with the bold question, "Is God Dead?" It was, undoubtedly, a newsworthy story. Here was a religious development tainted with scandal. These theologians were making waves precisely because they did *not* believe! This was rather like someone stumbling onto a chef who hates the sight of food or a surgeon who cannot stand the sight of blood.

It just so happened, of course, that this turn inward—God is found in the depths of our being—coincided with the turn inward that was happening in every Western culture at that time and which has continued down to the present time. In the 1960s this was allied to a robust secularism that was also rippling through the West. Indeed, so vigorous was this that many among the religious seriously thought that secular humanism might eclipse and then eliminate all believing. In these decades there was, as a result, a large literature both defending and attacking secular humanism.

However, the story did not end in the way that either side thought it would. Instead the West, against all expectations, suddenly turned spiritual. By the end of the 1990s, those who said that they were spiritual—though many of these were not religious—made up about 80 percent in each Western country. The feared secularism did take root in some pockets of society and, undoubtedly, continues to exert pressure on belief down to the present day. But it is not the pressure that once was feared. And all of the maneuvering on the radical left of theology to adjust the content of belief to this secularism by rejecting the God "up there" turned out to have been an exercise in futility. It attracted no one and it discredited Christian believing. As it turned out, many people began to yearn for something more in life than just its buying and selling, something beyond its struggles and confusion.

But now, by a strange twist of circumstance, we have come back to this earlier radicalism without even knowing it. The route back has not been through the older theologians like Bultmann and Tillich who fathered this movement in the 1960s, but rather, through our radical, cultural individualism with its therapeutic disposition. There is, for many people, no God "above" them who is relevant to their daily preoccupations. They intend no new radicalism and would be quite shocked to know how far out they really are. They simply are uninterested in a God who is other than themselves, who inhabits a realm that cannot be accessed by intuition. These are people deeply preoccupied with their own selves, and often with not much else. They are the harbingers of a new cultural narcissism. They are attuned to their own internal aches, pains, and confusions, and for them, the world "out there" is overshadowed by the world "within." Their wounds become the prism through which they see all of reality. It is through this prism that they see God. And the value that God has for them is simply his value in resolving these internal pains and wounds.

This is a therapeutic vision. It is not a moral one. And what is often missed is that evil can be defined only in a *moral* existence, not in one that is simply therapeutic and psychological. There is no evil in a therapeutic world. There is only pain.

The truth, though, is that behind our pain, behind our many troubles, there is radical evil even if there are many who are blind to it. And when we line evil up against the expressed will of God, we get something even more serious than evil. We get *sin*. Without an understanding of sin, life is simply beyond explanation. We are left simply with therapies to help soften the blows, while what we really need is redemption.

This therapeutic vision is but the contemporary version of the salvation from "below" that we considered earlier. And this cultural mood, which has its unwitting evangelical proponents, becomes a dagger aimed at the heart of God's actual disclosure of himself. This disclosure comes from "above," not from within or from "below."

That, at least, is the biblical affirmation. God is elevated over all of life. God is God. We are but a part of his creation and dependent on him. He is its center. We are its periphery. He is infinite. In our humanity, we are but fading and finite. Between Creator and creation is a boundary. There is no place for pantheism in a biblical worldview. All spiritualities that begin within the self, building on the self as their religious source, are false. The self cannot reach out, in, or up and find God in a redemptive way. All of these cultural spiritualities have assumed that the boundary set between Creator and creature, between the holy God and sinners, can be crossed from our side and crossed naturally and easily. It cannot. Only God, the infinite Creator and the one who is utterly holy, can cross these boundaries. They are crossed only from "above," and they can be crossed only by God himself. He rules; we are ruled. He acts; we are acted upon. He gives life; we receive it. We are sustained in his providence. We are not self-sustaining in our existence. We live in his world. He is not, therefore, an intruder in our world. In short, he is above and we are below.

Far but Near

And yet, this transcendence that Isaiah saw symbolically represented by the throne does not mean that God is remote from life, isolated from it, cut off from all that happens in this world. He has not turned his back on the world. He is not mute and withdrawn. This was often the case with the pagan gods and goddesses. Their names might be invoked, but they were often quite indifferent to those who offered them prayers and sacrifices. But Yahweh is completely unlike those deities. It is part of his greatness that he has turned toward his creation and spoken into it. He wills that his glory be known, that he be worshiped, that his greatness be honored. In this sense, he is "jealous," for his glory is unique and cannot be shared with another.

So it is that he has turned to us. God, Paul said on Mars Hill before his skeptical audience, "is actually not far from each one of us" (Acts 17:27). Not only are we providentially sustained by him, but his presence is made known to every person throughout the creation. As David had said long before, "The heavens declare the glory of God, and the sky above proclaims his handiwork" (Ps. 19:1). It is true, of course, that sinners do not "honor him as God or give thanks to him" (Rom. 1:21) even though the revelation of his power is evident in creation. And yet, despite this human rebuff, God does not withdraw this revelation of himself.

More than this, God has also disclosed himself, and disclosed much more of himself, in Scripture. "Your word is a lamp to my feet and a light to my path" (Ps. 119:105). God's word is a light because in Scripture, by the Holy Spirit's supernatural work, God has made known his character, his acts, and his will.

But supremely, God turned to the creation in the sending of the Son who, as we have seen, embodied this disclosure in himself. "You are from below; I am from above," Jesus declared. "You are of this world; I am not of this world" (John 8:23). He had come from "glory" (John 17:5), had left the presence of the Father (John 6:62; 8:38; 10:36), and he entered our human "flesh" in the incarnation. He had "descended from heaven" (John 3:13), having been "sent into the world" (John 10:36). Christ said of himself that he is the one who "comes down from heaven and gives life to the world" (John 6:33). He came down, descended, and had been sent into the world. He came from "above." This reiterates the truth that the triune God is other than the creation and is over against all that is fallen in creation, over against all that is now dying. It is only from this other world, the world "above," that we can find the bread that never perishes, the life that never ends.

Moral Otherness

An Awful Sight

To this vision, given to Isaiah, of the majestic otherness of God was also added the understanding of his moral otherness. Indeed, his moral otherness explains his majestic otherness. It was a vision of his holy and pure being. Not only do we hear this affirmed by the seraphim—"Holy, holy, holy is the LORD of hosts; the whole earth is full of his glory!" (Isa. 6:3)—but we also have the impact upon the prophet of seeing God, and this is instructive.

The angelic beings were in ceaseless praise before God but Isaiah was speechless. He stood on the doorstep of heaven, in the presence of God in his greatness, and he was mute. He was an intruder. He was like an alien who did not belong where he was. And the reason was that in this moment, the radiant beams of God's holiness had penetrated every nook and cranny within Isaiah's being, illuminating it all as if by a blinding flash of lightning. Isaiah cried out in desolation, "Woe is me! For I am lost; . . . for my eyes have seen the King, the LORD of hosts!" (Isa. 6:5). He was so overwhelmed by his sin, so mortified, that he was unable to lift his head and worship. That did not happen until his lips had been cleansed. That is, the lips gave expression to what was in the prophet's inner life, his heart, and all that was there needed to be cleansed by the coal, the divine fire, from the altar (Isa. 6:6–7).

In a later chapter, we will return to this theme of worship. Suffice it to say here that what we see in Isaiah's experience is the central, most important element in worship. It is coming face-to-face with God, standing in his presence, bringing forth our praise to him for who he is. This, of course, Isaiah could not do until he was cleansed, and neither can we.

If the greatest commandment is to love God with our whole being, then to come to him in worship is a duty central to living out that love. Worship is not primarily a social occasion as we gather with others to worship, though we are always grateful for the other believers with whom we gather. Worship is not primarily a time for our enjoyment, though being in worship is enjoyable. But worship is primarily an expression of the worth of God. It is a God-centered thing. It is primarily for God and about God; it is not primarily for ourselves and for our needs. Whatever social and psychological benefits it has are secondary. Worship primarily is for *God*. And that was what stood in Isaiah's way. The seraphim were ceaselessly worshiping but he was stricken and mute before God. Until, that is, God enabled him to join the heavenly chorus. This, though, had to be preceded by the terrible consciousness of sin that overwhelmed the prophet.

This experience was an awful, soul-shaking reminder that the nature of sin cannot be concealed in the presence of God's holiness. Its nature is exposed. It cannot hide, cannot evade, cannot change its dress, cannot pass itself off as something other than what it is. It is exposed. And that lesson is often learned the hard way. Those men of Beth-shemesh who irreverently handled "the ark of the LORD" were struck down. Those who survived, no doubt now in some awe, asked, "Who is able to stand before the LORD, this holy God?" (1 Sam. 6:19-20).

In life, sin often does mask its real nature. Indeed, Satan "disguises himself as an angel of light" (2 Cor. 11:14) and, by sleight of hand, makes evil plans and intentions seem good (cf. Gen. 3:4–6). But "God is light, and in him is no darkness at all" (1 John 1:5). God is pure with a purity that excludes the possibility of even the slightest taint of wrong. And this purity lights up everything else. It exposes all that is not pure. God's holiness is not simply reactive, like a boxer who is counterpunching. It is *active*. It goes forth from him. It differentiates who he is from everything that is fallen and all that opposes his will.

This is unmistakably clear in Ezekiel. Through the prophet, God declared that "I will manifest my holiness among you in the sight of the nations" (Ezek. 20:41; cf. 36:23; 38:16). This holiness was not simply a set of cold rules, distant, lifeless, and abstract. It was God himself in his self-revelation as pure, as the one who demands purity and in that demand also insists on separation from the ways of life that seemed so normal in the surrounding pagan nations. A little later God again said, "And they shall know that I am the LORD when I execute judgments in her and manifest my holiness in her" (Ezek. 28:22). This holiness is as present as God himself is. Indeed, it is God in his absolute, burning purity asserting his presence in our world. Sometimes his holiness is veiled, sometimes it is lost to us, but we should not be in doubt that where God is, there is his holiness.

Furthermore, there is not the slightest possibility that God can ever accommodate the evil he opposes. That is an idea we find in some Eastern religion, but it is as far from biblical truth as anything could be. "God," James said, "cannot be tempted with evil" (James 1:13). Evil is never an option for him and, indeed, it is ever and always opposed by him.

God's holiness, then, is not only the opposite of evil; it is the measure by which we know evil to be evil. It illumines everything, and everything is revealed by him for what it is: right or wrong, true or false, good or bad, righteous or evil. It is this holiness, Hannah said, by which "actions are weighed" (1 Sam. 2:3).

The imagery of light, then, is particularly apt in connection with God's holiness. Light dispels darkness and reveals all that darkness covers and conceals. God dwells in "unapproachable light" (1 Tim. 6:16). The psalmist said, "You are clothed with splendor and majesty, covering yourself with light as with a garment" (Ps. 104:1–2). On the mountain, Moses saw the glory of God "like a devouring fire" (Ex. 24:17). It was light that became like a fire that would consume all before it. Indeed, much later the author of Hebrews said specifically that "our God is a consuming fire" (Heb. 12:29). The simplicity of these images of God's character—light and fire—may mislead us. What they convey of God's character is actually many-sided.

In this chapter, we have been thinking about holiness as the comprehensive term that includes all of God's moral perfections. However, Scripture also distinguishes these perfections, sometimes speaking of his goodness, sometimes of his righteousness, sometimes of his mercy, sometimes of his patience, and sometimes of his wrath. These are like light which, in the rainbow, breaks into its several colors. This is true of God's holiness as it is of his love. Each is a complex of attributes.

Here, three of his perfections within his holiness will be considered: his goodness, his righteousness, and his wrath. His holiness sometimes meets us as goodness, sometimes as righteousness, and sometimes as wrath.

Goodness

God is not "the Good" as philosophers have spoken of it. There is no standard of what is good apart from him. He is the standard. Good is defined by who he is. God himself *is* good and he is *the* good. Goodness is a part of the moral purity of his character. It is the power of what is right in its opposition to what is dark and evil.

In the Old Testament, God's goodness was often paired with his "steadfast love." When, for example, the ark was brought into the temple by Solomon, the singers sang that God "is good, for his steadfast love endures forever" (2 Chron. 5:13). There was an obvious reason for this connection. The going out of God's love in redemption, through the covenant, is how our human flourishing is secured. Indeed, it is the only way. And, as we have seen, that flourishing has been secured for all time and eternity in the death and resurrection of Christ. This pairing, therefore, is as natural as the pairing of the sun's light and its warmth.

God's intentions have always and everywhere been good. "The LORD is good to all, and his mercy is over all that he has made" (Ps. 145:9). "For you, O Lord, are good and forgiving, abounding in steadfast love to all who call upon you" (Ps. 86:5). Again the psalmist urges us to give God praise because "the LORD is good; his steadfast love endures forever" (Ps. 100:5; cf. Ps. 25:8; Ps. 136:1). And this goodness spills out in an abundance of gifts in creation. Paul declared that God "did good by giving you rains from heaven and fruitful seasons, satisfying your hearts with food and gladness" (Acts 14:17), and he does so despite human rebellion (Matt. 5:45). Again and again the psalmist celebrated God's providential provisions in creation (e.g., Ps. 104:1–30). It was this that led him to say, "I will sing to the LORD as long as I live; I will sing praise to my God while I have being" (Ps. 104:33). "Every good gift and every perfect gift," James declared, "is from above, coming down from the Father of lights with whom there is no variation or shadow due to change" (James 1:17).

Although we understand God's bounty in creation, it is harder for us to understand exactly how good is the goodness of God. What we meet in life, on both sides of the moral equation, are usually shades of grey. We do not know evil as black as it can be or, for that matter, goodness as good as it really is in God. We see in human life some moderation of both good and evil.

There are, undoubtedly, evil people in every society, those who take undisguised pleasure in hurting, maiming, terrifying, and killing others. There are torturers, cold-blooded killers, those blind to their actions because they are conceited, arrogant, power-possessed, and self-deluded. However, it is not easy for anyone to act out these warped desires unremittingly, without restraint, and indefinitely. Others stand in the way. In contexts of tyranny, where much evil is done, assassins often lurk in the shadows and opponents begin to accumulate, and so the tyrants do not have the complete freedom they would like to have.

In other kinds of society, there are laws. There are law enforcement agencies at work. Invariably the truly evil take to the shadows and work from behind cover of one kind or another. We therefore catch glimpses of what deep evil looks like, but its expressions are usually limited in one way or another.

The same can be said of goodness. There are good people who "by nature do what the law requires" (Rom. 2:14). They can be principled and generous (cf. 1 Cor. 13:2–3). But we also have to say—and say even of those who are redeemed in Christ—that however good and kind they are, human virtue is always qualified. It is never virtue on a par with God's goodness. There is always a worm in the apple. Within the most seemingly selfless acts there can be concealed motives that are unseemly or self-serving. We are all complex creatures. Along with our high, redeemed intentions there linger low and base impulses. Our best thoughts, best actions, and best moments are never entirely free of sin's discoloration. We are, as Luther put it, simultaneously justified and yet sinners. We are, therefore, always ambiguous creatures.

The consequence of all of this is that it is almost impossible for us to imagine how good God's goodness is or how bad Satan's evil really is. In life, what we see most of the time, and what we experience in ourselves, is shades of grey. But in God, there are no greys nor, for that matter, are there in Satan. God's goodness is pure blazing white, and Satan's evil is unrelieved, horrible blackness.

However, imagine a world different from our own, where all of the greys have gone and have yielded before the blazing light of what is completely right. There are a thousand ways, Cornelius Plantinga has said, in which life can go wrong, and so there are a thousand ways in which it can be made to go right, too. And there are a thousand ways in which God is going to make it right, because he is good.

The prophets caught small glimpses of this remade world. They used images and word pictures to catch the thought of a world where harmony and wholeness had returned and where God's people lived amid the blessings that he would shower on them. It was a world where predators and their prey lay down with each other and the prey were untouched, a world where the poor were always judged righteously, where the blind were made to see, and cities were always safe. It was a place where deserts burst into flower, where wine flowed down the mountains, and where water once again ran along dry riverbeds.

Today, we do see some glimmers of this, not in our societies but in the people in whom God's redemption has taken root and in whom eternity has dawned. But there is an even greater day coming when this redemption will have run its course and these partial glimpses will give way to full sight. This is the moment Peter called "the time for restoring all the things about which God spoke by the mouth of his holy prophets long ago" (Acts 3:21). Then will the entire universe be cleansed. Swept away in judgment will be all that has brought ruin, rebellion, and heartache. The world then will be filled only with wonder upon wonder, delight upon delight, because this will be a world where God's goodness is finally and completely triumphant. There will be the music of joy and dance. The air will be filled with pure delight. All creation will sing before its Creator (cf. Rom. 8:20–23) and the redeemed will bow down in uninterrupted joy (Jude 24), "lost in wonder, love, and praise" as the old hymn put it.

This coming triumph, already inaugurated but not yet completed, flows from the cross. It is because of Christ's conquest on the cross that the back of evil was broken. And there righteousness was established—the righteousness that is at the heart of God's goodness (Matt. 19:16–22). This is what brings such wonder and delight.

Righteousness

God, Scripture often declares, is righteous (e.g., 1 John 2:29). Because of that, God acts uprightly (Gen. 18:25), is always just (Ps. 11:7), is always manifestly pure, is utterly faithful. He is "a God of faithfulness and without iniquity," Moses sang, "just and upright is he" (Deut. 32:4).

Indeed, this is exactly what we see manifested in the life of Christ. It was sometimes stated in the negative. Pilate found "no guilt" in him

(John 18:38); the thief on the cross next to him confessed his own guilt and then said that "this man has done nothing wrong" (Luke 23:41); the centurion who was responsible for Jesus's execution said "this man was innocent!" (Luke 23:47); and Judas despaired that he had betrayed "innocent blood" (Matt. 27:4).

On the positive side, Christ said that he had glorified the Father in his life (John 17:4) and that he always did "the things that are pleasing" to the Father (John 8:29). John, who had lived and traveled with Jesus, called him "Jesus Christ the righteous" (1 John 2:1), and Peter declared him to be "a lamb without blemish or spot" (1 Pet. 1:19). He was, the Scripture says, without sin. He was, therefore, without any consciousness of sin, fully human though he was. More than that, as we have seen, he was the embodiment of God's character, and in this he showed what human life had originally been intended to be. And at his second coming he will be the very Judge of all sin. It is he who, on the last day, will say to some, "I never knew you; depart from me, you workers of lawlessness" (Matt. 7:23). This theme of divine righteousness, then, which we see being lived out in the life of Christ, now needs to be unpacked a little more.

Righteousness is used more commonly of God's actions than of his character. Of course, the reason that he always does what is right, always renders true verdicts, is that he is righteous in character. His being and his actions are all of a piece. He could never act unrighteously because his character is always and everywhere upright and just.

However, the connection between God's righteous character and his righteous actions, especially in the keeping of his covenant with the people of God, has become a vexed one in the learned academy. The reason, of course, is that in the New Testament, the whole doctrine of justification hinges on what it means that "the righteousness" of God is revealed in the gospel (Rom. 1:17). What is the "free gift of righteousness" that Christ won at the cross (Rom. 5:17)? What does it mean that through Christ we have become "the righteousness of God" (2 Cor. 5:21)?

We will come back to this matter later. It is complicated. However, one thing we can say with certainty is that God does not impart his righteousness to us in order to make us covenant keepers, law keepers, in order that he can justify us at the end of time. That is the traditional Catholic way of thinking, and the Reformers were right to turn their backs on it. When Paul referred to "the righteousness of God," then, it is very hard to see that he meant that we have been made righteous. No, the thought is that we have been *declared* righteous and clothed in a righteousness that fully corresponds with who God is in his own righteous character. That is different.

But this fact creates a problem in our minds. How can sinners be clothed in a righteousness so completely alien to who they are in themselves? How can those who themselves confess their own unrighteousness be seen by God, who knows everything, as righteous? If he is the just Judge who always renders just verdicts, how can he also be our Savior in this way? If he were to judge justly, would he not issue a verdict that was injurious to every sinner? How, then, can his actions of redeeming lost sinners be seen to be just if, as seems to be the case, his redemption perverts the justice that is deserved? The dilemma, as Paul stated it, was how God might be "just and the justifier of the one who has faith in Jesus" (Rom. 3:26). And this is, of course, the glory of the doctrine of justification: that in Christ repentant, believing sinners are clothed with a divine righteousness that is entirely alien to who they actually are.

There is another side to this dilemma. If God is righteous, how could he *not* be a Savior?

After all, he cannot abandon the covenant that he made with Abraham. That would be impossible to do. Were he to do so, he would have acted in a way that was unfaithful to his promise. He would be shown to be fickle and unreliable. The reverse is true. He will "remember his covenant forever" (1 Chron. 16:15–17; Jer. 33:25–26). His righteousness, in fact, is often depicted as the way in which he is faithful to that promise. His righteousness is therefore connected to how he acts in grace and goodness to forgive sin. Through Isaiah, God comforted his people, saying, "My righteousness draws near, my salvation has gone out, and my arms will judge the peoples; . . . my salvation will be forever, and my righteousness will never be dismayed" (Isa. 51:5–6). His righteousness, then, is what makes us right with God (Isa. 42:6). So it is that he is a "righteous God and a Savior" (Isa. 45:21).

Much the same is said in Hosea. Israel was a child whom God "loved" (Hos. 11:1). God led these people out of Egypt, taught them, took them up in his arms, healed them, and fed them (Hos. 11:1–4). They, however, rebelled. They would not listen. They would not obey. So judgment was pronounced against them. "The sword shall rage against their cities . . . and devour them because of their own counsels" (Hos. 11:6). But then God's heart recoils within him. His compassion goes out to his own covenant people. "I will not execute my burning anger," he declares, "for I am God and not a man, the Holy One in your midst, and I will not come in wrath" (Hos. 11:9). Here, perhaps more than anywhere else in the Old Testament, is found this startling conjunction of the simultaneous demands of God's righteousness and of his love. It seems as if the one cannot be satisfied if the other is. This, of course, all points quite dramatically toward the cross, where righteous judgment and grace come together. The demands of each are resolved.

Wrath

In all Western cultures, I have suggested, the love of God is welcomed and the holiness of God is given inhospitable treatment. Western nations will tolerate almost anything except a hard truth like this. We therefore do need to do a little ground-clearing work—because this idea has been so widely misunderstood and is so easily caricatured.

If we are to understand the biblical teaching, we must distinguish between wrath in God and what we so often see in human anger. Human anger is often accompanied by malice, vindictiveness, retaliation, revenge, and hatefulness. God's wrath, of course, has no such defilements. It is a pure expression of his holiness. It is not an outburst of irrational temper. Temper, malice, revenge were seen in some of the ancient gods and goddesses. They could be capricious, bad-tempered, and destructive. God, though, is not. He is none of these things and never could be. His wrath is instead about restoring to an unchallenged position all that is good, pure, true, beautiful, and right. And it is about removing everything that challenges his rule because it is bad, impure, rebellious, repugnant, or otherwise evil.

This wrath is the way in which God's holiness finally engages all that is wrong, all that has defiled his world, all that has defied his law, all that has rejected his rule, and all that has spurned his love expressed in Christ. It is the pure reaction of God to all that is impure. It is the dissatisfaction that arises within God over all that is other than what it should be, all that is dark, all that still has a raised fist. Wrath is his repudiation of all of that. It is the way in which he upholds the moral order of the universe.

Luther spoke of this wrath as God's "strange" work and of his love as his "proper" work. The intention, no doubt, was to show that God's final word, and the word most representative of his deepest intentions, is grace, and that judgment is a deviation, however necessary, from his core intention.

This is, however, an unwise distinction. Wrath is quite as much God's proper work as is his love. God's wrath is not an aberration, not some kind of deviation from who he is. It is an expression of his holiness, and that holiness is what God has been like from all eternity. Indeed, the perspective of Scripture is that God's wrath solves moral dilemmas rather than creating them. The biblical writers had no difficulty in declaring that God will act in judgment. The difficulty would be if he did not act, for then evil would have triumphed. As it is, the day of reckoning is coming. When God finally acts to eliminate all evil, heaven will ring in triumphant shouts of joy. God has finally, and decisively, asserted his holy character! Until this moment, those in heaven are in suspense, saying, "O Sovereign Lord, holy and true, how long before you will judge and avenge our blood on those who dwell on the earth?" (Rev. 6:10).

When we speak of God as Judge, and of his actions in judging, we need to distinguish these, in some ways, from the court system with which we are today so familiar. This court system has a set of rules to ensure that justice is administered in a dispassionate way. The judge's main task is to ensure that the rules are followed. That is what secures impartiality. But this is entirely unnecessary with God.

In the Old Testament, since God is inherently fair and righteous, procedural rules do not have to be put in place. It is his *character* that secures the impartiality that we try to ensure in our court system. That is why his judgment is often mentioned side by side with references to his character. "Righteousness and justice are the foundation of your throne," the psalmist said, "steadfast love and faithfulness go before you" (Ps. 89:14). "I will sing of steadfast love and justice" (Ps. 101:1; cf. Ps. 111:7). And God said to Israel through the prophet, "I will betroth you to me in righteousness and in justice, in steadfast love and in mercy" (Hos. 2:19). There is in God's judgment both a love for people and a love for what is right. His justice arises within his character of love.

Already, though, two major differences are emerging when we compare God as Judge with our judicial system. First, his judgment comes from within one in whom is also found mercy, love, and faithfulness. It is a judgment that is qualitatively different from the cold, dispassionate working of the wheels of justice in our judicial system.

Second, when God acts in judgment, it is not simply an execution of law in the universe but it is, in fact, an encounter with God himself. It is, of course, true that God sometimes uses secondary means to bring about his ends. Often, he brought upon Israel in its moments of spiritual wandering the fierce oppression of other, marauding nations (e.g., Judg. 6:1–6; Amos 5:25–27). And certainly, sin brings its own immediate consequences. Sin is its own immediate judgment. Hosea said of God's people that "They shall eat, but not be satisfied; they shall play the whore, but not multiply, because they have forsaken the LORD to cherish whoredom, wine, and new wine, which take away the understanding" (Hos. 4:10). They were disobedient, they had no regard for the truth and commandments of God, and so they lost their way even more.

This is exactly what Paul said many years later when reflecting on how sin worked out in his own time. Because men and women had turned away from God and from what was right, God "gave them up," he says three times, to the captivity of their lusts, to degrading passions, and to a debased mind (Rom. 1:24, 26, 28). This was, and is, God's initial judgment. Not only so, but Paul even sees the state in this light. Wrongdoers in society will bear their punishment. But when the law is thus carried out, it is a bit more than simply the machinery of the legal system at work. It is also part of God's providence. The ruler "is the servant of God, an avenger who carries out God's wrath on the wrongdoer" (Rom. 13:4).

Sometimes, as we have seen, God works through people as he brings about his judgment. We should be in no doubt, though, that even when God so acts, this judgment is the judgment of our personal God. Judgment is about being encountered by this God in his holiness. It is an encounter as personal as meeting one's neighbor next door. It is personal because it is the reaction of God's holiness to sin—not to sin in the abstract, but to particular sin, particular dispositions, and ways of looking at life that people and nations have.

God's judgment is, therefore, a present reality. Indeed, part of the language used for divine judgment has the sense of ruling. When Absalom yearned to take his father's position he said, "Oh that I were judge in the land! Then every man with a dispute or cause might come to me, and I would give him justice" (2 Sam. 15:4; cf. 1 Sam. 8:20). Judging sometimes has this sense of ruling. And on a cosmic scale, God is ruling today. He is enthroned. He is exercising his sovereign rule, and part of this rule is moral. He is upholding the moral order of the universe in the face of all of the onslaughts of evil upon it. However, how he judges evil, and why he continues to allow it, and why he does not halt it, are all part of a mystery that has not yet been fully unfolded to us. It is clear, though, that Christ himself was in no doubt about his Father's moral rule. When he was reviled, we are told, Christ did not retaliate "but continued entrusting himself to him who judges justly" (1 Pet. 2:23).

It is the climax to this process, though, of which Scripture speaks the most. Its focus is on the moment when Christ returns and acts decisively to remove all evil from the universe and establish his rule in a way that will no longer be contested.

In the Old Testament, this was captured in the phrase "the day of the Lord." This was a battle as yet in the future when Yahweh would come to earth, redeem Israel, and rebuff all of her enemies. It was, therefore, a time that was greatly anticipated. "Then shall all the trees of the forest sing for joy before the LORD," said the psalmist, "for he comes, for he comes to judge the earth" (Ps. 96:12–13; Ps. 97:1). That would also be a day, Isaiah said, when all of the idols would be cast aside and people would head for hiding places, running "before the terror of the LORD, and from the splendor of his majesty" (Isa. 2:21; cf.

Mal. 4:5). This Day was, then, a two-sided moment that would bring ecstatic joy and terrifying wrath.

In the unfolding of God's truth as we move from the Old Testament into the New, we are given more light on this "day." It is now called the "day of the Lord" (1 Thess. 5:2; 2 Pet. 3:10), the "day of God" (2 Pet. 3:12), the "day of Christ" (Phil. 2:16), or simply "that day" (1 Thess. 5:4; cf. 2 Tim. 4:8). It will come at the end of time. Everyone, Peter says, "will give account to him who is ready to judge the living and the dead" (1 Pet. 4:5; 2 Tim. 4:1), and not simply Israel's enemies. It will be a terrible day of judgment, what Jesus called "the wrath to come" (Matt. 3:7). And, in fact, he is both the Judge on this day and the Savior who now "delivers us from the wrath to come" (1 Thess. 1:10). This is the day, "the day of wrath," Paul tells us, "when God's righteous judgment will be revealed" (Rom. 2:5).

This "day of the Lord will come like a thief," Peter tells us. It will be sudden and unexpected. Life will be going on in its normal routines as it has for millennia. But suddenly, God's redemptive plans will have been fulfilled and "the heavens will pass away with a roar" (2 Pet. 3:10). And so, "according to his promise we are waiting for new heavens and a new earth in which righteousness dwells" (2 Pet. 3:13).

God, then, is holy in his being. He is good and righteous in all of his actions. That righteousness will one day become the broom that sweeps the universe clean. Such is his holiness. The psalmist rejoiced in this holiness even as it filled him with awe. "Bless the LORD, O my soul, and all that is within me, bless his holy name!" (Ps. 103:1). Later, he says that the purpose of salvation is "that we may give thanks to your holy name and glory in your praise" (Ps. 106:47; cf. 1 Chron. 16:35). Still later, he encourages everyone to "bless his holy name forever and ever" (Ps. 145:21). "Worship the LORD in the splendor of holiness; tremble before him, all the earth." Let heaven and earth say, "the LORD reigns!" (1 Chron. 16:29–31).

Through a Lens

God—this God of holy-love—is not simply a subject about whom we can talk. He is not simply a theme in a book of doctrine. No. He now stands before us. But what we see, the one who we think is before us, may be vastly different from who is actually there. Our experience in this culture creates in us ways of thinking and ways of wanting that may take us into a very different place from where Scripture wants us to be. We see God, very often, through the lens of our culture. And that may even change the meaning of our faith.

Our culture, as I have suggested, fills us with plenty and then empties us out. In so doing, it often forces our hand. It shapes the way we see things, what we see, and what importance all of it has to us. It allows us our own private reality because it inclines us to live only within ourselves and to see all of reality from behind this peephole. We see everything from the position of the self with its senses and aches and needs. This shapes everything else. In this psychological world, the God of love is a God of love precisely and only because he offers us inward balm. Empty, distracted, meandering, and dissatisfied, we come to him for help. Fill us, we ask, with a sense of completeness! Fill our emptiness! Give us a sense of direction amid the mass of competing ways and voices in the modern world! Fill the aching emptiness within! This is how many in the church today, especially in the evangelical church, are thinking. It is how they are praying. They are yearning for something more real within themselves than what they currently have. This is true of adults and of teenagers as well. Yes, we say earnestly, hopefully, maybe even a little wistfully, be to us the God of love!

Those who live in this psychological world think differently from those who inhabit a moral world. In a psychological world, we want *therapy*; in a moral world, a world of right and wrong and good and evil, we want *redemption*. In a psychological world, we want to be *happy*. In a moral world, we want to be *holy*. In the one, we want to *feel* good, but in the other we want to *be* good.

In truth, the God of love inhabits a moral world because he is also the God of light. His is a consuming love but he is also a consuming fire. We cannot know his love except in its union with what is holy.

God therefore stands before us not as our Therapist or our Concierge. He stands before us as the God of utter purity to whom we are morally accountable. He is objective to us and not lost within the misty senses of our internal world. His Word comes to us from outside of our self because it is the Word of his truth. It summons us to stand before the God of the universe, to hear his command that we must love him and love our neighbors as ourselves. He is not before us to be used by us. He is not there begging to enter our internal world and satisfy our therapeutic needs. We are before him to hear his *commandment*. And his commandment is that we should be holy, which is a much greater thing than being happy. It is a commandment to be holy but not a promise that we will be made whole. We will not be made whole in this life. We will carry life's wounds with us, and we will be beset by painful perplexities and our own personal failures. It is true that there are psychological benefits to following Christ, and happiness may be its by-product. These, though, are not fundamentally what Christian faith is about. It is about the *God* who is other than ourselves, who is the infinite and gracious God. But let us never forget, it is this God who also summons us to come and die at the foot of Christ's cross.

God begins to have weight in our lives only when we begin to hear his summons from outside ourselves. He summons us to stand before him, to hear his Word, to know him as he is in his holy-love. When we begin to do so, reality enters our soul. It begins to replace our wishful thinking, our illusions, our dreaming, our many futile and fumbling attempts at remaking our private world.

In the famous opening lines of his *Institutes of the Christian Religion*, Calvin observed that our highest wisdom consists of two parts: knowledge of God and knowledge of ourselves. He was thinking of the knowledge of ourselves in light of God's self-disclosure to us. We know ourselves to be wanderers from the path of what is true and right, to be rebels who lift up fists in defiance of God's rule in life. And it is only when we have plumbed our own weaknesses, our own waywardness, our willfulness, and have done so in light of who God actually is that we are ready to see the depths in his goodness, righteousness, and grace. We will not see him clearly in these ways until we *long* to see him. And we will not yearn to see God in this way until we have stood terror-struck in his presence. Strange as it sounds, our relationship to God is established, as Luther said, not on the basis of our holiness but on the basis of our sin. That is our *entrée* into the knowledge of God. And it is this thread that will lead us into our next chapter.

CHAPTER 6

A Sight Too Glorious

Crown Him the Lord of love! Behold His hands and side,
Those wounds, yet visible above, in beauty glorified:
No angel in the sky can fully bear the sight,
But downward bends his burning eye at mysteries so bright.

MATTHEW BRIDGES

It was a death that many others had also suffered. In fact, it was an event so common in the first-century Roman world that Jesus's crucifixion almost passed unnoticed. For the soldiers who carried it out, it was an unexceptional part of their routine. As for the Jewish leaders who had opposed Christ, it was a fitting end to their problem. Soon, they were back to business as usual. And although the resurrection was to happen shortly thereafter, and although the disciples were to be emboldened in their preaching, and although the Holy Spirit was to authenticate what they said by miracles, the historians of that day also missed the significance of this event. By the time the Roman empire awoke under emperor Nero, by the time the night sky over his garden was lit by the bodies of burning Christians, it was too late. The gospel had already traveled far and wide.

The spread of this gospel was both geographical and social. It moved not only out but also up. It went from slaves like Onesimus, to the wealthy like Lydia, to the well-connected like Manaen, and on to the powerful like the Ethiopian eunuch. The gospel quickly penetrated all layers of society. Even as early as Paul's day, it had already entered Caesar's household. But what is remarkable is that this gospel message was grounded in a death that was common and ignominious. It had happened with very few even noticing.

However, even those who did notice, those who stood around that wooden cross on that day, could not see its real significance from the outside. Looking was not enough. Let me explain.

There is a distinction between the crucifixion and the cross. The former was a particularly barbaric way of carrying out an execution, and it was the method of execution that Jesus endured. The latter, as the New Testament speaks of it, has to do with the mysterious exchange that took place in Christ's death, an exchange of our sin for his righteousness. It was there that our judgment fell on the One who is also our Judge. Indeed, he who had made all of creation was dishonored in the very creation he had made. And yet, through this dark moment, this fierce judgment, through this dishonor, there now shines the light of God's triumph over sin, death, and the Devil. And in this moment, this moment of Jesus's judgment-death, God was revealed in his holy-love as nowhere else.

This, however, was not seen from the outside. Besides Christ's cry of dereliction—"My God, my God, why have you forsaken me?" (Matt. 27:46)—there was little to indicate what was really happening. For that we need to think back to the Old Testament with its prophetic foretelling of the cross and to Jesus's own expressed understanding of it, and we need to look on to the apostles for their more complete exposition of it. Without this, the meaning of Christ's death is lost on us. We would see the execution but, without God's explicating revelation, it would remain mute. It would be a death like any other death except for its disgrace. God must interpret his own actions, and so he has. Without this, we too are mute.

That is why dramatic presentations of Christ's death, such as on TV and in movies, so often miss the point. They give us the crucifixion, not the cross. They show the horrifying circumstances of his death. These circumstances may be shown accurately. But this can take us only so far. It leaves us with only a biographical Christ, who may be interesting, but not with the eternal Christ whom we need for our salvation. The crucifixion without the cross is an incomplete picture, a half-told story. What is omitted is the *meaning* of the event. We do not carry this meaning within ourselves, nor can we find it in this world. What eludes us is something we have to be *given* by God himself, for only he can say what was happening within the Godhead as Christ was killed and, in his death, atoned for our sin. This is indispensable to the meaning of Christian faith. Without it, Christ's death is only a martyrdom and Christian faith is just a nice, moral religion but one that is neither unique nor uniquely true.

This chapter is going to show how the crucifixion became the cross. In order to do this, I need to build up the argument in four steps. First, we must see that Christ's incarnate life was no random sequence of events. There was nothing accidental about it. Rather, in Christ's life and death we see the sovereign, eternal, steady purposes of God being worked out. Second, in his death, he was a *substitute* for us. Third, we need to see how the apostles ransacked their imaginations to find word-pictures that would show us how this substitution accomplished God's purposes. Finally, we must think about how Christ's death magnified the holiness of God that required it and the love of God that provided it.

Born to Die

Judas

In *Jesus Christ Superstar*, a disillusioned Judas says disparagingly that every time he looked at Jesus he wondered why he had allowed things to get so out of hand. Christ, he suggests, should have done some better preplanning. He should not have chosen as his venue such a strange people and he should not have come in such a backward time.

It is true, of course, that the story of Christ in the Gospels does seem to move to its climax somewhat chaotically. Someone reading the gospel accounts for the first time today might have no idea how the story will play out. There is high, built-in drama as it nears its end, though. The opposition gathers force, political calculations are made, actions are taken, and the story ends.

However, what this modern version of Judas apparently missed was the fact that Jesus was driven by a deep, eternal purpose. It is quite clear that Jesus would follow this purpose through to the end despite the growing animosity. As a boy, for example, when he had lingered behind in the temple, he said to his parents, "Why were you looking for me? Did you not know that I *must* be in my Father's house?" (Luke 2:49). And then, in different contexts and times, he re-iterated the fact that he "*must* go to Jerusalem and suffer many things from the elders and chief priests and scribes, and be killed, and on the third day be raised" (Matt. 16:21; Mark 8:31; Luke 9:22; 17:25; 24:7). And afterwards, when he walked with the befuddled disciples on the way to Emmaus, he asked: "was it not *necessary* that the Christ should suffer these things . . . ?" (Luke 24:26). Many times, he said he had been "sent" into the world (e.g., John 4:34; 5:23, 30; 6:38–40, 44), and it is clear that he had come in order to die. The reader of the Gospels catches this truth. A divine purpose was driving the mission of Christ. At the ground level, though, the events did seem chaotic, unplanned, merely the product of human machinations, the outcome unclear and unpredictable. The reality was, however, that there was a mysterious conjunction occurring here between God's sovereign purposes and the choices that sinful people were making.

The case of Judas is especially striking in this regard. This much we know for sure about Judas as he actually appears in Scripture. He was among the original twelve chosen to be apostles (Matt. 10:4). He was with Jesus from this point onward. He heard Christ's teaching, witnessed the miracles, and must have seen the glimmers of an oth-erworldly reality in Christ, as did the others. Yet Christ was deeply disappointing to him. It is not clear why. It has been speculated that Judas was a revolutionary and imagined that Jesus would lead the over-throw of Roman power. When it was clear that this would not happen, Judas became disaffected. This might have been the explanation, but the narrative does not throw a lot of light on his motives.

The evening Judas set off on his errand of betrayal, he was at a dinner. His disappointment with Christ had been kept so private that none of the other disciples had any idea what he was thinking. At this dinner, though, Jesus announced that he was about to be betrayed and then, by passing the "morsel of bread" to Judas (John 13:26), in-dicated who the betrayer would be. How did Jesus know? The other disciples were so unsuspecting of Judas that they imagined that he had been sent by Jesus on a mission of mercy to the poor (John 13:29).

In this moment, Judas was at the edge of his own personal precipice. Now, there could be no question that he was in the presence of God-incarnate. But he had closed his heart to Christ long before this time. Step-by-step, he had hardened his own descent into evil. At this dinner, this descent was sealed. "Satan entered into him" (John 13:27). The narrative closes with the simple words, "And it was night" (John 13:30).

It was night in more ways than one. It was night in Judas's soul. He went on to betray Christ for reasons that seemed good and sufficient to him. Perhaps he thought he was making an astute political calculation. We know that he was an unprincipled man. Deception, apparently, was second nature to him (John 12:1–8), so he may well have been in it initially for what he thought he might get out of it. Perhaps there was an element of revenge for the disillusionment he had suffered. Maybe there was conceit: Christ was not worthy of his loyalty. There was the money, too. This is the point, though. The dark motives—whatever they were—became the very means God used in working out his sovereign purpose. A little later, at Pentecost, Peter declared that "this Jesus, delivered up according to the definite plan and foreknowledge of God, you crucified and killed by the hands of lawless men" (Acts 2:23). Delivered up by God? In the Gospel accounts, he was delivered up by Judas's definite plan! How do we resolve this?

Divine Sovereignty

What we should see, quite simply, is that God used the evil in Judas's soul to accomplish his own ends. Through the betrayal by Judas, for which Scripture condemns him, God's settled will, fixed in eternity, came to be realized.

We see the same kind of thing much earlier in Scripture in the life of Joseph. His brothers betrayed him, but God, in his sovereign purposes, worked through that evil to bring much good. "You," Joseph said to them later, "meant evil against me, but God meant it for good" (Gen. 50:20; cf. Gen. 45:8). So it was here with Christ. Herod, Pilate, and the others responsible for his death did "whatever your hand and your plan had predestined to take place" (Acts 4:28). "Christ," Peter said elsewhere, "was foreknown before the foundation of the world but was made manifest in the last times . . ." and then betrayed into his death (1 Pet. 1:20–21). That betrayal was the means by which the sovereign purpose of God was worked out. We are clearly at the edge of deep mystery here.

How could God brush so close to evil? How could he come so close to the flames without ever being singed? And how could Judas act freely in doing what he did so that he was held accountable while also acting as the instrument of God's will?

It is as natural as it is mistaken for us to think that God's sovereignty and our responsibility are mutually exclusive. That is, we are inclined to think that the only way our freedom of will can be preserved is if God does not interfere with its exercise. Or, to look at the other side of this dilemma: if God acts sovereignly in a situation, and works through our desires, we think that we cannot be held responsible for what then takes place. The case of Judas, though, completely exposes our fallacious thinking. God did act sovereignly in delivering up Christ, and Judas did act freely in betraying him. As Augustine observed a long time ago, the Father gave up his Son, Christ gave up himself, and Judas gave up his master. The Father and Son acted righteously. Judas acted wickedly. Divine sovereignty and human responsibility, it turned out, were not mutually exclusive, or mutually limiting, but both were there and both were fully real. And it is in this strange conjunction of things that the crucifixion did not remain just another crucifixion. It became the cross.

It is, then, also quite mistaken to think, as some have, that God had to improvise his plan along the way, that he had not foreseen the hostile reception that awaited Christ, and that he had to make adaptations to it. Once he saw what the actual situation was, the argument goes, he devised a new plan that he then wove through the events as they were unfolding. But this reading of the Gospel accounts could not be more mistaken. The truth is that God's "definite plan" was fixed in eternity and was never subject to revision. It was because of this plan that the second person of the Godhead was incarnate. It is why he was compelled to go to Jerusalem and to the death that awaited him there. This was his mission. It was the purpose for which he had come.

This means that our redemption arose in the far reaches of eternity and in the Father's heart. Let us make no mistake about this. Many have been the proposals that have seen Christian faith to be a mere human construction. Historians have searched for its origins, and some have found them in the mystery religions. Others have seen its origins in human longing and need. Christian faith, they think, is a mere projection of these longings. It is the result of our desire to see ourselves in a greater universe than just our own private, internal worlds. They have made Christianity a thoroughly this-worldly affair.

But we need to say, with respect, that Christian faith was neither a product of other religions nor a psychological projection. Nor yet was it an invention of the apostles against what Jesus himself had taught, as the older liberals once declared. Nor did it begin even in the Gospels. It did not begin with the young unmarried mother for whom no one would give up a bed. It did not begin with Jesus's life, with his teaching, or with his death. It did not begin with his resurrection, or with his ascension.

We must look behind all of this, behind that bare stable, the cold night, and the inn's closed door. We must look into eternity past. We must look to that place where Christ was in the Father's presence, where he shared the Father's glory "before the world existed" (John 17:5). We must look back to the moment in the eternal counsels—if we may be allowed to use this kind of time language—when redemption was conceived and Christ took it upon himself to become incarnate. That is when Christian faith began. It began in the eternal counsels of God. Without the incarnation, death, and resurrection of Christ there would be no Christian faith. But without the eternal counsel of God, there would have been no incarnation, atonement, and resurrection.

That God has thus planned our redemption from all eternity delivers a declaration louder than any thunderclap. It is that he is *for* us, that he has always been *for* us. He was *for* us in the far reaches of eternity. It was there that he took thought of us even before we existed. It was there that he planned to act for us. This plan was there from the very beginning. He planned to do this knowing that once we fell into the disorder of sin our fist would be raised against him. But his grace preceded us. It preempted our refusal to submit to him. He did for us what we could not do for ourselves. He refused to abandon us as orphans in the world. On the contrary, from all eternity he planned

135

to effect our rescue and adoption. Can we find a more reassuring word than this?

Indeed, can we describe this in any other way than grace? This is, indeed, the whole meaning of grace. It is his unearned favor extended to those who can make no claim on it, who must receive it as a gift, with hands open and outstretched. That is how we come, and this is ever the posture of faith. But the only reason we come, the only reason we *can* come, is that before we do so God has already come to us. He was there before us. He was there before all time. He was there for us in eternity past. And because of this he acted before we could act. Indeed, he acted because we cannot act for ourselves. In eternity past, within the counsels of the Trinity—Father, Son, and Holy Spirit—our creation and redemption were conceived.

In Our Place, For Our Sin

This divine plan for our redemption is revealed in Scripture. However, it was not revealed all at once. In fact, its unfolding happened only very slowly and across great epochs of time.

The first hint of what was to come is heard in the judgment God pronounced on Satan: "cursed are you . . . dust you shall eat all the days of your life" (Gen. 3:14). This is figurative language describing conquest, submission, and humiliation (Ps. 72:9; Isa. 49:23; Mic. 7:17). Satan's "head" was going to be bruised under the heel of Adam and Eve's offspring (Gen. 3:15). Much later, Paul could see this already being inaugurated because of Christ's conquest on the cross. To the Roman Christians he offered the encouragement that the "God of peace will soon crush Satan under your feet" (Rom. 16:20; cf. Rev. 12:1–17). But of course this crushing, this conquest, the final and total humiliation of Satan, has not been completed. It is still in process. At the cross, the back of evil was broken but evil was not itself eliminated. It will continue its perverse, rebellious, God-hating, dark work until the return of Christ, the end of time, and the final judgment when the universe will be swept clean of all that has darkened and ruined it.

But thus began the movement toward the cross. It would pass through Abraham and the promise made to him. It would pass on down through time in a stream of electing grace. It would come to its destination in Christ. This was why he came and why he *had* to go to Calvary. This river would then flow on from the cross and into our world. It has created a vast, multinational people of God from every tribe and nation. This is the City of God that lives amid the earthly City of Man, to use Augustine's language. It is God's kingdom, the kingdom in which we see the dawning of the "age to come," though it is not yet consummated. And the church, which is the result of this dawning age, is called to live out its life amid all of the fallen kingdoms of this world.

But how was God's plan made effective? It is on this that we must now focus more fully.

In Our Place

We can divide the passages of Scripture that speak of Christ's death into two groups. In one group, he is said to have died *for* us. That is, his death was substitutionary. His death was for our benefit and for our sake. It was on our behalf and, more precisely, in our place. In the other group of passages, this substitutionary death is interpreted for us. Christ died in our place for our sin, because of our captivity, and to spare us from God's wrath. The first set of passages simply state the *fact* of his substitution. The second *interpret* this fact. We will take them in order.

In a large number of passages, Christ's substitution, his death *for* us, is stated. The good shepherd, Christ said, "lays down his life *for* the sheep" (John 10:11). Greater love has no one than this, that "someone lay down his life *for* his friends" (John 15:13–14). We are those friends for whom Christ died. Christ "died *for* the ungodly" (Rom. 5:6). He "died *for* us" (Rom. 5:8; see also Rom. 8:32; 1 Thess. 5:10; Titus 2:14; Heb. 6:20, 7:24; 1 Pet. 2:21; 1 John 3:16). He died *for* all" (2 Cor. 5:15). "Christ loved us," Paul says, "and gave himself up *for* us" (Eph. 5:2). "Christ loved the church and gave himself up *for* her" (Eph. 5:25). Christ died, "the righteous *for* the unrighteous" (1 Pet. 3:18). He tasted death "*for* everyone" (Heb. 2:9). The Communion wine represents his blood, his life in sacrifice, "which is poured out *for* many" (Mark 14:24). It was, then, for his sheep, for his friends, for the ungodly, for us, for the church, for the unjust, and for the many that he died. That is the fact.

137

For Our Sin

In the second set of passages, the fact of Christ's substitution is interpreted for us. For example, Paul said that "Christ died *for our sins*" (1 Cor. 15:3; cf. Rom. 8:3). He gave "himself *for our sins* to deliver us from this present evil age" (Gal. 1:4). He became "a *curse for* us" (Gal. 3:13). He was made *sin for* us (2 Cor. 5:21). He "gave himself as a *ransom for* all" (1 Tim. 2:6). The writer of Hebrews said that Jesus "offered for all time a single *sacrifice for* sins" (Heb. 10:12). John used a different Greek preposition but he made the same point when he wrote that Christ "is the *propitiation for* our sins . . ." (1 John 2:2).

In a striking statement, Jesus said that the Son of Man "came not to be served but to serve, and to give his life as a *ransom for* many" (Mark 10:45). This is a different Greek preposition than those mentioned above, but it clearly carries the same meaning. Paul used it, for example, when he said that we are to "repay no one evil *for* evil" (Rom. 12:17). We are not to engage in retaliation, which seeks to return as much pain as has been received. That retaliation would be *for* the injury received. It would be the one for the other. Similarly, Hebrews tells us that Esau "sold his birthright *for* a single meal" (Heb. 12:16). It was an exchange: his birthright *for* that meal. This is clearly the sense in which Christ here speaks of his own death. His death was not simply on behalf of others but it was *instead* of others. It was *in place* of the "many."

This highly unusual expression, Christ giving himself as a "ransom," might be seen against the backdrop of warfare, of prisoners who were captured and then released by the payment of a price. This certainly is a motif in the New Testament understanding of his death. But far more likely, Jesus had in mind the Old Testament guilt offering and the suffering servant. It "was the will of the LORD," we read, "to crush him; he has put him to grief; when his soul makes an offering *for* guilt" (Isa. 53:10). This servant was entirely innocent (Isa. 53:9) and yet he is a sacrifice in place of others. On him were their sins laid (Isa. 53:6). The thought, then, is that Christ, the predicted suffering servant, surrendered his life in atonement, doing for sinners what they could not do for themselves, and from this substitutionary self-surrender he gained the release of the "many." Jesus stood in their place, their place of captivity to sin, guilt, death, and judgment. Because he has stood there for them, the many can now stand in his place, the place of freedom from the guilt of sin, freedom from the hold of the law, and therefore freedom from divine condemnation. This all rests on Christ being our substitute in the divine treatment of our sin. As Paul would put it later in a key text, Christ "who knew no sin" was made "to be sin" for us (2 Cor. 5:21).

Christ, who made our sin his own, entered a place that should have been ours. He entered our existence and made it his own. He entered our world and made our plight his own. He took up our cause. He took up what was not properly his so that we might have that to which we have no right. He stood before God, at the cross, as our representative. He tasted death for us by dying in our place. In a strange and beautiful paradox, he who is our Judge submitted to the penalty for our sin. And in this moment, this moment of judgment, our sin was no longer ours. It became his. That righteousness which was and is his became ours by a transfer that is as mysterious as it is real.

This substitution is not only at the core of the gospel; it is at the center of God's revelation of himself, of his character, and of his saving intentions. It is the center of Christian faith and the center of our knowledge of God. Without it, we have neither gospel nor faith. Without it, much of what we know of God's character would be far less clearly etched in our minds than it now is.

That being the case, we need to think, step-by-step, what this divine self-substitution entailed and what it means. How does the New Testament plumb these depths of Christ's death *for* sin?

In the New Testament, this idea of Christ being our substitute in the divine remedy for sin is explained through a series of word pictures. Here we will select just three of these. They come out of the spheres of the law court (justification), human relations (reconciliation), and warfare (ransom).

These are analogies. That is, there are both similarities and dissimilarities between Christ's work and how the legal system works and how human conflict unfolds and warfare happens. It is important for us to understand this lest we press the parallels too far. There is not, for example, an actual heavenly courtroom, with a robed judge, a prosecutor, an accused, a jury, and then a verdict followed by sentencing. It is therefore foolish to argue, as some have, that since no earthly court would tolerate one person substituting for another and taking the guilty party's punishment, nothing like this was happening on the cross! The parallels help us to understand God's work but the dissimilarities also need to be respected.

The New Testament does not offer these pictures as alternatives one to another. Rather, they complement each other. Although they are all different, they have in common the same core idea of the Son's substitution. That is why they are not alternatives. Each of these pictures gives us a different angle of vision on this same central, core idea of what Christ did for us as our substitute, and therefore in our place.

Justification

First up, then, is the law court. The Old Testament's legal framework of thought was taken over by the New Testament writers when they thought about our justification. They therefore set up a parallel between the law courts we know in our earthly life and what happens between sinners and God. This other "law court" is presided over by the "one lawgiver and judge" (James 4:12), who is God himself. But the parallels do not end there. For sinners, their standing before God parallels that of the guilty who stand before an earthly judge. However, in this other "court," before justice can be carried out there is an intervention by the Judge himself. The accused, against everything that they actually deserve, are cleared of all charges. They are given a righteousness, a standing before the law, which is not their own. In light of this, the charges are dropped. "Who shall bring any charge against God's elect? It is God who justifies" (Rom. 8:33), cries Paul. "Who is to condemn?" (Rom. 8:34), Paul continues rhetorically. No one. There is not now, nor can there ever be, "condemnation for those who are in Christ Jesus" (Rom. 8:1).

Different Meanings

In the New Testament, this language of justification is used in two ways. One is primary and the other is secondary. The primary use is that of being *declared* righteous and thus innocent before the law. The secondary use is that of this righteousness, this right standing, being *exhibited*. This distinction will help us to understand the unusual passage in James 2:18–26. There, James uses "justified" in this secondary sense, while Paul always uses it in the primary sense.

Let us first look at a few examples of the secondary sense of *justify*. On one occasion, Jesus was accused of being a drunk, whereas John the Baptist, who was abstemious in all ways was, for that reason, accused of having a demon. Having observed this, Jesus said, "Yet wisdom is justified by her deeds" (Matt. 11:19). Clearly, what he meant was that wisdom is demonstrated to be wise in its works. It is seen for what it is in the things that are said and done. Wisdom could not have been declared to be righteous!

Likewise, in a hymn to Christ that is embedded in the New Testament text, Paul said that Christ was "manifested in the flesh, vindicated [Paul's Greek is *justified*] by the Spirit . . ." (1 Tim. 3:16). Christ clearly did not need to be declared to be righteous! Rather, this expression comes amid this hymn of adoration in which the realms where Christ was revealed are contrasted. In the earthly sphere, he was incarnated ("in the flesh"), then "proclaimed among the nations," and then "believed on in the world." In the heavenly sphere, he was revealed to be who he was. He was, as it were, exhibited (or vindicated/justified) "by the Spirit," then was "seen by angels" and then "taken up in glory."

This is the way in which *justify* was used in James's most enigmatic statement, in which he asked, "Was not Abraham our father justified by works when he offered up his son Isaac on the altar?" (James 2:21). This statement so troubled Luther that he said that he had been tempted to stoke his furnace with James because of it! James was, he declared, an epistle of straw. And again he said that if anyone could reconcile Paul and James on this subject he would be glad to give that person his doctorate. That would have been an easy doctorate to obtain!

What James did was to relate Abraham's justification to an event that happened many years after the moment of his original acceptance by God, when "he believed the LORD, and he counted it to him as righteousness" (Gen. 15:6). The offering up of Isaac (Gen. 22:1–19) happened after Abraham was already justified. James, then, must have been using this language in its secondary sense. That Abraham had been declared righteous was *exhibited*, or demonstrated, or made known, or revealed in his later obedience. James's argument was that if there is no such obedience manifest, if there is no such evidence, then there are grounds for asking if a spiritual transformation has ever happened in the first place.

Alien Righteousness

The primary meaning of "justify," though, is a righteousness *declared*. It is the verdict of a judge. The verdict itself does not make anyone either guilty or innocent. It is simply the verdict of the court. Sometimes in our human courts the guilty are declared to be innocent and so they evade justice. And sometimes the innocent are declared to be guilty despite their innocence and so justice miscarries.

With respect to Christ's death, we see how this declaration of the sinner's innocence works from Paul's statement that, "For our sake he made him to be sin who knew no sin, so that in him we might become the righteousness of God" (2 Cor. 5:21). How was Christ "made sin"?

Clearly, he did not become a sinner. On the cross, he did not become morally guilty of sin, for he was, and remained, sinless. Rather, he bore the *penalty* of our sin as if it were his own.

In the same way, we are not accepted by God because we have actually been made completely righteous in our lives. Plainly we have not been. Rather, we have been judged and *declared* righteous. We have been clothed in a righteousness not our own, one which is alien to us, and in this righteousness we stand before God. We stand before him as people who are still in their sin and yet, despite that, have been made entirely acceptable to God. As Christ was made sin, just so are we made righteous. He did not become morally guilty, and we do not need to become actually righteous in order to be accepted by God. Our sins were the ground on which Christ was judged, and his righteousness is the ground on which we are declared free from all condemnation. Our sins were imputed to Christ, and his righteousness was imputed to us.

We cannot stand before God without this alien righteousness, because we can never justify ourselves. We do not have our own righteousness. That is why Paul insisted that this justification has to be given by grace alone, for "by works of the law no human being will be justified in his sight" (Rom. 3:20; cf. Rom. 4:2; Gal. 2:16). This is entirely consistent with what James said. After all, when Paul laid out the specifics of his gospel for some of the apostles, including James, they "gave the right hand of fellowship" (Gal. 2:9) to Paul.

Imputation Disputed

This thought of imputation is much disputed today in the academy. However, it is a construct that grows irresistibly out of the New Testament texts. There are three passages in particular that lead to this understanding: 2 Corinthians 5:21, Romans 4:3, and Romans 5:19. In *Jesus' Blood and Righteousness*, Brian Vickers has shown that while Paul has not spelled out his complete doctrine of imputation in any one of these passages, the idea is inescapably there when they are considered together because each takes up an aspect of it.

Because Abraham believed the promise of God, it was *"counted* to him as righteousness" (Rom. 4:3). For Abraham, as for us today, justification is something conferred, received only by faith, and it can never be earned.

There are, though, two kinds of "counting"—two kinds of reckoning. One is where something is credited to our account which we have earned and therefore deserve. There is, for example, the just recompense for labor given (Rom. 4:4). It is the paid wage. But there is another kind of reckoning that is quite different. It is unearned (Rom. 4:5). It is a gift. It is true that Paul does not say here in this passage that this gift is *Christ's* righteousness. He does say, though, that it is the righteousness of God, and we know that our only access to this righteousness is through Christ (Rom. 3:21–22). And the only way we can thus receive this justifying righteousness is by faith. What we thus receive is righteousness not our own, and what Christ receives, in our place, is sin that was not his own.

The second passage we need to note is Paul's statement that because of Christ's obedience, "the many will be *made* righteous" (Rom. 5:19). It is a statement found in the comparison Paul makes between the two heads who represent others. When Adam was judged for his sin, that condemnation passed on to all of humanity because he represented them (Rom. 5:18–19). And when Christ obeyed, the benefits of his obedience passed on to all whom he represented. There is an exact parallel here in how this representation works.

The "obedience" of Christ (Rom. 5:19) was, most immediately, what we see in his work on the cross. But inasmuch as Christ in his life was completing what Adam had left undone, as we have seen, and in his death was undoing the wrong that Adam had done, it seems that Paul had in mind more than just the cross when he spoke of Christ's "obedience." It would seem that it is Christ's own fulfilling of the law that is imputed and then conveyed to us by the Holy Spirit as righteousness, even as it is by Christ's death on the cross that we are declared righteous. We need Christ's righteousness for both our justification and our sanctification.

Finally, Christ went to the cross in order that "in him we might *become* the righteousness of God" (2 Cor. 5:21). In this text, Paul seems to be completing a thought. He had just said that when Christ acted to reconcile sinners to God he did so by "not counting their trespasses against them" (2 Cor. 5:19). Reconciliation, in part, happened by the non-imputation of sin to believers. But the other part, which is just as necessary, is the imputation of Christ's righteousness to them. But, in place of the familiar language of imputation, Paul substituted "become the righteousness of God." It is the same thought in different language. Christ was "made . . . to be sin" (2 Cor. 5:21) in that, as our sacrifice, he bore the full penalty of our sin. And as our representative, from him has come the righteousness of God by which we stand.

Righteousness is "counted" to us, we are "made" righteous, and we have "become" the righteousness of God. If we are "reconciled to God by the death of his Son, much more, now that we are reconciled, shall we be saved by his life" (Rom. 5:10). There is no other way to encompass Paul's thought in these passages than to say that our sins were imputed to Christ, and his righteousness—both from his life and in his death—was imputed to us. It was to accomplish this double imputation that Christ died *for* us, and he died *for* our sin, in our place, and for our benefit. We are therefore joined to Christ in his death; we die with him, receive his righteousness, and rise with him. On the ground of what he did at the cross as our substitute, on the ground of his victory over sin, we are declared to be righteous.

If all of this is true, then it is impossible not to think of Christ's death in penal terms. Christ took that penalty upon himself. He took our place, we who are rebels and law breakers. In that place, he absorbed in himself the just judgment that should have fallen on us. As T. S. Eliot observed, "we are redeemed from fire by fire." Christ's death is incomprehensible if it was not also penal in its nature. Some evangelicals are now thinking that this word, *penal*, is unhappily old fashioned and limiting. But if we dismiss what it stands for, we will be dismissing what the cross is all about.

Reconciliation

If the law court was a familiar institution in the ancient world, as it is in ours, so were human squabbles and conflicts. It is, perhaps, remarkable that Paul would take up such a down-to-earth, familiar, unhappy experience to draw parallels that shine light on some of the deepest truths that we know regarding Christ's death. But that is exactly what he did.

In the human context, people fall out with one another because offenses have been caused or injuries have happened. Perhaps harsh words or insults have also been traded. However the conflict happens, and however it proceeds, the outcome is inevitable. Alienation results. That alienation is not overcome until it has been replaced by reconciliation. This involves an exchange of relations. Hostility must be replaced by friendship, animosity by accord. The two parties must have their relationship put on a new footing so that the source of the conflict is removed. Thus they are able to move into the future with a clean relational slate.

Double Alienation

Paul used the analogy of human conflict in developing what Christ did on the cross (Rom. 5:10; 2 Cor. 5:18–19; Eph. 2:16). As we consider Paul's picture of our conflict with God, however, we might overlook the fact that, while we are alienated from him by our sin, he is also alienated from us by his wrath. It is a two-way alienation. Indeed, Paul even spoke of our having become God's "enemies." Once, he said, we were "alienated and hostile in mind" (Col. 1:21). "We were enemies . . ." (Rom. 5:10). Elsewhere he says that those who refuse the gospel are "enemies of the cross of Christ" (Phil. 3:18).

In what sense might we speak of God being alienated from us by his wrath? What we are thinking about is the fact of his moral over-against-ness. As we have seen, this wrath has nothing in common with the defilements that are so often part and parcel of human anger: selfish irritation, irrational outbursts, malice, hatred, and vindictiveness. Rather, God's anger is his holiness asserting itself against what is morally wrong. It is the way in which he upholds what is right in the face of what is wrong. It is how he preserves what is good against the assault of what is evil.

All of this being so, then, for us to be reconciled to God requires that this double alienation be reversed and our relations with God be put on a whole new footing. The consequences of our sin have to be removed and God's anger has to be turned away. Despite our sin, we have to be able to look on God with confidence and without fear, and he has to be able to look on us with acceptance and without disapproval. How, then, does this happen?

How Reconciliation Happens

There are two New Testament passages in which the language of reconciliation is used in other than a doctrinal sense. These passages, though, help us to understand how the language is used when it comes to Christ's death.

In the first of these passages, Jesus addressed a situation in which an offense had been caused by insulting, angry behavior (Matt. 5:22). What should happen then? Jesus said that before the offender comes to worship, he or she should first "be reconciled to your brother, and then come and offer your gift" (Matt. 5:24).

The second passage parallels this. If a married woman leaves her husband, she should either remain unmarried or "be reconciled to her husband" (1 Cor. 7:11). In both cases, the offender is spoken of in the passive. He or she must *be* reconciled to the person who has been offended. The offender can only confess their fault, offer to make amends, and then ask for forgiveness. Whatever the offender may do to mend relations, the prerogative to restore the relationship really rests with the person who has been offended. It is in his or her power to extend forgiveness and so to restore the broken relationship as the offender asks for it.

This pattern in restoring broken human relations is carried over into our relation with God in one important respect. In another, though, it is not.

First, the prerogative to forgive, pardon, and restore our relation with God rests wholly with him. We have to *be* reconciled. In this, we are completely in the passive. Reconciliation is something that happens *to* us, not something that we can do ourselves. We can seek him and humble ourselves before him, but we cannot reconcile ourselves to God. We cannot restore this breached relationship by anything we do. We are helpless and empty-handed. It is God alone who can reconcile, while we have to *be* reconciled. It is true that Paul says, "We implore you on behalf of Christ, be reconciled to God" (2 Cor. 5:20). However, we would be quite mistaken if we thought that, from our side, we could go about restoring this breach on our own. This statement should be read in the light of what Paul says elsewhere, that "we have now received reconciliation" (Rom. 5:11). We *receive* the reconciliation by faith; we do not make it happen by our works. That is the consistent message of the New Testament.

Second, unlike the human situation, God, whom we have offended, does not wait for us to seek pardon. Indeed, because we are sinners we would never seek a reconciliation that is not on our terms. But he does not wait for an approach that will never happen. Rather, it is he who takes the initiative, even though he is the party against whom the offense has been committed. "In Christ God was reconciling the world to himself, not counting their trespasses against them . . ." (2 Cor. 5:19). It is he who, as it were, turned the other cheek and reached out in grace to those who were his enemies.

This peacemaking requires that there be an exchange of righteousness for sin and forgiveness for wrath. Neither happens without Christ's substitutionary work. Reconciliation means that our sins were imputed to Christ and his righteousness to us. He reconciled us by "making peace by the blood of his cross" (Col. 1:20), and by that same cross is God's wrath turned aside.

The language used of this typically is "propitiation." God put forth Christ, Paul said, "as a propitiation by his blood" (Rom. 3:25; cf. Heb. 2:17; 1 John 2:2). The New Testament never uses this language in the way that the pagans used it. The apostles never thought that they, or anyone else, could appease God by bringing gifts and offerings to him. Rather, God himself provided his own propitiation in his Son. "In this is love, not that we have loved God but that he loved us and sent his Son to be the propitiation for our sins" (1 John 4:10).

This, then, is the second way in which Christ's substitutionary work is explained. He is the reason we have been brought near. We have had our inward hostility to God exchanged for acceptance and our alienation for reconciliation. We have been moved from a position of peril under his wrath to one of privilege as his reconciled children. None of this would have happened had Christ not died *for* us and *for* our sins.

Conflict and Conquest

Our third word picture is one that often comes from the battlefield, though it also applies to the context of slaves finding their freedom. On the battlefield, troops who are engaged in conflict are sometimes taken captive. The experience of captivity followed by rescue and release illumines some aspects of Christ's death. In a modern idiom we might think of a situation in which passengers on an airplane become captives when a hijacker takes over the plane. They are held by him under severe threat. Once the plane lands, though, he is overwhelmed by police and taken into custody. The passengers then breathe a sigh of relief because now they are free.

Captivity

Captivity, of course, is of different kinds when we are thinking about the Christian faith. Paul, for example, says we are "imprisoned" under sin (Gal. 3:22) and "held captive under the law" (Gal. 3:23). The law has been our jailor. But here we are thinking of a different kind of captivity: captivity to Satan.

However, it would be a mistake to see this theme as the dominant one of the New Testament, as some have argued. It is a mistake to displace justification from the central place it holds. Nevertheless, this aspect of spiritual captivity is undoubtedly there. And, as it turns out, it correlates seamlessly with justification and reconciliation if we will simply let the New Testament speak for itself.

Satan, this dark power of evil, rules over the world. This is where we start. "The whole world," John says, "lies in the power of the evil one" (1 John 5:19). This was almost certainly in Jesus's mind when he spoke of the "strong man." No one can enter a house to plunder its goods unless its owner, this "strong man," is first overcome (Mark 3:27). Jesus set up his mission in these terms, and though he provided no detail it seems inescapable that the "goods" he was about to wrest from Satan's control were those people who were held in the bondage of sin and under Satan's control. Later, John would say that the "reason the Son of God appeared was to destroy the works of the devil" (1 John 3:8).

The picture is rather clear and straightforward. We who are sinners belong in a realm over which Satan presides. We should not think of this as meaning that all sinners are demon-possessed, for that is not the case. Yet all live within this realm where sin and death reign, and behind that sin and death is the power of darkness.

We should not speculate about how this situation came about. The early church fathers were fascinated by this and offered some quite graphic images to explain it. There was, one Father suggested, an original deal between God and Satan that led to the whole of humanity falling into Satan's hands. But, as it turned out, God got the better of it in the end. Satan was like a fish who saw a tasty morsel in the water. He went for it not knowing that inside this bait—the humanity of Christ—was the hook of Christ's divinity. So it was that he was caught and disempowered!

It is enough to say that this power of evil is real and that it is part and parcel of life. Indeed, it is our fallenness, our "flesh" that makes us vulnerable to Satan's designs, for he has within each of us an internal ally. And this "flesh" also resonates with the external "world," with our culture, with the system of values, expectations, and ways of looking at life that arise from our own fallen natures and which are projected publicly and fill our public environment. These values are there in the movies we see, the workplace where we spend much of our time, in TV ads, and in the talk around our neighborhoods. This is the "wisdom of this age" (1 Cor. 2:6), as Paul puts it elsewhere, and along with it we encounter the "rulers," "the authorities," the "cosmic powers over this present darkness," and "the spiritual forces of evil" (Eph. 6:12) against which we wrestle. And behind all of this, and keeping this whole complex web of evil plans, strategies, and assaults in place, is the source of all darkness, Satan himself.

Victory

According to Paul, the world, the flesh, and the Devil are the three-pronged enemy that we must overcome if we are to be released. And that has happened. God, "being rich in mercy, because of the great love with which he loved us, . . . made us alive together with Christ" (Eph. 2:4–5). He overcame our captivity when we were "dead in . . . trespasses and sins" (Eph. 2:1), when we followed "the course of this world" (Eph. 2:2) and when, for these reasons, we were following "the prince of the power of the air" (Eph. 2:2). Christ, Paul said, "gave himself for our sins to deliver us from the present evil age" (Gal. 1:4).

Once again, we see the substitution motif. It was *because* Jesus gave himself for our sins that he can deliver us. And he delivers us not just from this "present evil age" but also from Satan, who sustains this evil age. In a pivotal text, Paul declared that Christ "disarmed the rulers and authorities and put them to open shame, by triumphing over them" at the cross (Col. 2:15).

The captivity of which Paul spoke in Colossians 2:14–15 was twofold. First, there is "the record of debt that stood against us with its legal demands" (Col. 2:14). Paul had in mind here the moral law (cf. Eph. 2:15), and one of the ways in which our shortcomings are explained is through this idea of debt. In the moral sphere, as it were, we have run up a credit card debt that is so enormous that it can never, ever be paid off. God's moral law shows up our bankruptcy, our complete inability to pay. It shows us for what we are beneath the surface images, self-projections, rationalizations, and protective masks.

On the other side of our captivity are these "rulers and authorities" (Col. 2:15). It is best to see these as the ranks of evil beings, malignant in intent, who are arrayed against us. Here is the ultimate opposition to God, Christ, his Word, his law, and his truth. For our captivity to them to be broken, three things must happen. First, our sins need to be forgiven (Col. 2:13). Second, the "record of debt" needs to be cancelled (Col. 2:14). Third, these evil powers need to be disarmed (Col. 2:15), their powers stripped from them.

This triumph, we need to see clearly, has not come about simply by force, the greater power of God being arraigned against the lesser power of Satan. Were it that simple, Christ would not have had to go to the cross. The point about Paul's argument is that the power of evil is broken only when the instruments through which it is exercised are disabled. Those instruments are sin and the culture whose air we breathe. And therefore, this conquest motif correlates exactly with justification and reconciliation. For how is the penalty that stands against us resolved? How is the debt paid? How is our broken relationship restored? How is God's wrath turned aside? How is Satan's hold on us broken? The answer is given in the doctrines of justification and reconciliation. When we are justified and reconciled to God, the power that Satan once had over us is completely broken. Evil was crippled at the cross. And now we look with eager anticipation to that moment when God will take his broom and sweep the entire universe clean of all of Satan's work.

Incarnation and Cross

The Imitation of Christ

Christ's incarnation and his atonement need to be understood in light of each other. He came to die, and he died that we might live. At Christmas, we celebrate Immanuel, "God with us." At Easter, we celebrate the cross, "God for us." There is a seamless history that runs from Christ's incarnation to his cross and on to his resurrection.

However, there has been a long tradition in and out of the church which has keyed in on the "God with us" and then overlooked the "God for us." Wherever this has happened, Christ has been seen mainly as an example. On the Christian side of things, this has led to a literature in which people try to imitate in their own lives what Christ did in his life. Christ's life is seen as an object lesson, a pattern that should and can be followed, a model of piety that can be replicated in our own lives. Thomas à Kempis's *The Imitation of Christ* is an example of this, albeit a pious one.

Especially within Catholicism, this has been an honored tradition. Although there is much that is admirable about it, it tends to be built on the idea that our wills are only wounded and therefore what they need, and what will suffice for our spiritual growth, is an inspiring example. This inevitably turns into legalism. The moral demands of trying to imitate Christ come to crush those who cannot meet those demands. The truth is that we need grace before we can follow such an example. It is not the imitation of Christ that makes us children of God, Luther said rightly; it is being children of grace that enables us to be Christ's imitators.

There are, however, far less pious versions of this kind of thinking. Some have reached significant audiences. In these, there is a Christ, or a Christ figure, who has flaws and weaknesses, even sins. These are more of an attempt to show how Christ is identified with us than they are attempts to show how we should imitate him. In 1988, for example, a Nikos Kazantzakis novel was turned into a film, directed by Martin Scorsese, called *The Last Temptation of Christ*. In this movie, Christ is disoriented, uncertain, inwardly shaky, a little lost, and lustful. And there is no understanding of how he bore our sin in atonement. How could there be? We are shown the crucifixion, but there is no cross. Christ, then, becomes a "model" because he suffers as we do, is as confused as we are, and often knows no more about how to deal with life than we do.

So, how should we really be thinking of Christ as our model? It is perfectly correct that he picked up the threads of humanity where Adam had dropped them. He has, indeed, given us a model humanity. This is so because he was sinless. In fact, in the New Testament, there are several passages that urge us to follow his example.

The Corinthians, for example, were urged to be generous in their giving, seeing in Christ's self-giving an example to be followed (2 Cor. 8:8–15). Paul urged the Romans not to please themselves, for "Christ did not please himself" (Rom. 15:3). Paul commanded the Ephesians to "walk in love, as Christ loved us and gave himself for us" (Eph. 5:2). In the hymn found in Philippians 2, Paul urged squabbling Christians to find the same humility that we see in Christ's descent from heaven, his taking on of our flesh, and his entering into our death (Phil. 2:5–11). All of these injunctions can be summed up as saying, in John's words, that we "ought to walk in the same way in which he walked" (1 John 2:6). However, the imitation of a perfect life is a forlorn possibility until God has begun to remake us by his grace. That is what we must understand.

We cannot, therefore, separate the "God with us" theme from the "God for us" theme. And, indeed, his death is as much a model in its humility and obedience as was his life. His life and death are all of a piece. Christ took our humanity so that he might take our sins. The incarnation was for the cross. The incarnation cannot stand on its own. Together, but only together, these themes are God's answer to our fallen world.

Real Events

There is another angle to this that we should not forget or overlook. It is that all of this happened within our space-time history. It is all as real, as objective to us, as any other event from this or any other time. Because God took upon himself our flesh in a real human biography, because Christ was no phantom, because he was crucified at a specific place and time, because he rose from the dead, because he was seen afterwards and did not simply disappear, because all of these things are true, we are confronted by a set of facts that must be answered. We cannot evade them. They speak to us even when we wish not to listen. They speak to us of how God has shown himself to us and what he has done for us in Christ. They speak to us from outside our own private worlds. This revelation crashes into our subjectivity. It enters our inward world from the outside. Its truth is alien to us as fallen people but its reality is unmistakable. It demands to be heard. And no greater assurance could ever be given than this. The God who was *with* us in our history is the God who is *for* us throughout eternity.

Needless to say, what I have been describing collides head-on with the way postmoderns tend to see things. For them and, indeed, for some in evangelical churches, there is no objective reality that we can know. There is only the way people see things. For postmoderns, there is no Truth, only truths. There is only our internal radar. There is no metanarrative of meaning that arches over all of life. There are just our own personal stories.

This inward orientation, this absorption in our own interior reality, is what feeds the burgeoning contemporary spiritualities of our day. Spiritual reality, people believe, is accessed from within themselves, intuitively. That being the case, the biblical redemptive history, this disclosure of God outside of ourselves, in a distant place and a faraway time, strikes many as simply too remote. They cannot relate to it. Besides, it is redundant. They have far more confidence in their innate powers than in their ability to access the meaning of this ancient history.

This results in a kind of religion that is without an atonement, for it does not need one. Such thinking may end up with a sense of God, but it will never have the knowledge of the God who redeems. It sees the importance of being spiritual, but misses the greatness of the God who condescended to enter our existence. It may speak of love, but it knows nothing of the depths of divine love next to which human loves pale by comparison. Those who are thus spiritual may know some of their own weaknesses, but they know nothing of how their weaknesses appear before the eyes of God. And they will not know the God who humbled himself to take their sins upon himself at the cross.

God's Holy-love

When Paul came to ponder all of this, he accented the fact that it was "while we were still sinners" (Rom. 5:8), it was when "we were dead in our trespasses" (Eph. 2:5), that God sent his Son. It was God, acting into our world from "above," who initiated this redemption, and it was so initiated precisely because we could not enter the presence of God from "below." Only God could initiate this and carry it through. Only he could take up our cause. Only he could prosecute it. Only he could bring it through to a triumphant conclusion, for we have been stripped of our ability to do any of this. And all of it he did in his Son.

This is what shows his love and what assures us of his love for all time. It was because God "so loved the world, that he gave his only Son" (John 3:16; cf. 1 John 4:9). God, "being rich in mercy, because of the great love with which he loved us," sent Christ (Eph. 2:4–5). God did not spare "his own Son but gave him up for us all" (Rom. 8:32). And in this act of self-giving, this substitution of himself for us, he defined what love is: "In this is love, not that we have loved God but that he loved us and sent his Son to be the propitiation for our sins" (1 John 4:10). This is the love that Paul prays we might be able to understand in all its breadth and length and height and depth (Eph. 3:18).

This love grieved over our predicament. God did not abandon us. He did not leave us as we were—waifs, strays, rebels, and orphans. Indeed, from all eternity he had planned on not doing so. But God's mercy, his love, could not deal with our situation unless he also intervened for us in his righteousness, for it was our unrighteousness that was the root cause of our situation.

We were in Christ when judgment fell on him in our place (Rom. 5:9–10). Nothing affirms God's holiness more than this. Christ *had* to die. Nothing shouts out the demands of that holiness more loudly. Nowhere are its demands seen more clearly. Indeed, these demands are so clear, so incontrovertible, that only a righteousness from God himself will suffice to meet them.

And nowhere do we see the graciousness of his grace more clearly than when those demands are accepted by Christ, satisfied on the cross, and his righteousness imputed to sinners. And wherever God's holiness has not swallowed up sin in Christ, it will confront sin outside of Christ. That there was a cross means that there will be a judgment. But that there was a cross also means that God's mercy toward his people is bottomless. The God who is righteous is the God who is the Savior. He is the one who forgives.

However, we misconstrue the nature of God if we imagine that the cross was the resolution of competing and conflicting attributes, his holiness and his love. It is true that they are different because Scripture speaks of them in different ways. And yet, are we to suppose that the holiness of God did not long for our redemption as much as his love? Does not all holiness long to see a world cleansed of sin? And would not God's love look to see his holiness triumph in our redemption,

155

too? And is not God himself equally and fully present, in all of his splendor, wherever his love is present and wherever his holiness is present? The character of God is not splintered into parts that compete with one another. But, rather, it is God in his holy-love who engaged our sin at the cross and in Christ vanquished all that has fractured and broken our world.

Scripture's redemptive narrative has here reached its destination. The will of God, conceived "before the foundation of the world," has now been carried out in Christ in all of its finality. The God who was with us, the One who came near, who entered our life, is also the God who was for us. He was near, but in that nearness lay hidden a majesty. Indeed, everywhere we look there are the strange conjunctions that faith must hold together. In his grace we have found his righteousness, in his mercy a burning holiness, and on the other side of his love there is a wrath. Strange and mysterious as was the path that took Christ from the glory of heaven to the rough wood of that cross, the outcome is clear, simple, and unmistakable: Christ took our penalty, stood in our place, and paid the price. He overcame our sin, God's wrath, and our captivity to Satan's designs. We see here God's grace, his tender heart, and his boundless love. We see, too, at the same time, his awesome, burning purity. So it is that we lift up our voices in worship, for he is our God—Father, Son, and Holy Spirit.

CHAPTER 7

Walking with God

See, the streams of living waters,
Springing from eternal love,
Well supply thy sons and daughters
And all fear of want remove.
Who can faint while such a river
Ever flows their thirst to assuage?
Grace, which like the Lord, the giver,
Never fails from age to age.

JOHN NEWTON

In eternity, God turned to us. That is the theme we have just explored. Now we must take up the other side to this truth. It is that God turned to us so that we might turn to him. More exactly, he turned to us despite our rebellion, and then he turned us to himself despite our sin.

This required that Christ descend to us so that we might ascend *through* him. And ascending through him means that we not only entered into his death but now we are already sharing in his resurrection. We have been raised to a new kind of existence. That is what we must now explore. What is this new life? Now that we are justified, reconciled, and redeemed, what does it mean to be sanctified? If we now know God, how does that knowledge get translated into how we think and what we do?

In this chapter, I first need to explain where and why we have sometimes gone so wrong in our thought about sanctification. And, of course, we are asking ourselves this question because it gets at the more constructive issue of how we *should* be thinking about sanctification. Second, this will then lead us back to the central theme of this book: how should the holy-love of God define and shape our sanctified lives? And finally, how will we sustain a sanctified life in the context of our chaotic and distracted world?

Roads and Ditches

Like most roads, this theme of sanctification has a ditch on both sides. And many are the wrecks that have found their way into one of these two ditches! On the one side are those who *separate* the gospel and sanctification. On the other side are those who *confuse* justification and sanctification.

The gospel—the proclamation of Christ's self-substitution as articulated in doctrines such as justification, reconciliation, and redemption—should be distinguished from sanctification but not separated from it. Those who have separated them have driven off the main road into a ditch on one side. That is the first mistake. Those who have confused them, making justification no different from sanctification, have made the second mistake. We need to look at both of these mistakes.

No Separation

First, there are those who, one way or another, have ended up with a gospel belief that does not lead on to sanctified life. So, what am I thinking about?

Today, in the evangelical church, there are apparently many who have made decisions for Christ, who claim to be reborn, but who give little evidence of their claimed relationship to Christ. Something is seriously amiss if, as George Barna has reported, only 9 percent of those claiming rebirth have even a minimal knowledge of the Bible, if there are no discernible differences in how they live as compared with secularists, and if the born-again are dropping out of church attendance in droves. If these numbers are anywhere close to being accurate, then the gospel has become a stand-alone thing, and many who say they have embraced it have never entered the Christian life to which it was supposed to be the entry point. The gospel has, in fact, become the end point. It did not inaugurate a life of growing sanctification. Sanctification was either never a part of the Christian life or it has dropped away. This is an expression of the antinomianism that has, from time to time, plagued the church. It is the thought that, once we have been justified, sin is no longer something to which we need pay attention, since it has already been forgiven in its entirety.

Given this kind of situation, we need to ask ourselves again why it is that we cannot "continue in sin that grace may abound" (Rom. 6:1) after we have believed the gospel. Why should we not make a commitment to Christ and then get on with our lives as we always have and as we want? The answer, of course, is that if this is how we are thinking about Christian faith, we have completely misunderstood what it is about.

One with Christ

In justification we are not merely acquitted but that acquittal is the ground for our being joined to Christ. We are joined to him in his death and resurrection. We cannot, therefore, live any longer for ourselves. We must live "for him" who died and was raised for us (2 Cor. 5:15). Paul turned his back on his old habits of self-justification. That, I think, is what he meant when he said that he was "crucified with Christ." Henceforth, he said, "it is no longer I who live, but Christ who lives in me" (Gal. 2:20). If we belong to Christ, we will have "crucified the flesh with its passions and desires" (Gal. 5:24). If we suffer, it is so that "the life of Jesus may also be manifested in our mortal flesh" (2 Cor. 4:11). All of this is written into the way the New Testament sets up the relation between the gospel and sanctification. We believe the gospel, not only so that our guilt might be forgiven, but so that henceforth, on a daily basis, we might live for Christ, walking in his ways, living by the power of the Holy Spirit, who leads us into the paths of godliness.

Our coming to faith in Christ, through the truth of the gospel, was the moment in time when God declared his acceptance of us and welcomed us into the family of the covenant by imputing our sin to Christ and his righteousness to us. We may not have known the depths of despair before God that Luther did, but we must have known our estrangement from God. And we may not have experienced the same depth of terror before God's wrath that Luther knew, but we must have known ourselves to be in peril because we were on the wrong side of the moral law. Then it was, when we considered Christ and his death, that we knew that God had turned to us. He pardoned us in Christ, declared us righteous in him, reconciled us to himself, and liberated us from the hold of death and Satan.

God not only turned to us, but in that turning he claimed us for himself. He made us his own. Our justification was the entry point to this, but God's action did not end with our justification. Along with that declaration was another action. It was distinct from justification, but it was also in continuity with that action of grace that brought us pardon. God justified us and then tore us from what we were, from the existence we once lived, and transferred us to a new existence entirely. Paul was not exaggerating when he said that God "delivered us from the domain of darkness and *transferred* us to the kingdom of his beloved Son" (Col. 1:13). In this kingdom, we put off "the old self with its practices." We have already put on "the new self" (Col. 3:9–10). Sanctification is about living in ways that are consistent with what we already are in Christ. Nor was it an exaggeration to say that "if anyone is in Christ, he is a new creation. The old has passed away; behold, the new has come" (2 Cor. 5:17). The "new" is the inbreaking of the "age to come," which we are already experiencing through our new, regenerate natures. Our experience of this coming "age" is not yet full but it is nevertheless real.

If, therefore, there is no clear evidence from how we are living that the old self has been put off, if we do not know ourselves to have been transferred into Christ's kingdom, if we do not have as our deep, unremitting purpose to live as one who is already in Christ, then there are good reasons to doubt whether we have ever been received by him. After all, "what good is it, my brothers, if someone says he has faith but does not have works?" (James 2:14). Claims to faith unaccompanied by the evidence of that faith are worthless (James 2:26). We are justified by faith alone, but faith, if it is genuine, never stands alone. It always brings forth works.

Can we be more precise now in saying exactly what the connection is between the gospel and sanctification? I think we can. But to do this, let me retrieve a distinction that has now mostly passed out of use. It is the distinction between positional sanctification and conditional sanctification.

Position and Condition

Positional sanctification is what we are already in Christ. It has to do with our being separated to him and separated for him. Conditional sanctification is about our own level of spiritual maturity in our daily walk with Christ at any point in time. This is an important distinction because positional sanctification underscores the essential bond between the gospel and the new life that blossoms from gospel-believing. It secures their unity. It makes it impossible, at a biblical level, for anyone to think that they can believe the gospel, be born again, and then settle back into their former way of life once their "decision for Christ"—what 72 percent of Americans apparently now claim to have done—has been made. So what is meant, more precisely, by positional sanctification?

Our justification, reconciliation, and redemption arise from a single completed act wrought by Christ on the cross. This is what was applied to us by the Holy Spirit. But the New Testament also sees our sanctification—positional sanctification—as bonded into this act. This is why some New Testament passages speak of sanctification in the past tense. It, too, has already happened. It is quite as much a completed act as is our justification. When God pardoned us, he created for us this new existence. It is no less of grace, no less dependent utterly upon his goodness, than is our justification.

How else can we understand Paul's statement to the Corinthians, whose flaws and sins were glaring, that Christ "became to us wisdom from God, righteousness and sanctification and redemption" (1 Cor. 1:30)? Justification and sanctification are here linked. Both are seen as completed events. These are the believers who, despite their warts, are already "*sanctified* in Christ Jesus" (1 Cor. 1:2). Despite their prior, degraded life which lingered on in unhappy ways, Paul still could say to them that "you were washed, you were *sanctified*, you were justified in the name of the Lord Jesus Christ and by the Spirit of our God" (1 Cor. 6:11). How can this be? How could these Corinthians be seen as already sanctified when they were acting in ways that were so plainly and painfully wrong?

The answer is that their sanctification had already been fully secured in Christ even if, in their actual lives, they were far from acting as those who were in Christ. There is a background to all of this that will help us to understand it.

In the Old Testament, many things were said to be holy or sanctified, and we need to know in what sense this was meant because it explains what we find in the New Testament. For example, Israel was called a "holy nation" (Ex. 19:6). This may not seem to square with the history we know because Israel was quite often very unholy. Moses spoke of "a holy Sabbath to the LORD" (Ex. 16:23; cf. Gen. 2:3). There were things that could be holy when consecrated as "holy gifts" (Ex. 28:38). The sanctuary was "holy" (Lev. 16:33). Even a person's house could be dedicated as "a holy gift to the LORD" (Lev. 27:14). Fruit was sometimes seen as "holy." The people of God were instructed not to eat fruit from trees until three years after they were planted. In the fourth, the fruit could be picked but not eaten. It was to be considered "holy, an offering of praise to the LORD" (Lev. 19:24). The next year, the fruit could be eaten. There was, then, a widely established practice of thinking of certain things, times, people, and places as being holy or sanctified. Why were they considered holy?

The temple was not considered holy because of its impressive construction or its costly materials. Sacrifices were not seen as holy because there was anything unusual about these animals. The priests in the temple were holy but not because they were without sin. The Sabbath was not holy because, in some way, its hours were different from the hours of the other days. No, in all of these cases what was holy became so because it had been *separated* from common use and given to the Lord for his use. It was a double action: separation from and separation to.

The action of God in calling Christian believers, justifying them, and giving them the Holy Spirit to indwell them, is what he had to do to *separate* them from fallen human life and from their own fallen selves. It is also what he did to separate them to himself. It is a double separation: separation *from* the world, the flesh, and the Devil accompanied by a separation *to* God. This is why, in the New Testament, all be-lievers are called "saints," or those who have been made holy. They have been separated from fallen human life and separated to God through Christ's death. At the present time, said Paul, "I am going to Jerusalem bringing aid to the *saints*" (Rom. 15:25; see also Rom. 1:7; 1 Cor. 1:2; Heb. 13:24). He was thinking of all of the Christian believers there. They were God's "holy ones," or saints, or those who had been sanctified.

This language of "saint" has been co-opted by the Catholic Church to speak of those who, in its judgment, have reached extraordinary levels of personal piety and sanctity. They are eventually declared to have been saints, and forever after they bear that title. In the New Testament, by contrast, all who have been called to know God in Christ are saints. They are saints because they have been separated to God and separated from fallen life by their union with Christ. That is why even the Corinthians were called "saints."

This is positional sanctification. And it is really important to see this truth. How utterly impossible it is to think that in and with our embrace of the gospel we were not, at the same time, launched upon a life of discipleship. We can, and should, distinguish between justifi-cation and sanctification. But we cannot separate them one from the other. That there are those who claim to be born again who show no evidence of their inward renewal, of having been torn from the past life and relocated in an entirely different spiritual existence, is a trav-esty and a scandal.

Power

We have seen, then, that in our positional sanctification we are already sanctified in Christ. Now we need to consider its companion truth, our conditional sanctification. We are to become in fact, in the midst of life with all of its conflicts and temptations, what we are already in Christ. Our condition, what we actually are, must move ever closer to who we are in Christ, to our position in him. However, this does not happen by bare effort. If we see it as a venture only of human will-ing, we are doomed to fail. It is a serious mistake to think that God's grace takes us up to the moment of gospel belief and then after that we are on our own.

As we come to faith in Christ and enter into the Christian life, we carry our fallen selves with us. A conflict rages within. It produces a fearful ambiguity. There is a conflict between the new nature that we now have in Christ and the fallen nature that we have not yet left behind. Conditional sanctification is about learning, against all that we are in sin, how to live consistently with who we are already in Christ (e.g., Gal. 5:16–25). Sanctification in this sense, as our condition, is what Jesus had in mind when he prayed for the disciples that God would "sanctify them in the truth; your word is truth" (John 17:17). And Paul prayed, "may the God of peace himself sanctify you completely, and may your whole spirit and soul and body be kept blameless at the coming of our Lord Jesus Christ" (1 Thess. 5:23). And we can expect no success at all in this inward struggle unless we are greatly aided by the Holy Spirit.

But that is not the same thing as saying that we can expect no gain in Christlike character at all! Unbelief can defeat us here, too. There are some whose great virtue is that they understand the darkness of their own hearts, they know their own willful sinfulness, and they have acknowledged all of this before God. Nevertheless, they are so overwhelmed by this truth that they are unable to think that God the Holy Spirit can, indeed, transform them, can build character within them, and can successfully lead them in the paths of godly living. They feel that because of this sin, they are forever compromised.

Sinful and rebellious though we are, we are also the children of grace in whom the Holy Spirit resides. Christ's redemption is not going to be stopped cold by the very sin he went to the cross to overcome! Scripture gives abundant evidence of the fact that we can, indeed, please God, do what is right, and become, in our characters, men and women of God. Paul confidently asserted that as we all look to Christ in his glory, we are "being transformed into the same image from one degree of glory to another" (2 Cor. 3:18). Our fallen *imago Dei* is being progressively transformed!

To the Romans Paul said, for example, that he was satisfied that "you yourselves are full of goodness, filled with all knowledge and able to instruct one another" (Rom. 15:14). The kingdom of God, he said, is all about "righteousness and peace and joy in the Holy Spirit."

And then he added, "Whoever thus serves Christ is acceptable to God" (Rom. 14:17–18). And to the Ephesians he wrote that they were to render "service with a good will as to the Lord and not to man" (Eph. 6:7). This is all quite possible.

But here undoubtedly this double action must be at work: separation from and separation to. We are, indeed, to "put to death the deeds of the body" (Rom. 8:13) though we do so, Paul said, "by the Spirit." We put to death "what is earthly" within ourselves (Col. 3:5) such as sexual impurity. We have "died to the elemental spirits of the world" (Col. 2:20). We are to purify ourselves as we look for the return of Christ (1 John 3:3). We have definitively "put off the old self with its practices" (Col. 3:9; cf. Rom. 6:6). This is all about separation *from*.

But there is separation *to* as well. We are to present our body to God "as a living sacrifice" (Rom. 12:1). We are to "put on the Lord Jesus Christ, and make no provision for the flesh, to gratify its desires" (Rom. 13:14). If we have put off the practices of the old self, we have also "put on the new self, which is being renewed in knowledge after the image of its creator" (Col. 3:10). We are, therefore, to build up virtue in ourselves. Make every effort, Peter said, "to supplement your faith with virtue, and virtue with knowledge, and knowledge with self-control, and self-control with steadfastness, and steadfastness with godliness, and godliness with brotherly affection, and brotherly affection with love" (2 Pet. 1:5–7; cf. Col. 3:12). We are to give ourselves to everything that is true, good, wholesome, and right. We are "to pursue righteousness, faith, love, and peace . . . from a pure heart" (2 Tim. 2:22).

So, then, we are to separate ourselves from sin and in every way separate ourselves to God, for his arms are open wide to us. In Christ, God has done everything that needs to be done for us to be able to turn from our old self-centered, self-serving ways and begin to live a God-centered life, for with such a life God is pleased.

Our focus here is on seeing the *continuity* in God's saving work from the gospel into our sanctification. Although the Galatians had their own set of issues, it is not difficult to see some parallels to what we are thinking about here. "Are you so foolish?" Paul asked at one point. "Having begun by the Spirit, are you now being perfected by the flesh?" (Gal. 3:3). Beginning with the Spirit meant for Paul acknowledging their own personal bankruptcy, depending utterly on God's grace, believing his promises, and looking only to Christ for pardon, acceptance, and standing. However, these very principles carry through into sanctification. Having begun with grace, are we going to depend only on self-effort after that? Have we been abandoned by God to make our way through life as best we can after we have believed the gospel? No. The Spirit continues his work. Paul could say to the Philippians that he was confident "that he who began a good work in you will bring it to completion at the day of Jesus Christ" (Phil. 1:6). If that is the goal, how could we think that, along the way to that goal, God would have lost interest in our sanctification or would have withdrawn his enablement?

The truth is that he who began this good work does indeed persist in bringing it to fruition. He works behind, within, and through our own responses, connecting us with Christ's work and pointing us to him. The Spirit illumines within us where the impulses of sin are at work, nudging us toward those things of which God approves; he illumines the Scripture as we study it and lifts up our eyes to see Christ, who is the center of reality. Paul prayed—and he so prayed because what he was asking for is what ought to be—that the Ephesian believers would be "strengthened with power through his Spirit in your inner being" (Eph. 3:16). Elsewhere, he said that our transformation "comes from the Lord who is the Spirit" (2 Cor. 3:18). It is "the Spirit of life" who has set us free "in Christ Jesus from the law of sin and death" (Rom. 8:2). Let us therefore "keep in step with the Spirit" (Gal. 5:25).

Work and Grace

In a striking passage, Paul told the Philippians to "work out your own salvation with fear and trembling, for it is God who works in you, both to will and to work for his good pleasure" (Phil. 2:12–13). We are, he said, to work out what God, in his grace, has worked in. Paul's language of "work" was used of almost any activity that took effort, such as laboring in a business enterprise, or finding fish in the ocean, or plowing a field. It was used of any labor in which energy was expended with the goal of making something productive, fruitful, or worthwhile. However, having given this instruction, Paul then gave an argument for it that seems to go against logic. Why are we to work out this salvation, making it productive in all areas of life such that we "shine as lights in the world" (Phil. 2:15)? The answer is because it is "God who works in you, both to will and to work for his good pleasure" (Phil. 2:13).

There have been those who have assumed, or implied, that after justification we are more or less on our own. The grace that brought us into belief peters out shortly thereafter. The reason we must work at our sanctification, therefore, is that if we do not, no one will. God has done his part, and now we must do ours. But that is directly contradicted by Paul's argument here. In fact, it is *God* who is always at work within us both in "the willing" and "the working." This is Paul's exact language. God works and we work. He works in our willing and in our working. His work is behind ours. It is present in ours. His sovereign action is entirely consistent with the exercise of our responsibility. And yet we would miss Paul's point entirely if we did not see that without God's initiative, we would not be doing this willing and working. It is *because* he infuses our desires, our ambitions, our inward nature with his gracious, sanctifying power that we work. It is because of this that our regenerate nature brings forth its sanctified fruit.

At the end of time, we will be able to look back and see that whatever sanctity has come to expression in our lives all goes back to the grace of God. He was there at the beginning of our redemption, and he turned us from our sin to belief in Christ as our sin-bearer. He was there along the way, sustaining us and energizing us to do whatever good we have done. And he will be there at the end, when we will know, as we do not yet know, what it is to share fully in the resurrection life of Christ in heaven.

No Confusion

On the other side of the road of sanctification, there is another ditch. It is the opposite of the one we have just been considering. This other ditch is the second great mistake in the way that some have related justification to sanctification. This used to be the one into which traditional Catholics had driven. In recent days, though, there are evangelical vehicles in this wreckage as well.

This mistake makes justification a part of sanctification. It sees justification as but the first step in *same* process of becoming righteous. It is a mistake that rests on two assumptions.

First, it sees our salvation as a single process, not a process divided into two distinguishable phases—justification and sanctification. Second, it assumes that Luther and the other Reformers misconstrued justification—that justification, too, is a process and not a moment. Justification and sanctification in this understanding are therefore merged into each other. If God is active in opening the front door through which we enter, we nevertheless make ourselves acceptable to God along the way by bringing the divine life he imparted to us to fruition. This happens through our "works," such as our effort, self-discipline, diligence, acts of piety, self-sacrifice, and labor for the kingdom of God. At the end of time, all of these works will be weighed on the divine scale and the verdict will then be rendered as to whether or not we are justified.

This, in fact, is what the Protestant Reformers like Calvin and Luther opposed. Justification, they countered, is not a verdict about how well the divine life *imparted* to us in regeneration has come to fruition. It is, rather, a verdict based on righteousness—Christ's righteousness—that is *imputed* to us before sanctification even begins. The Catholic belief that justification comes only at the end of life was once considered mightily injurious to biblical teaching. It was seen as the enemy of the biblical teaching about grace, faith, and justification. But it is now being given a friendly acceptance by some evangelicals, though they have come to it by a different route.

I have already spent some time on justification, and it is unnecessary to repeat what has been said. The issue, though, has an importance that cannot be overestimated.

The church is always in danger of losing this distinction between justification and sanctification because fallen human nature is always partial to the thought that it is able to commend itself to God. But when this distinction is lost, so too is the gospel. And so too is the need for the grace of God. And so too is the cross as the New Testament frames it for us. What remains then is only a moralism—justifying ourselves by our obedience. That is the very thing from which the gospel rescued Paul.

There is, though, something else lost when we confuse justification and sanctification. This has received far less attention than have these other themes. It is the matter of motivation.

When the gospel is made to be but the first step in the obedience of sanctification, then the only motivation for living the Christian life is that of law. The whole of Christian faith, from beginning to end, is placed under the demand of what we *ought* to do and be. However, law is not a strong motivator. When we understand justification, when we know that in that moment we have been forever declared free from condemnation, there arises within our souls an entirely different motivation for doing the will of God. It is a motivation that comes from knowing what debtors we are to grace. This leads to gratitude. And gratitude is an extraordinary motivator.

When Paul wrote to the Corinthians that "you are not your own, for you were bought with a price" (1 Cor. 6:19–20; 7:23), he spoke to this issue. What was the ground of their obligation to Christ? It was not only that they had been commanded to obey him but, additionally, that they had been *bought* by him so that they could do so. When we see with clarity the necessity of what Christ has done for us, we also see our immense obligation, because he redeemed us when we were helpless. Once we see that, the obligation to do what is right becomes more multifaceted.

It is still the case that "we make it our aim to please him," because "we must all appear before the judgment seat of Christ" (2 Cor. 5:9–10). And yet there is more to our walk than just this "ought" of law. Now there is the gratitude for grace. Certainly, we do what is right because it is right. But we also do what is right because we *want* to do it. This is what we see in the Psalms. "I will delight in your statutes," the psalmist declared. "I find my delight in your commandments, which I love"; "Oh how I love your law!" "Your testimonies are wonderful; therefore my soul keeps them" (Ps. 119:16, 47, 97, 129). Many of our hymns have caught this sense of obligation because of the one to whom we belong. Isaac Watts, for example, has a final stanza to "When I Survey" that declares, "Were the whole realm of nature mine, / That were an offering far too small; / Love so amazing, so divine, / Demands my soul, my life, my all." It is this kind of gratitude that fuels the godly life, even as it is the moral law that structures it.

Sanctification, then, is the life of godliness that arises on the foundation of God's grace in the gospel. It grows up from that foundation, under the power and internal working of the Holy Spirit. The Spirit's work is to separate us from our former fallen life and separate us to God so that we might know him, worship him, love him, and serve him. If we are thus being separated, then in our sanctification we will be shaped more and more into the character of God, to whom we have been separated. And that character, as we are thinking about it here, can be summed up as holy-love. This holy-love should be reflected in those who know God.

Holy-love

The Soul of Sanctification

If sanctification is all about becoming more like God in his character, then clearly this can happen only as the lost moral image of God (Eph. 4:22–24; Col. 3:10) begins to be restored. It is restored in Christ. Indeed, Paul says that we have been "predestined to be conformed to the image of his Son" (Rom. 8:29). And Christ is himself "the image of the invisible God" (Col. 1:15). But this process of transformation is a lifelong and complex one, with quite a few stops and starts along the way. How could it be otherwise? We are very complex beings. We are, within ourselves, deeply contradictory. Indeed, we often struggle to understand ourselves and we struggle to understand the world around us. Learning how to walk with God in this world is learning to walk by faith, but that is easier said than done. And yet, in principle, what that walk should look like is rather clear. So, we now need to go to the heart of the matter. In its most central, fundamental way, what does it mean to be sanctified? The question, of course, has to do with our conditional sanctification.

Fortunately for us, this question as to what is in the center of sanctification has already been debated and, more than that, answered by Jesus himself. He was asked, on one occasion, "Teacher, which is the great commandment in the Law?" (Matt. 22:26). It was a sly, futile attempt to get him to commit what the questioner hoped would be seen as a blunder among the religious specialists of the day, for this had been a topic of much discussion.

And what was Jesus's answer? In Mark's Gospel, he began with the text repeated twice a day by the Jews: "Hear, O Israel: The Lord our God, the Lord is one" (Mark 12:29; cf. Matt. 22:34–40; Luke 10:25–27). To this, he then added that love of God is at the center of everything. "And he said to him, 'You shall love the Lord your God with all your heart and with all your soul and with all your mind.'" Then Jesus added a second command. "You shall love your neighbor as yourself. On these two commandments depend all the Law and the Prophets" (Matt. 22:37–40; cf. Lev. 19:18). Love for God and love for neighbor are at the pinnacle. The motivation of love, to God and to neighbor, is what gives the reason for, and the weight to, all of our obedience. The keeping of the law loses its vitality, indeed its soul, if that keeping is not initiated, sustained, and directed by love. It is this connection between love and obedience to the law that we need now to explore a little further.

The second commandment that Jesus cited comes from a chapter in Leviticus in which God's laws for living were spelled out. There, we are not left in doubt about what love for our neighbor means. It is far more concrete than what we moderns might assume. We are inclined to think of this love only at an attitudinal, psychological level—having benign feelings, being positive, not being judgmental, always being accepting, being tolerant about life—but in Leviticus it is down-to-earth, concrete, and specific. It has to do with not stealing, lying, slandering, committing injustice, or acting unkindly. This love has much to do with acting justly.

This kind of justice has a far greater range of application than what we typically think of when we hear the word *justice*. Today, this word usually comes up in the context of the courts, when laws have been broken and punishment is handed out. But in this passage from Leviticus, acting justly has the sense of acting ethically, of being fair, being upright, caring enough for the other to do what is right by him or her. Indeed, we may take this even further. This love not only acts justly but will want to see that justice is done for others.

This is what has driven some of the great reforming movements in history. It is what moved some Christians to press for the end to the mistreatment of children in factories at the beginning of England's industrial age, the emancipation of slaves in the United States, and communist rule in some of the European countries. After all, the young, the oppressed, those on the fringes of society, the despised, and the outcast all bear the same image of God. They have the worth that every other human being has, and this worth is cited in Scripture as one reason why they should be treated ethically (Gen. 9:6; James 3:9–10).

Love, Paul said, "does no wrong to a neighbor; therefore love is the fulfilling of the law" (Rom. 13:10; cf. Gal. 5:14; James 2:8). Just how far removed we are today from both Leviticus and even our own Christian history is evident in the way this statement from Paul is so commonly misunderstood. Love "is the fulfilling of the law" is often taken to mean that those who intend no malice can do whatever they want. But this is a serious misreading because it divorces love from holiness. It imagines that if we just feel right about doing something, it will pass as right. It allows our therapeutic habits to trump what is ethical. Indeed, it makes that inward sense itself what is ethical. Feeling good becomes better than being good. Feeling good is the substitute for being good. The objective standard is replaced by the subjective disposition.

How far can we be from what Scripture actually says? God's holiness includes his love, and therefore love for God requires that we respect what is right and do what is ethically upright. An alibi of love can never be the justification of what is un-holy. There is no opposition between love and holiness. Indeed, there is only a mutually reinforcing union. Love is holiness in attitude and in action.

That this is so is evident from the fact that this command to love our neighbor in Leviticus was placed under the overall commandment, "You shall be holy, for I the LORD your God am holy" (Lev. 19:2). So, under holiness, and as a requirement of that holiness, and as an expression of its essential nature, is the demand that we love. This is the rule in Scripture, not the exception.

Nowhere is this truth made more evident than in the Johannine epistles. There had been a landslide away from apostolic belief and practice when John wrote to the churches in and around Ephesus. "Fierce wolves" had indeed entered the flock and had "twisted" things were in fact being said (Acts 20:29–30). John's response was simple and direct. Within the biblical framework of the gospel, authentic Christian faith will always be evidenced in the practice of holy-love. That was exactly his argument, and it was premised on his twofold description of God: "God is light" (1 John 1:5) and "God is love" (1 John 4:8). God, in other words, is holy-love.

So it was that John then insisted that the presence of holiness in its bond with love is the prime test of our spiritual authenticity. How do we know that we know God? The answer is "if we keep his commandments" (1 John 2:3). If we do, "truly the love of God is perfected" in us (1 John 2:5).

The genuineness of our knowledge of God is revealed by whether or not we are obeying the truth that we have from his Word. This love grows in the soil of obedience. We may be tempted to separate love from holiness, to think that love can flourish apart from holiness, but John will have none of it. We can no more allow this separation in ourselves than we are able to see it in Christ. Whoever claims to know Christ "ought to walk in the same way in which he walked" (1 John 2:6). Later, John wrote that "this is the love of God, that we keep his commandments" (1 John 5:3). And, again, "whoever does not practice *righteousness* is not of God, nor is the one who does not *love* his brother" (1 John 3:10). It is, then, both love and holiness. It is love as an expression of holiness and holiness in its bond to love, because there is no divorce between them in the character of God.

The command to love, John said, was an "old" one, a commandment "that you had from the beginning" (1 John 2:7). Presumably he was thinking about the commands to love God and neighbor that were there in the Law and the Prophets. Certainly the command to love was also in Jesus's teaching. But, paradoxically, it was also a "new" commandment, John said. Indeed, Jesus himself had called it new: "A new commandment I give to you, that you love one another: just as I have loved you, you also are to love one another" (John 13:34).

In what sense was this commandment to love "new"? It was new in the sense that it had in Christ a real-life model of what this great virtue looked like in practice. He gave to the commandment a fresh exegesis and application in actual life that had never quite been seen before in the same way. And this application had no limits. We are to love, not simply the loveable, or those like ourselves, but even our enemies and persecutors.

But more importantly, it was new because through the cross and resurrection, Christ was making redemptively present to us, and in us, the "age to come" in which love endures forever. That age is breaking in on this world. The "darkness is passing away and the true light is already shining" (1 John 2:8). We are experiencing in ourselves another world, another reality, one that will never fail, will never fade, and will never cease. We know ourselves to be anchored by sight, sound, and inclination in an age that is passing away, to which we are connected through our fallen human nature. But at the same time we also know ourselves to be part of that world that is coming. We taste and experience this other world even now. And this ability to love, even as Christ did, is a sign that we have made this transition from a world doomed to pass away and into a world that will be there for all eternity.

This holy-love of God, then, is at the core of all reality. It was there in eternity past and it will be there in the eternity that for us is yet to come. It is what we see in the life of Christ, what was at work in his death as he bore our sin for us, in our place, and as he rose triumphantly over all of the enemies whose work and character are dark. He now waits until all of these enemies are put under his feet. Then his conquest on the cross will ring throughout the entire cosmos, and that "age" that for us is yet to come will indeed come in all of its splendor. And this holy-love will reign unchallenged because God himself will be without challengers.

Looking Further

We have been thinking about the heart of sanctification, its very core, as consisting in loving God and loving our neighbor. These twin loves, these two commandments, are at the same time an expression of holiness. God's character is that of holy-love, and that is what the Holy Spirit is working to restore to us through the process of sanctification.

It is, though, worth lingering on this thought a little more because we all find it hard to hold together these two aspects of God's character. They seem, at times, to be incompatible, though of course, they are not. And we often surrender one side or the other. There are those,

I suggested earlier, who may affirm both sides but then lose sight of love. They become preoccupied with holiness but this is then reduced to rules, some of which can be quite petty and have little to do with Scripture. This preoccupation then slides into a graceless legalism.

There are others who are consumed by the thought of the love of God but lose its connection to his holiness. That leads into an anti-nomianism or, worse, into the kind of liberalism that was once wide-spread in American Protestantism. Its gospel, as H. Richard Niebuhr put it, in *The Kingdom of God in America*, was that a God without wrath, brought man without sin, into a kingdom without judgment, through a Christ without a cross. When God's love is thus disengaged from his holiness, the church is left without a gospel.

Legalism and antinomianism, in their different ways, damage Christian life because they undo the connections between love and holiness. At their base, in both cases, is a misunderstanding of the character of God. Or, at least, an inability to live consistently in the light of both holiness and love.

If we think of God's holiness as his perfect, burning, moral purity, then how can we conceive of that purity as not including love? If it did not include love—his patience, long-suffering, compassion, and kind-ness—would it be the holiness of which Scripture speaks? Without his love, God's holiness would be incomplete. It would be lacking half of its character. It would not be perfect holiness.

At the same time, what kind of love would we have if it were dis-engaged from God's holiness—his righteousness, goodness, truthful-ness, and justice?

Disengaged from holiness, love would be indifferent to sin. It would be unmoved by what is *wrong* except, perhaps, that it might be sympathetic to the suffering that comes from what is wrong. Would it be God's kind of love, then, if it were willing to overlook despicable human behavior? Would it really be love if it were untouched by what is cruel and depraved? This looking the other way might masquerade as loving forgiveness. But is this not actually moral indifference? Let us not forget that those who are unmoved and untouched by cruelty are psychopaths. No. This is not love! Nor is it love to allow any ac-commodation to what is wrong simply because we do not want to be "judgmental." This kind of moral weakness, one that wants always to be "tolerant," is at best a soft, boneless sentimentality.

Think about how this works out in practice. Are we to suppose that love without righteous character has ever driven Christian missions? The love that has motivated missions has, in fact, never been indifferent to the human plight. This care for others begins with their fallen and lost condition and with the wreckage that has resulted among humans because of sin. Why would missionaries and evangelists have gone out into the highways and byways of life, and into far-off places, taking with them the gospel of Christ's redemption, if they were not engaged in a conflict with what is wrong? Why would some of these missionaries have put themselves in peril to do this if they were not moved by *both* love for the afflicted and a passion for what is right?

Among those who have thus gone forth with the gospel are some who have also worked in truly dark places in the world. Besides carrying the gospel with them, they have also picked up abandoned children and cared for them, and rescued some in the sex trade, some consumed by drugs, those forgotten on the fringes of society, children being misused, the desperately poor, those of the lowest caste, and the otherwise despised of the earth. Why? Was it because love was untouched by the injustices these people were suffering or, in some cases, the wrongs they were inflicting on others? No. The truth is exactly the opposite. Real love is never morally indifferent because it is always part of the vision of what is *right*. It can never be untouched by what has gone wrong in life. It can never be uncaring at a moral level. And the reason is that God's love is never indifferent, uncaring, or disengaged. It is forever bonded to holiness. Love, indeed, is an expression of that holiness.

We must have both love and holiness, and we must have them in the union that they have in the being of God. This is exactly what the Holy Spirit begins to replicate in believers in the process of sanctification.

Ground Level

So, if love for God and for neighbor is at the center of sanctification, what does it mean to love in practice at the place where the proverbial rubber meets the road? When Paul wrote his lyrical and famous description of love, was he just dreaming as poets sometimes do? Was he just imagining what a perfect world might look like? I doubt it. Would it be far afield to suppose that 1 Corinthians 13 is an application of what Paul knew of God's character from Scripture? That, I venture, is the answer.

Certainly, Paul wanted the Corinthians to major on the love that comes from God rather than on the gifts he had given, with which they were so infatuated (1 Cor. 13:1–4). It is, indeed, possible to exploit God's gifts, for our own gain, while forgetting from whence the gifts come. The antidote to this is understanding more deeply, and practicing more consistently, the nature of *agape*-love—because it cauterizes all self-serving attitudes.

Paul's description of this love in 1 Corinthians 13, it has often been said, is both positive and negative. It is negative in that love opposes sin and positive in that it embodies beautiful virtues like patience, kindness, and generosity. This, though, is not very apt. There is nothing negative and everything positive in love's opposition to sin.

It would be better, then, to speak of the two sides to love as being rather like the two sides to a coin. The so-called negatives, the coin's one side, all express God's holiness. Love "does not envy" but is generous. It does not "boast" but, rather, is humble and seeks, as we have seen in the Godhead, the praise of the other. It is not "arrogant" but, as we see in the incarnation, is willing to take a lowly position. It is not self-centered but is other-oriented, so it "does not insist on its own way." Indeed, had love not been this way in eternity, there would have been no incarnation at all. Love is not "irritable or resentful." It takes no pleasure in "wrongdoing" (1 Cor. 13:4–6). Love here is a name for God's holiness. Indeed, as we have seen, Paul says that because love does no harm to others, it is "the fulfilling of the law" (Rom. 13:10).

On the other side of the coin, there are the so-called positive dimensions of love. It is "patient and kind." It rejoices in the "truth." It "bears all things, believes all things, hopes all things, endures all things" (1 Cor. 13:47). Who can read these brief descriptions and not remember the many statements in Scripture of God's gracious, patient, and long-suffering love? For us to begin to love in this way is to be

God-like, for this is what God is like. While never accommodating himself to our sin he is, nevertheless, slow to judge it and willing to wait for our repentance. He waits for us to come to a better mind. He shows compassion to us, the psalmist says, because "he knows our frame; he remembers that we are dust" (Ps. 103:14). And so we are. Not only is our life fleeting, not only are we subject to all of life's perils, diseases, and catastrophes, but internally we are frail and shaky, too. Where would we be without a compassionate God who remains compassionate despite knowing our every thought, weakness, and sinful disposition?

Is it, therefore, too much to ask that, where this same love of God has reached us in Christ, where it has taken hold of us through the gospel—that we, too, should be patient and kind? Is it too much to expect that we would be slow to take offense, slow to resent the behavior of others toward ourselves, and that we will be quick to pardon it as we ourselves have been pardoned? This is exactly what is expected of us. We should be "forgiving each other . . . as the Lord has forgiven" us (Col. 3:13; 2:6).

This *agape-love*, rooted in and arising from the character of God, is constantly undoing what is done in the world. At least it undoes the consequences of sin in the context of personal relations. When unkind, nasty, demeaning, or despicable acts occur, they do have an indelible nature. What is done has been done. It stands there. It is a kind of irremovable witness that will not be silenced. "The Moving Finger writes," observed Omar Khayyam, "and, having writ, / Moves on: nor all thy Piety nor Wit / Shall lure it back to cancel half a Line, / Nor all thy Tears wash out a Word of it." And yet, while this is true, it is not the whole story.

The past is, indeed, indelible. In the one afflicted, it lives on in the memory, maybe for a lifetime. But kindness, patience, and forgiveness reach across the divide to the other. And by so acting within their nature as virtues, they remove the presence of that irremovable witness. It is as if that witness is no longer there. And to the one who is forgiving, this act itself dissolves the poisonous inward consequences of the bad things that have been said or done. To the one forgiven, it opens a new chapter.

It is natural for us to love our country, our children, and our friends. It is natural to fall in love. But it is not natural to love with *agape-love* those who are unlike ourselves, or those who offend us, or those for whom we have lost all respect for one reason or another, or those who speak ill of us or do us other kinds of harm. Furthermore, it is natural for us as sinners to love ourselves. That is, we have an eye out for our own interests; we protect those interests, seek advantages for ourselves, become irritated when we do not get our own way, and we are willing to step over others in pursuit of that self-interest. All of this comes quite naturally to us.

What is unnatural in a fallen world is this *agape*-love. Indeed, it is *so* unnatural that Reinhold Niebuhr thought it to be an impossible ideal. He thought it could only be for another age and time! In a way that he did not quite understand, he was right. This love is of another "age," but this other "age" is now breaking into our world and is being made redemptively present through Christ's cross. That is what lies behind this other-oriented kind of love. It puts others ahead of that self-interest which is so persistent and so loud in our fallen nature. It has an open hand with itself. It gives itself away. It genuinely wants the other's good and happily promotes it. This love works in, with, and through the virtues like goodness, truthfulness, and faithfulness. This is all quite unnatural, but this is what God's kind of love is like.

Love, in its very nature, bears all things and endures all things. This is surely exemplified in the cross. That Christ bore sin that was not his own is of the essence of the gospel. And that he bore the assault of evil upon himself is clear from the narrative. The point about love, his love, is that it was *willing* to bear this assault and bear this penalty. That is what love is like. But we also see that, as defenseless as love seems, it is also the way of victory. In this strange and awful moment on the cross, when all that was true and right in Christ was in the process of being maligned and destroyed, defeat turned to triumph. Love triumphs because it is part of the moral fabric of life that God not only preserves but will also make victorious.

It was "for the joy that was set before him" that Jesus "endured the cross, despising the shame, and is seated at the right hand of the throne of God" (Heb. 12:2). This has set us an example. Paul could say, "I endure everything for the sake of the elect" (2 Tim. 2:10). We can endure insults, threats, opposition, being demeaned and put in danger because this is what God's kind of love does: it "endures all things." The only reason there can be endurance is that behind it, in the love that motivates it, there is great strength.

This is why it is so mistaken to reduce this kind of love to what is commonly thought of as love. It is not only sympathetic. It is not only kind. It is not only forbearing. It is not only generous. It is all of these things but it is so much more. It is holy and it is eternal. It thinks from the starting point of the Holy about the world, about individuals in the world, about their well-being, and about God's glory. It has eternity as its framework. And as P. T. Forsyth said, the church needs, above all, people who have been there and have been "naturalized" as citizens of that country.

It is these strong fibers in love that sustain the virtues that become so beautiful, even in their very fragility, in a fallen world. Love brings, as a part of its life, a self-control, a gentle courtesy. It brings the totally different perspective of eternity to our fallen world. How very different it is from the in-the-moment volcanic eruptions of anger, dislike, and resentment that are heard so often in the workplace and in homes. Such love has a gentleness that only the strong have. And when truth speaks in the company of love, it speaks to the most effect. And when righteousness walks with love, as it always should, it is less likely to be read as mere self-righteousness.

We need to have our eyes fixed, then, on what will endure forever. What endures are not the gifts, but love. That was Paul's starting point, and it is where he also ended in this chapter. What endures is "faith, hope, and love," but "the greatest of these is love" (1 Cor. 13:13). Faith, hope, and love are frequently mentioned together and in association with one another (e.g., Rom. 5:1–5; Eph. 4:2–5; 1 Pet. 1:3–8). But of these, it is love that "endures," for faith will be swallowed up in sight, and what we have hoped for will have come in its fullness. But love endures because it reflects what is eternally true of the character of God. God is love.

Not So Fast

Another Inconvenient Truth

These truths about God are always easier to see than to live by. And this is especially so, given the difficulty we all have of living in this highly pressurized, haste-filled, faster-than-fast, here-today-and-gone-tomorrow, impermanent, noisy, and intrusive kind of world. Let us not think that such an environment leaves us unscathed or that it has no impact upon our ability to know and love God.

This God, against everything our culture judges to be reasonable, against everything we judge to be reasonable, actually comes to us and bids us die. We cannot know him unless we die. We cannot walk with him unless we are constantly dying to all that is perverted, dark, willful, self-centered, and self-serving within ourselves. We are not our own but have been bought, and therefore our goals, ambitions, desires, and patterns of life all fall under the rule of Christ. They are all to conform to his will and not to the patterns of life that seem normal in the culture. There is a world of iniquity at work within us, and it is this world that must be put to death. Those "who belong to Christ Jesus have crucified the flesh with its passions and desires" (Gal. 5:24), writes Paul. This self-crucifying is "in order that the body of sin might be brought to nothing, so that we would no longer be enslaved to sin" (Rom. 6:6). It is "the passions of the flesh," our fallenness, that "wage war against your soul" (1 Pet. 2:11) and therefore need to be rejected, repented of, and inwardly outlawed.

The Puritans called this "mortification." It is perhaps a sign of how far removed we are from the temper of that kind of godliness that this language no longer rings a bell with us. That would not be so bad if we had our own language and our own equivalents for what they had in mind. But we do not. This is not something about which we talk much. It does not show up in our sermons except when preachers mumble and then move on to more positive things. It is not what authors write about much or what readers mostly want to read.

But how else can we speak of the rejection of "the desires of the flesh" (Gal. 5:17) or "the works of the flesh" (Gal. 5:19)? In Galatians 5:19–21, Paul saw these as working out in several different areas. Some are sensual ("sexual immorality, impurity, sensuality"). Some are doc-

GOD IN THE WHIRLWIND

trinal ("idolatry, sorcery"). Others are behavioral ("enmity, strife, jealousy, fits of anger, rivalries, dissensions, divisions, envy, drunkenness, orgies"). The "works" of the flesh are the fruit, the outworking, of the "desires" of the flesh. No one will see an end to the fruit unless they can get at the root, the inner compulsions. And that is what inward "mortification" is all about.

Mortification is, of course, the language of the *moral* world, the world defined by God's holy-love. Where we so often live in our minds, as I have been arguing, is in a world that is *psychological*. The former is a world where faith is required and where the death of Christ is at the center. The latter is where self-help techniques replace faith. Where we once had redemption, we now have therapy. The one is all about dying to the morally deformed parts of the self. The other is all about finding, cherishing, and realizing the self, even in its deformed parts, if it makes us happy. An age whose temper is therapeutic and self-focused will find this language of mortification quite quaint. More than that, it will sound disagreeable. Indeed, some may see it even as an obscenity, perhaps the only one that now remains.

The age in which believers live, however, is already "the age to come." It is totally different from the culture in which they also live. All believers live in both of these worlds. They cannot escape the one to live in the other. That is the miscalculation that both mystics and monks have made. Nor yet can believers simply curse the darkness in this world, for they can still see all the marks of its divine creation. They must live in this world and light a fire for it because it is cold and dark. They live in the midst of their culture but, to change the image, they live by the beat of a different Drummer. They must hear the sounds of a different time, an eternal time, listening for the music from a different place. For that world is theirs. It is Christ's world. It is the "age to come." They have been received into this world. It penetrates their existence even now. They live in their own culture in order to be the outposts of this other world. In the one world, they are but sojourners and pilgrims. In the other, they are permanent residents.

Sound and Fury

But how are we to do this? How are we going to hear this music? How are we going to hear the divine Drummer whose beat gets lost in all of the noise of our modern world? We are constantly distracted, always under pressure, constantly bombarded by e-mails. We have unwanted telephone calls. We are alerted to the arrival of text messages. Families have music lessons and football games, and there are hikes to be organized. Parents have demanding jobs; some have endless traveling to do. And we are all besieged by the world into which we are wired. It has become a great temptation even as it is a great fascination to us. Indeed, in 2013, almost half of the American adults surveyed acknowledged this.

Like everything in the modernized world, our information technology has two sides to it. It blesses with one hand and then takes away with the other. And, most importantly here, what it takes away is our capacity to have a functioning worldview. Without that, our doctrine of God becomes emasculated. An emasculated view of God will never be able to sustain the life of sanctification to which we have been called.

Information and entertainment technologies have annihilated distance, enlarging the circle of our knowledge and, indeed, of our presence. Or, would it be truer to say that the entire world with all of its events, movies, and music has entered our homes? Once we had to be where the events were happening, where the music was being made, to know about it. Now, all that is needed is a camera and it is splashed across the whole world. This instant access to information worldwide, to all of its sights, sounds, and happenings is an extraordinary benefit. It has made us citizens of the entire world with an ability to communicate with any other citizen in this world instantaneously. It has the capacity to lift us beyond our naturally parochial boundaries.

At the same time, though, as our knowledge of the world grows—indeed, at an exponential rate—our capacity to have a worldview becomes much diminished and our ability to pay attention to God and his truth is often undermined. God, we need to remind ourselves, is not just an experience or an idea. The saving knowledge of God comes within a framework which God himself has disclosed. It is a framework of ideas that corresponds to what is there in the world, in reality, in God himself. If this worldview breaks down under the bombardment of news, e-mails, videos, blogs, and music, then what is lost is also what is at its center. It is God himself or, I should say, it is our understanding, our ability to make sense of the world in the light of who God is that breaks down. And that is where our sanctification breaks down, too.

Technology greatly expands and enlarges our abilities and it mightily expands what we can know. But this is a two-way street. If it enables us to be everywhere, it is also the case that the whole world—at least its sounds and sights—can enter our minds, too and, once in, it can then enter our souls. This potentially imperils any functioning worldview. Why is this so?

It is partly because of the sheer volume of what is coming in. It overwhelms us. Since 1960, the amount of data and information individuals are absorbing, because of all of our new technology, has tripled. If this technology expands our capacity to know things, it also multiples the things that are thrown at us to know. When all of this was just taking shape, Neil Postman warned about "information glut," and a little later David Shenk spoke of "data smog." They were right. That is what we now have. Our minds are choked with too much to know. And things are only intensifying.

What allowed all of this to happen only keeps expanding. The iPad and iPhone now massively increase our capacity to access media while we are on the run. The iPod and MP3 massively increase the amount of music we can consume. With the ability to multitask, American teenagers are now packing in an additional two hours of media consumption per day, bringing their total to more than ten hours.

In addition to the sheer volume is the rapidity with which the whole of the media-filtered, technology-delivered world is changing. It never stands still long enough for us to take our bearings on it. What is important and what is not, what is weighty and what is ephemeral, what is tragic and what is trivial, meet us with about the same intensity. It becomes hard, sometimes, to tell which is which. Our world blurs amid the rapid flow of facts, factoids, images, voices, laughter, entertainment, and vapid commentary. We slowly lose the capacity to see the connections between things. Life seems to have no shape. It looks like a sequence of fast-moving but random experiences with no center and little meaning. Not only does a Christian worldview disappear; the very capacity for such a thing becomes tenuous. How, then, will we hear this other music from another place? How will we hear that Drummer's beat above the sounds of this world?

I will say only this. There are no easy answers and there are no painless ones. But, at the same time, it is not impossible. It is not impossible for us, if it is important to us, to choose what we are going to do and then to focus on doing it. The real question is how deep—or how shallow—is our desire to know God?

We need to begin by asking what is at stake. What might we be in danger of losing amid the noise and frenzy of our modernized societies here in the West? We are in danger of being squeezed into the mold of the modernized world with its low horizons of knowing, its relativism, and its superficiality. This threatens our identities as knowers of God, those for whom he is the center, for whom his holy-love defines what moral reality is, and before whom we stand. It threatens how we see life and how we live in the world. It threatens all of that.

Recognizing this danger, we need to carve out space for ourselves in which we can daily attend to God's Word, to study it, mark it, learn it, and inwardly digest its truth. This truth must shape our whole understanding of life as we recognize from whom this truth comes and why God has thus given it to us. This must take precedence. It must take precedence even at the cost of phones, e-mails, the Internet, texts, TV, Facebook, music, and all of the other ways that our technology wires us into a major competitor for our time and attention. Innocent though these things may be, they stand in the way of our knowing God if they steal from us the time that we need for that pursuit.

And we do need time. This kind of daily discipline used to be an undisputed part of Christian practice. But it appears to have fallen on hard times. And the result will be, once again, that we will be in danger of "forgetting" God. In the Old Testament, as we have seen, this had to do with the disobedience of not paying attention to God and his truth. And today, we are in danger of reaching the same end, though by a different route. Now, we are simply too preoccupied, too frenzied, living simultaneously on too many fronts, so that we just do not have time. We are not able to find this central space in our lives.

When David spoke of the "meditation of my heart" (Ps. 19:14; 49:3; cf. Ps. 119:15, 23, 99), he was speaking of being in God's presence, reflecting on his truth, learning how to walk with God, being before the face of God. This Word he stored up in his heart "that I might not sin against you" (Ps. 119:11). That is what we need to do and where we need to be every day. This will happen only if we are deliberate about it and are willing to give up whatever stands in our way to this end.

Let us make no mistake about this. If we do not do this aright, if we are not daily seeking God's face, if we are not pondering the truth he has given us in his Word, if we are not daily being nourished in our souls by it, and if we are not daily repenting of our sin where we need to, our faith will wither and our walk with God will disappear. If, however, we carve out this center for our lives, we will be in the place where Paul's prayer for the Thessalonians can be realized in us despite our very modern lives: "May the Lord direct your hearts to the love of God," he wrote, "and to the steadfastness of Christ" (2 Thess. 3:5). That is what God, the Holy Spirit, will do.

CHAPTER 8

Come, Let Us
Bow Down

Praise, my soul, the King of heaven,
To his feet thy tribute bring;
Ransomed, healed, restored, forgiven,
Evermore his praises sing: Alleluia! Alleluia!
Praise the everlasting King!

HENRY FRANCIS LYTE

Prelude

Worship is essential to our sanctification. It is, at the same time, an essential expression of our sanctification.

God's grace in Christ has turned us from our former ways of unbelief into the ways of belief. We therefore aim to make God and his truth central to all that we do. And part of being centered on him is that we join in with the celestial worship that rings out, day and night, in adoration, praise, and thanksgiving before God. Yes, "sing, choirs of angels, sing in exaltation . . . all glory in the highest," and let us add our voices to yours! Unlike the angels, though, we come as redeemed sinners, and that makes our worship different. What is not part of the angels' worship is central to ours. Indeed, this is something into which they "long to look" (1 Pet. 1:12).

So, what should this worship, this worship of ours, look like? How should we do this in our churches? Private worship is one thing; corporate worship is a little different because there has to be agreement

187

on what we do together. In recent years, though, this agreement has been hard to find, at least in many evangelical churches.

Worship Wars

There are really two issues here. The one has to do with the *content* of our worship. The other has to do with its *form*. Worship is about expressing the "worth" or the "worthiness" of God. That is what the word *worship* means. Its content, therefore, is what God has disclosed to us of himself, his character, and his redemptive work. It is both a response to who he is and a celebration of what he has done especially in our redemption. The form of our worship has to do with how this praise is shaped as a vehicle for the church's corporate praise.

Most people assume that on the content of worship there is a widespread, commonsensical accord, at least in the evangelical world. We gather every Sunday to worship *God*! It is, people assume, the forms that create all the disagreements. At least this was the case in many of the discussions that reverberated around the church in the 1970s, '80s and '90s.

This, though, was a mistake, and there are now growing indications that more and more people are seeing this. In the context of Western culture, and because of growing biblical illiteracy in our churches, the content has often become highly eroded. It has been made light and insubstantial, replaced by a set of self-focused interests. There is often not enough substance to direct, discipline, and shape the forms through which this content is expressed. It is the content, after all, that gives us the reason for our worship, and it should, therefore, also suggest the ways in which we should worship.

It is true, of course, that the church has never had an entirely common mind on how its corporate worship should be done. And these historic differences continue today. In some churches the form for each Sunday is prescribed, but in others it is not. Some are liturgical but others are not. Some have a more traditional feel while others are more contemporary. Some have preserved prayers and litanies from the past while others invent them in the present, sometimes in the very moment of worship. In some, the thought of the congregation acting together is important. But in contemporary worship the focus moves more toward the individual. Each expresses his or her own worship in his or her own way.

Contemporary worship forms really took shape with the Jesus Movement of the 1960s. But this coalesced with other things that were happening. Most important here was the inward turn that our culture took, sometimes coupled with an antiauthoritarian mood. This was then intensified by the surging charismatic movement that followed in the 1970s, '80s, and '90s. During this same time, churches were often moving into a marketing mode. Adapting to pop culture became a key ingredient in outreach strategy. The result of all of this was that worship was more likely to be led by a worship team made up of musicians than by the pastor(s) as was the case in more traditional churches.

And there is another complicating factor here. Most people understand that even the best forms of worship do not themselves secure the best worship. What the worshiper brings to worship is an indispensable part of the mix. Without the knowledge of God in those who worship, without active faith, without reverence, without gratitude in the worshiper, even the best forms of worship simply fall flat.

But today this relationship between the form of worship and the disposition of the worshiper is vexed for a reason that is altogether more contemporary. It is music. Those who come to church often feel that they cannot worship adequately if they dislike the music, its style, its beat, or the instruments that are being used. This may not be because they have thought carefully about what kind of music is appropriate to worship. It may simply be a matter of personal taste.

Somewhere along a line of musical styles, taste for most people has settled down. That line goes from Patti Page, Frank Sinatra, and Dean Martin; to the Beatles and Rolling Stones; to Pink Floyd and The Who; to Led Zeppelin and Janis Joplin; to the Grateful Dead and AC/DC; to Pink and Fiona Apple; to jazz, country, blues, and bluegrass; and on to . . . Debussy . . . to Mozart, Chopin, Bach, and Beethoven. Somewhere along this line, taste comes down. Once there, for so many, it is reinforced daily by hours of listening. Our ability to hear music, to hear exactly the kind of music that we want to hear, is unprecedented. Because taste has thus been reinforced, and because our listening becomes habitual, our preferences become fixed, immoveable, and invincible. Wherever taste has come down along this line is where we are comfortable. This—or something like it—is what we want to hear in church on Sunday (or, perhaps, Saturday night).

The problem, of course, is that we come down at different places. In the church, we are nowhere near to having a common mind on this matter. We do not have a common set of taste buds when it comes to music. And we have not reached any agreement as to what musical styles are appropriate for worship. We only know what we like and dislike. So it is that we are engaging with ourselves in a bit of a tussle.

I suspect, though, that our worship wars, which are almost wholly music wars, are really obscuring the larger issues that are in play. These lie below the surface. They are more in the *content* of our worship and less in its outward forms. The most fundamental of these issues is whether the focus will be on the triune God or on our experience of ourselves as worshipers, whether our worship will be God-centered or needs-driven.

This may seem like an unfair dichotomy. After all, it is uncommon for people to go to worship who have no intention of worshiping God! And who has come into a church to worship who has not had needs?

However, needs-shaped worship is invariably self-focused. When worship begins from this premise, it quickly becomes a carnival of competing desires, demands, tastes, and private aches in the congregation. It easily descends into the therapeutic world. Sermons, in this atmosphere, are almost always aimed simply at providing a lift, some inspiration, from whatever source help can be had. And this also inclines pastors to infuse the worship with flourishes from the feel-good entertainment world. Is it not striking how, in contexts like these, we can be in worship without being aware of the centrality, goodness, and greatness of God, of his grace, and of Christ's self-giving in the incarnation and cross? Not even once. Or, if we are aware, it is because we have brought this awareness with us into church and not because the worship service itself has directed us to these great truths.

These are all theological themes, of course, and that may be the problem. In so many churches today, theological themes have been forsaken for inspirational, therapeutic, and practical ones. These are what are considered "relevant." Worship, as a result, then becomes a blend of inspiration and entertainment offered up in a musical form that correlates with the generational niche into which the particular church wants to settle.

This, I believe, is where the real worship war is going on. It is far more profound than what music we like and how loud the drums should be. Because our current debate is so much focused on the forms of worship, we are often overlooking the far more basic questions about its content.

In this chapter, then, I will not be discussing musical instruments, the order of service, or whether prayers should be extempore or liturgical. I need to go beneath the forms. I will be thinking more about some of the theological substructure under the surface than about the actual practice of worship on the surface.

The way into this subject, I am proposing, is to begin with the nature of the church, the church that is worshiping. I do so given what has been said thus far in this book. There would be no church without God's gracious initiative, and so to begin with the church is to acknowledge this prior action. The church has a nature and a unity that are alike the result of God's supernatural work and his grace. This is where we must start when answering the question as to what worship is and how we should do it.

Those who come to worship in a local church are not simply a voluntary association of people. A church is neither a club nor an organization. It has an organizational aspect to it, but it is fundamentally much more than an organization. It is a called-out people. And the worship itself is not simply a get-together, a gathering where people can express themselves. It is not simply what we like. It is not like going to a concert. There is a purpose, a different purpose, for the church's gathering. It is to give glory to God, to be renewed in his presence, to be instructed, to remember Christ's death, and to remember again our place among the people of God. This purpose should shape everything that happens both in the service of worship and in the worshipers. It is here that I will begin, and then I will move on to think about how God is central in, and present to, the church as it worships.

Call to Worship

On the eve of his death, Christ prayed for the disciples. In that prayer he also included the church that was yet to come. This prayer, now so familiar to us, contains the request that the Father would keep those whom he had given to Christ, "that they may be one, even as we are one" (John 17:11). What did Christ mean?

The answer, it seems clear, is that the church is ever exposed to the world, ever vulnerable to its alternative reading of reality, its system of values, its outlook, its habits, its prejudices, its temptations, its counterfeit gospels, its fraudulent hopes, its dangers, its pressures, its distractions, its dark holes, its conflicts and persecutions. With the church thus ever in danger, Jesus prayed that it would be kept in the Father's "name." That is, the wall of separation between Christian faith and this spiritually dangerous and intrusive world is what we know of God's character, his holy-love. When the church lives deliberately within this boundary, within this knowledge, it is not only in a good place but it also finds its definition of itself as the people of God. It finds its purpose, its mission, and its end. It is to be God's people who live before him faithfully, contentedly, productively, and joyfully. And it is also here that the church finds its reason for worship. It is here that it finds the *way* to worship. And here, this people becomes "one."

In the days when the ecumenical movement was still in full swing, this prayer—and, indeed, this request—was perhaps the most frequently reiterated biblical text of the time. It was assumed that, since Christ had prayed that Christians might all be one, there was a mandate for setting aside all theological differences to get to this destination. Matters of doctrinal belief were often dismissed as being secondary, as unhappily divisive, and they came to be seen as an impediment to the church's flourishing. They needed to be set aside if this visible Christian unity was to be achieved.

What was missed, though, is that in the New Testament this unity is not primarily ecclesiastical. The church's outward unity is certainly desirable and to be pursued. We need to do everything we can to preserve it. However, outward unity is impossible in the absence of inward unity. This inward unity arises from the nature of God and his redemptive purposes. That being so, it must be expressed in ways that are theological because this is how the New Testament itself frames what God has done in Christ. This unity is never about simply engineering church structures.

This is exactly the point that Paul made. Since there is only one Spirit, there can be only "one body." Since there is only one Lord, there can be only "one faith, one baptism." There is only one God and Father, "who is over all and through all and in all" (Eph. 4:4–6). In thinking of the church's unity, Paul began with the triune reality of God and with his redemptive work. That has to precede our understanding of the church, and without it there is, in fact, no church.

Christian unity, therefore, is not something we *create*. It can be created only by God, because it exists only in Christ. This unity is the result of the redeeming work initiated by the Father, carried out by the Son, and applied by the Holy Spirit. Because this is so, the church's spiritual unity is as inviolable as is the nature of the Trinity. This is what gives reality to the church as the *one* people of God. This is the only reason we have for worshiping our triune God. And this is the underlying unity that should come to expression in our worship. Indeed, what God has done constitutes our call to worship *together*.

These divine actions explain why the church is spoken of in the singular in the New Testament. It is true, of course, that we find references to local churches as well. Phoebe, for example, was "a servant of the church at Cenchreae" (Rom. 16:1), or there was the "church" that met in the home of Prisca and Aquila (Rom. 16:5). And Paul wrote to "the church of God that is in Corinth" (1 Cor. 1:2) as he did to "the churches of Galatia" (Gal. 1:2). But he also spoke of the church in universal and singular terms.

All things, he declared, have been put under Christ's sovereign control, and he is "head over all things to *the* church" (Eph. 1:22). Paul clearly was speaking of the whole church and not simply a particular church in a particular place. Christ "loved *the* church" and will "present *the* church to himself in splendor" (Eph. 5:25, 27). It is his only bride (2 Cor. 11:1–2; Rev. 19:9; 21:2). Give no offense, Paul counseled, "to *the* church of God" (1 Cor. 10:32). And elsewhere the church is spoken of as "*the* assembly of the firstborn who are enrolled in heaven"

(Heb. 12:23). This theme is carried through the New Testament in a rich set of images that were employed to describe the church.

The church is the extension of the Old Testament people of God, in whom God's redemptive purposes have reached their end. There is, though, only one people of God. Christ, Paul said, gave himself "to purify for himself a people for his own possession" (Titus 2:14; cf. Heb. 4:9). But we need to see this statement in its full biblical context. The Corinthians were reminded of the promised Old Testament covenant blessings. As Paul reminded them, God had said of his own people that "I will be their God, and they shall be my people" (2 Cor. 6:16). It is a single people. As Peter said to some persecuted Christians, "Once you were "not a people, but now you are God's people" (1 Pet. 2:10; cf. Rom. 9:25). This covenant, which had created this people, rested upon the principles of God's initiating grace. It excluded works as a basis of acceptance, and it set out the need for faith in the God who promised. That is why Paul argued that being a "Jew" was no longer a matter of ethnicity—at least not for those thinking biblically—or of religious rites and rituals. A Jew "is one inwardly, and circumcision is a matter of the heart, by the Spirit, not by the letter" (Rom. 2:29). The logic from here was inescapable. Those who have been justified on the basis of Christ's work, be they Jew or Gentile, constitute the one "Israel of God" (Gal. 6:16). The church, then, is not only in continuity with the Old Testament people of God but is today *the* people of God.

The church is also Christ's "body" (Eph. 1:23), and there is only "*one* body" (Eph. 4:4). All who are believers have been baptized into this single "body" (1 Cor. 12:20). They are all "*one* body in Christ" (Rom. 12:5).

Once again the images change and, indeed, even get mixed! The church is "God's building" (1 Cor. 3:9; see also Matt. 16:18). But this building grows—it grows!—"into a holy temple in the Lord" (Eph. 2:21). And yet Paul spoke of this as a singular building. From here it was an easy transition into seeing the church as a household. It is the "household of God" (1 Pet 4:17; 1 Tim. 3:15) or, more simply, "God's house" (Heb. 3:6).

This was a metaphor that was well understood at the time when the New Testament was being written. Besides the family, well-to-do households also had a steward and servants. The steward ran the household. He oversaw its accounts, ordered its provisions, supervised the servants, and cared for guests on their arrival. All of this was then seen as a picture of the church. God is the owner of the house, and the redeemed people of God are his family. And the preacher is analogous to the steward. The preacher, though, does not provide for the church any more than the steward provided for the household out of his own pocket. The provisions we have from God for his church are in his Word. The important point here, though, is that there is *one* building, *one* household.

Finally, there is one flock. This, too, was a familiar image, and it was immediately picked up by Jesus. He declared himself to be "the good shepherd" (John 10:11, 14). Once the Gentiles had heard and embraced the gospel, there would be, he said, "one flock, one shepherd" (John 10:16). We have all been straying from God like lost sheep (Isa. 53:6; Luke 15:1–7) but "have now returned to the Shepherd and Overseer" of our souls (1 Pet. 2:25). Christ, in fact, is "the chief Shepherd" (1 Pet. 5:4) and "the great shepherd of the sheep" (Heb. 13:20).

These are just some of the images that are used of the church, and they are drawn from every aspect of life. There is, though, no one dominant image. They each highlight something a little different. The body image, for example, speaks to the church's unity and interdependence, the bride to Christ's self-sacrifice and covenant-love, the temple to the unique dwelling place of God. But as diverse and as varied as these images are, they all point back to the same fundamental reality: it is the reality of the triune God and the centrality of his redeeming work which explain why there is a church and why he is present to the church.

There is, then, one church, one people of God, one body, one bride, one building, one household, and one flock because there is only one God, one Redeemer, and one gospel. It is, in other words, God's initiating grace and the consequent knowledge of God that constitutes the church. It is upon these truths that the church is built. They are at its center. The church exists only to celebrate, declare, and live out these truths in a genuinely countercultural way wherever they are in tension with what is taken to be normative in the culture. This, after all, is what Jesus asked. He asked that the boundary between those who know the character of God and the world outside that does not know God would be preserved (John 17:11). It needs to be preserved in every church. It needs to be preserved in every worship service.

If we were to look for a single word that captures this thought of what makes the church "one," as Jesus asked in his prayer, it is *fellowship*. This is a word, though, that has mostly lost its biblical meaning today. When we say that we had "good fellowship," we mean that we had a good time, or that it was fun, or that we left with warm feelings. None of this is wrong, but it is all quite removed from what the biblical writers had in mind.

In the biblical world, the word *fellowship* was used of the relationship people had as a result of something they had in common. For example, there might be a piece of property that was jointly owned that, in this way, brought two people into relation with each other. Or, two people might have been in a business venture together, and in this they had fellowship. It was the thing that they had in common—the property or the business—that tied them together. These people might, in fact, not have had much else in common personally—they may even not have liked each other particularly—but because of their mutual interest, they worked together for their mutual benefit.

That is why Paul warned believers not to marry unbelievers, for "what *partnership* [his Greek is *fellowship*] has righteousness with lawlessness?" (2 Cor. 6:14). What, in other words, do they have in common if they do not have Christ as the foundation of their marriage? Likewise, after Paul had journeyed to Jerusalem and met with the young church's leaders—James, Peter, and John—they "gave the right hand of *fellowship*" to Paul (Gal. 2:9). They found that they and Paul shared in the same gospel truth, the same understanding of Christ. It was this that bound them together and gave them all a common mission.

It is this understanding of *fellowship* that passed into New Testament usage. Because of God's grace and faithfulness we have been "called into the *fellowship* of his Son" (1 Cor. 1:9). Christ is the bond among all of his people. We declare this in the Lord's Supper. It is our *fellowship* "in the blood of Christ . . . in the body of Christ" (1 Cor. 10:16). Joined to Christ by faith, we have "*partnership* in the gospel" (Phil. 1:5). This language emphasizes what we have in common, what we share *in.* It does not speak primarily to our feelings of unity, though these may be there, or our friendship with one another, though that may be there as well. It speaks to what created our unity. It is out of this grace-created bond that our common purpose, our reason for being united, arises.

Our *koinonia*, our fellowship, arises from the fact that we are "one" in Christ. We are not "one" in the sense that we do the same work, have the same interests, share the same musical tastes, have the same disposition, speak the same language, live in the same culture, belong to the same ethnic group, are part of the same generation, or have the same network of friends. We are one in *Christ*. The common grounding that we have is in this divine work, this antecedent grace, this uniting bond by the Spirit, in the Son, and before the Father. This is why we are summoned into church to express our common praise and adoration. We have received and believed the same gospel. We share the same faith. We worship before the same triune God. We belong in the same universal church. We may not use the same language in our praise, but we praise the same triune God. We come to worship from different places in our life, with different challenges, but we come to be instructed by the same Word of God. All of this is symbolically represented as we gather to share in the same Lord's Supper. It is these truths that give our worship its content.

Here, in this one word, we have captured both the vertical dimension of our worship and the horizontal. Worship is centrally about bringing our praise and adoration to God—Father, Son, and Holy Spirit. And yet it is the gathered church, in a specific location, that does this. We also speak to *one another* as we worship God. We join our voices as we sing and hear each other sing. We participate together in the praise, confess our sins together, and with one voice join in the prayer that is offered publicly. That prayer is not an individual's prayer that the rest of the congregation overhears. It is the *congregation's* prayer, voiced by an individual on its behalf. We hear in each other's presence the words of assurance. We listen together to the exposition of God's Word, and together we receive the benediction. Today, though, the prospect of this wonderful, intergenerational, multiethnic experience, the experience of the *one* people of God, has fallen before so many cultural impulses.

If we look at the way in which many evangelical churches have actually been worshiping since the 1970s, it is rather different from what I have been describing. It has become far more culturally defined than biblically. It has often catered to generational niches. It has been about marketing a "product" in a way that attracts new customers. The new customers, though, tend to belong to one of the generational tribes. Christian faith is pitched to them often without doctrinal truth. Pastors who have been in this business have mistakenly thought that doctrinal truth is "off-putting" to believers and unbelievers alike. And the outreach that has been done often has far more in common with the entertainment world than with the truths at the core of Christian faith. Too often it has been about the worshipers, and giving them a pleasant experience as they express themselves, rather than about the God whom they have come to worship.

Why, one wonders, did so many churches go down this road in the 1970s, '80s, and '90s? I think the answer is rather clear. It is that the individualism latent in much evangelical believing has been mightily strengthened by our postmodern self-focus. Furthermore, we have this eerie sense that the church is losing its ground, that its forward momentum has been halted, that it is beginning to be looked at as a relic.

The great strength of the gospel preachers who have gone out into life's highways and byways in the past to win men and women to Christ is that they made faith *personal*. It required each person to repent of their sin, believe the gospel, and exercise faith in the Redeemer. However, this faith which is personal all too often became individualistic. It was but a short step to take, then, for pastors to begin appealing to this individualism, in whatever form it took, in order to attract a congregation. When we appeal to consumer instinct in this way, and to what are often generational prejudices, the truth of the church is lost as the common denominator among the many individuals is lost. When this happens, local churches seem not to be part of the same bride, body, and flock. Consumer impulses so strongly appeal to self-interest that they destroy what believers have in common across generations, cultures, and races.

Now, along the edges of the evangelical world, this disposition is producing a lot of bleeding. It has propelled an exodus out of evangelical churches. Some have moved out into Eastern Orthodoxy, Anglo-Catholicism, and Catholicism. Others have simply moved home. Born-againers, in significant numbers, are dropping out of church. This is not true everywhere, or of everyone, or of every church. But many who were once part of the born-again world are now turning away from evangelical churches. In one study done in 2013, it was found that in the recent past, 70 percent of the young people who had been raised in evangelical youth groups had dropped out of church attendance once they became independent adults. Why?

When churches lose their central focus, when that focus is then displaced by generational tastes, when it is defined more by the culture of consumption than by who God is, it loses its seriousness. It also loses the sense of transcendence for which the human spirit longs. And, most importantly, it loses reality. Are we surprised, then, that Eastern Orthodoxy and Catholicism now begin to look like oases in the desert for those who still want to go to a church? And is it surprising that other churchgoers find that it is not worthwhile to go at all? The more churches become like their own culture, the less reason there is to be in a church. What the church offers can be had from the culture far more conveniently and perhaps at less cost.

Those who dropped out of church in the 1970s and '80s turned to televised worship services or simply to those preaching. But now these televised services have been largely supplanted by live streaming on the Internet. A church service heard in either of these ways, in the comfort of one's home, is certainly more convenient than going to an actual church. But individualistic "worship" of this kind has simply lost its connections to the one body and bride, the one people of God. How can we possibly be "addressing *one another* in psalms and hymns and spiritual songs, . . . submitting to *one another* out of reverence for Christ" (Eph. 5:19–21) if the "other" on the television or computer screen is mute and in a faraway city?

This, I suggest, is why there are wars about the way we should worship. If the way we worship is defined more by the worshiper than by the reality of the God who is being worshiped, then chaos breaks out. This is so because what is at the core of the church's existence is made to retreat before the church's human diversity. And diversity unchecked can only lead to fragmentation and disintegration.

Worshipers today not only bring their own postmodern individualism to church, but they also bring their own part in our human diversity. Human diversity is a gift of God. But in the church it can become divisive if the purposes of worship are not clearly preserved and given priority.

After all, one of the extraordinary things about the body of Christ is that what so often divides people in society is actually healed in redemption. The fault lines in society should disappear in church: old and young, men and women, educated and unschooled, affluent and poor, this generation and that generation. We should find all of these in local churches or, at least, they should all find a welcome there in Christ. And the different cultural dispositions we have, different tastes, and different social habits should be made secondary to who we are in Christ. That is the ideal. After all, we come before the same God through the same Christ, because of the same gospel, to be instructed by the same Word, and to be his one people.

Here, in fact, is unity in diversity. But what makes the church diverse is so much less than what makes it one in Christ. In life, it is a rare moment when a cause, or center, is powerful enough to overcome what pulls people from one another, be it ethnic, generational, or gender-based. Today, all of the forces in Western societies are pulling people away from any center and toward the edges where they coalesce around their own kind. In the church, the exact opposite should be happening. And this should be seen and heard in its worship.

It would be foolish, of course, to think that for this reason it should be possible, even if it were desirable, for every Christian everywhere to worship in exactly the same way by singing the same hymns, to the same music, with the same instruments, and saying the same prayers, and in the same order of service. That is not possible. It is not possible unless we do what the Catholic Church once did, which was to prescribe the whole service and offer it all in the same language, Latin. But the Second Vatican Council decided to forgo this even if it meant that the thought of the one true church expressing itself in exactly the same way worldwide also had to be abandoned.

What is possible, though, is what we are often missing today. Simple as it may sound, it is that *God* must be central to our worship. This is where the church's unity is created. It is where our differences and diversity are tamed. It is he who must be central. His character and works must be the focus of our worship. And his greatness must shape the tone of the worship as well as the attitude in the worshipers. In many evangelical churches, the focus has been elsewhere. The arguments about whether or not we should toss out the pews, abandon the pulpit, bring in the drums, or offer coffee, important though they are, are not as important as why people are in church in the first place.

"Oh come," then, "let us worship and bow down; let us kneel before the Lord, our Maker!" Why? Because "he is our God, and we are the people of his pasture, and the sheep of his hand" (Ps. 95:6–7). There could be no simpler and more direct encapsulation of the argument that I have been making so far than this. But how are we going to do this? What actually goes into our worship?

I want to answer these questions by first exploring a little further how we should think about the presence, the centrality of God, in worship. Making God central to our worship is about conforming what we think and do to what is true and real. Second, I need to take up the place of the Word of God in this. I do so because, as I shall argue, it is through Scripture that God becomes present to us in his character. And it is by this truth that we are addressed, corrected, instructed, encouraged, comforted, and lifted up to see the greatness of God in his holy-love.

The Presence of God

The God Who Is There

There are two themes that have run through this book which now need to be brought to the forefront of our minds again. They can be distinguished, but because they are also intertwined I am going to consider them together here. They are, first, that God is objective to us. And, second, God is "above." It was from "above" that Christ came to be incarnate. These two themes are really the presuppositions of Christian worship.

Nothing is more important to our understanding of worship than this: we come to the Lord, not because it is our idea to do so, or because we need to do so, or even because we like to do so, but because he first came to us. Worship is our response to what he has done. Worship undoubtedly can have its benefits. However, it is not primarily about our finding comfort, inspiration, or social connections, or being entertained. It is primarily about adoration and praise being directed to God simply for who he is and what he has done. Worship loses its authenticity when it becomes more about the worshiper than about the God who is worshiped.

This principle was established early in Israel's life. God prescribed how he was to be approached in worship. If these conditions were met, he promised, "I will dwell among the people of Israel and will be their God. And they shall know that I am the LORD their God, who brought them out of the land of Egypt that I might dwell among them" (Ex. 29:45). Later on, the temple was built in accordance with God's instructions. It was to be the place where he would uniquely meet with his people. But then this people divided into two after Solomon's reign. It was God's judgment on Solomon (1 Kings 11:9–13). Jeroboam then established rival places of worship in the northern kingdom. He feared that if the people went south to Jerusalem to worship, he would lose his hold on them (1 Kings 12:25–33). In Jeroboam's actions we see prototypical self-made religion coming into full bloom. He had "devised" this strategy, we are told, "from his own heart" (1 Kings 12:33). It was a response, not to God as he had revealed himself, but to *need*. In this case, it was Jeroboam's political need. From this point onward, northern kings were judged by whether they perpetuated this self-made religion, this idolatry, or not. Many were the casualties that followed. Jehu "did not turn from the sins of Jeroboam, which he made Israel to sin" (2 Kings 10:31); Jehoahaz "followed the sins of Jeroboam" (2 Kings 13:2); Joash's son, another Jeroboam, "did not depart from all the sins of Jeroboam" (2 Kings 14:24); finally, "the people of Israel walked in all the sins that Jeroboam did" until the time of the exile, when "the LORD removed Israel out of his sight" (2 Kings 17:22–23).

This is where we must start. We start with God and not with ourselves, with his reality and not with our needs. Without his first action, rooted in his eternal counsels and involving Father, Son, and Holy Spirit, we could not come. We would not come. At least, we would not come to worship *him*. We might worship, as many do in the world, but it would not be the triune God who was being worshiped. It might be the worship of idols, or the forces of nature or, as in the West, the self. But true worship is the worship of the triune God, and that worship can arise only from redeemed people, and it is acceptable only if it is in accordance with God's self-revelation in Scripture.

When we begin with the God who is objective to us, and when we start "above," our worship is different from what our culture would incline us to do. It is the starting point that makes this difference. Biblical worship is of the God who is *outside* of us, before whom we come. We acknowledge who he is before we think of what we need or want. And to know him in our worship is, necessarily, to know him in his character. It is to know him for what he has done in redemptive history. Worship must center on what we know of God in his holy-love. It must return to him who is holy-love, and it must celebrate the works of this holy-love. That, after all, will be the eternal song (Rev. 5:9–10; 7:15–17; 19:6–8).

Early Days

For the church in the days of the apostles, all of this was new. Of course, across the ages God's people had known of his loving-kindness, his mercy, and his patience. They had also known of his holiness, which required regular sacrifices if he was to be approached. They had known of his wrath. Again and again, we encounter these themes in the Old Testament. But God's people had not known of his holy-love as revealed in and personified by Christ. And so now a transition began to take place in the way Christians worshiped.

The disciples initially "were continually in the temple blessing God" (Luke 24:53), Luke tells us, but the death and resurrection of Christ had also changed everything. So, while they were "attending the temple together" they also began to break bread in each other's homes (Acts 2:46). More than that, "they did not cease teaching and preaching

Jesus as the Christ" (Acts 5:42). Outside of the temple, home churches began to be formed (Acts 12:12; 1 Cor. 16:19; Col. 4:15). This was not all. They now began to see that the sacrificial system had culminated in Christ, who "had offered for all time a single sacrifice for sins." The result was that "there is no longer any offering for sin" (Heb. 10:12, 18). Now, there was only the remembrance of Christ's atoning sacrifice in the bread and wine.

But this was part of a much larger transition. The church, which Paul described as "a holy temple in the Lord" (Eph. 2:21; cf. Matt. 26:61), was to be a transformation of what the temple had been. In AD 70, in fact, the Roman general Titus marched on Jerusalem and destroyed the temple. It has never been rebuilt. But sometime before this, Jesus himself had hinted at things to come. In his conversation with the Samaritan woman he said that henceforth worship would not be tied to any particular place. It would be tied to the fact that the Father sought worshipers who would worship "in spirit and truth" (John 4:23). And then he told her that he was the Messiah (John 4:26). As this history unfolded, it became clear that it was not the place where the worship was to take place that was important, as it had been in the Old Testament; what was now important was the person who was to be at the center of the worship.

And so it was that when worship became regularized, Christians began to meet, not on the Sabbath, but on Sunday. They met on Christ's day of resurrection. This was "the Lord's day." Worship was to be a gathering around the Lord, and it was a celebration of all that had become possible because of his death and resurrection. Every church service is, in fact, an Easter service. So am I being narrow-minded when I ask, are we doing the right thing to cater to convenience by offering worship on Saturday evenings, on the old Sabbath? Does this not depart from the important symbolism which the apostles insisted on preserving? They worshiped on Sunday, the Lord's day.

God-centered worship, no doubt, can be done in a variety of ways. However, it is what makes the people of God one, what makes them Christ's bride, his body, his flock that should be at the heart of what we do. These are the truths that make the church *the* church. There is only one God, only one Christ, only one cross, only one biblical Word, and only one gospel.

These core beliefs were at the center of the early church's worship. Luke mentioned four activities within which these beliefs were affirmed. They were: first, "the apostles' teaching"; second, "fellowship"; third, "the breaking of bread"; and finally, "the prayers" (Acts 2:42). Here are the rudiments of Christian worship, though Luke did not elaborate. From these we may structure for ourselves an order of service for Sunday morning. These four elements give us four essential activities. They should be in every worship service (though not many churches today practice the Lord's Supper with that degree of regularity!). But what Luke does not tell us here is how these elements should be related to one another. For that, we need to think more widely and integrate into our worship the understanding Scripture gives us as to who we are as worshipers, why we come to worship, how we can secure the centrality of our triune God in that worship, and how we should comport ourselves afterwards as those who have worshiped the one true God.

There is at least one point in Luke's brief account that we should not miss. It is that these activities all took place within the sensed presence of God. Luke tells us that, as they met, "awe came upon every soul" (Acts 2:43). It would be quite mistaken, therefore, to think of the four elements he mentions as activities that, in a way, can stand on their own almost like agenda items for a committee meeting. They cannot. They can function appropriately only in the context of God's holy-loving presence. After all, it is the truth of *his* Word that has formed and that instructs the church; it is *his* supernatural working by which human nature has been regenerated; it is *his* provision in Christ that makes this possible; it is *Christ's* cross that is celebrated in the Lord's Supper; and it is before *him* that we come in supplication and thanksgiving. Unless God's Holy Spirit enables worship, sermons fall flat, prayers are mechanical, the Lord's Supper is merely a rite, fellowship is just proximity, and the church is only an association.

Being Before God

However we decide to do our worship, in whatever language, with whatever forms old or new, there can be only one objective in mind. It is that we bring ourselves together to focus on our triune God, on his character and his attributes. We come to rejoice in his greatness, to be encouraged in his sovereignty, to be comforted by his promises, and to be instructed in his Word. We come to experience the awe of being in his presence and to seek that blessing without which we all wither and become unproductive in his service.

Worship, then, is all about refocusing our lives. It is about pulling ourselves away from the distractions of life, from all of its competing interests, from its corruptions, from its superficialities and false goals, from its incessant talking and false hopes, and once again making God central. It is about confessing our sin together—for God is holy—and once again hearing the words of assurance that Christ has borne sin's penalty. It is about remembering the resurrection of Christ, his grace, his holy-love, and his reign that will one day sweep away all that has broken life and defied God. There is no other reason to be in worship than to remember and celebrate these truths. They will endure for all eternity because they all correspond to what happened in the cross and to what is there in God's character. They will be celebrated in eternity. They will be our eternal song.

The Word of God

God Acts

There are many Americans, apparently, who think that because they have God in themselves, they do not need the church. At least, that is what they say. And, no doubt, they also believe that they do not need the Bible, either, and for the same reason. But is it true that God has hidden himself in our intuitions? Are we to listen to the little voice within that speaks to us, a voice we immediately recognize because it is really our own? Is this where we hear God's words of comfort and reassurance? Has God entered our self and is he there now, waiting for us to discover him?

As commonsensical as this may now seem, it is as wrong today as it has ever been. God did not enter the human self in creation. What he has done is to enter our world for our redemption. There is a stream of redemptive history that runs through the Bible, culminating in the birth, death, and resurrection of Christ. This history is external and objective to us. It was in this history, recorded and interpreted in the Word of God, that God made known his character and will. And now he makes us capable of knowing him as he has thus revealed himself because he has given us his Word and his Holy Spirit. He comes to us from outside our own private worlds. And he comes to give us truth from his Word, truth that may well intrude on our private world but which we can never find in ourselves.

We need to start, then, with the history which was the medium for God's self-disclosure. It is a long history, stretching all the way from the call of Abraham to the ascension of Christ. Within it are four high peaks with connecting terrain and quite a few valleys in between them. The peaks in the Old Testament are the call of Abraham, the exodus, and the Davidic kingdom. In the New Testament, the peak, of course, is the incarnation, death, and resurrection of Christ. The Old Testament people of God, in their good moments, looked back to their three defining moments: Abraham, the exodus, and David's monarchy. The New Testament looks back to Christ, in whom the promises made to Abraham are being finally and fully realized, the exodus has been reenacted on an even grander scale, and David's kingdom is now being established in a way that will endure forever. It was to all of this that Jesus himself appeared to allude on one occasion. His Jewish contemporaries were searching the Scriptures for eternal life, he said, but they had missed the point because they did not see that these Scriptures "bear witness about me" (John 5:39). They therefore refused to come to him. Nevertheless, he was and he is the end point, the culmination, the final conclusion to this long story of God's redemptive acts.

Abraham, of course, was important because the Jews owed their existence to his call. It was because of this call that they knew of God's promise that "I will make of you a great nation" (Gen. 12:2). And because of the covenant made with Abraham, God was forever after identified as Abraham's God. "I am the God of Abraham, the God of Isaac, and the God of Jacob" was language that passed into Israel's understanding, endured across the ages, and was recalled by Peter shortly after Pentecost (Acts 3:13; cf. Matt. 22:32). And as we have seen, it is this promise of a progeny as numerous as the stars that is being realized today through Christ.

The exodus was remembered because it marked the nation's emergence as a free people subject only to God and the covenant he had made with them. While they were in captivity in Egypt, as Stephen later recounted, God heard their "groaning" and came "to deliver them" (Acts 7:34). To do so, he had to "perform wonders" (Ps. 78:12), as the psalmist put it, in opening up the sea so that the Israelites might escape. But he did so, as God had earlier explained to Moses, "that I might dwell among them. I am the Lord their God" (Ex. 29:46). That was the purpose of the exodus, and that is why Israel's unbelief and unfaithfulness is recorded in such excruciating detail in the history that followed. But what the exodus also declared, and what pious Israelites took from the event, was that God, who had so acted, could be counted on to act again in comparable ways. The exodus was a foretaste of the many victories that Israel could count upon God to give her (e.g., Ps. 135:8–12; 80:7–9, 14–19). And that, the New Testament writers saw, was being realized afresh, and in an even greater way, through Christ.

David was important, not only because he was a model for the kings who followed, not only because of the many victories God granted him whereby the monarchy was established, but because of a promise made to him. The prophet Nathan assured him that "your house and your kingdom shall be made sure forever. . . . Your throne shall be established forever" (2 Sam. 7:16). This assurance seems to have been read initially as a promise of stability (Ps. 89:3–4; 132:11) but in time a far deeper meaning began to be seen in it. Paul picked this up much later. It was to Christ, he said, that "the holy and sure blessings of David" (Acts 13:34) had been given. David, "after he had served the purpose of God in his own generation," died, and so this promise could not be realized in him. Christ, by contrast, had been raised from death (Acts 13:36–38), and that is why his kingdom will endure forever.

God Speaks

The meaning of these three peaks, however, would not have been self-evident to a casual bystander. Abraham, who went out "not knowing where he was going" (Heb. 11:8), would have seemed like an aimless wanderer. The exodus undoubtedly involved some remarkable, inexplicable events, but in every other aspect it was no different from the pattern of other migrating tribes evident elsewhere. And David was a highly successful warrior-king but he was not the first and by no means the last of these in history. And this, as we have already seen, was true of Christ's cross as well. What a bystander would have seen was just one more instance of a public execution by crucifixion, of which there were many in that day. Events such as these were in and of themselves mute. They could not speak for themselves. They did not explain their own meaning. It was the prophet who did this. Without Moses, we would not know the meaning of Abraham's call, nor would we know the meaning of the exodus. Without the divinely inspired narrators of Kings and Chronicles, without Jeremiah and Ezekiel, we would not know the meaning of the exile. Without the apostles, we would not know the meaning of Christ's cross and resurrection.

This history in which God has acted redemptively is therefore made up of both his acts and the interpretation of those acts. The fact that God has so acted in the flesh and bone of history secures the *objectivity* of his revelation. If that self-disclosure is tied into events that have already happened—and it is—then it can no more change than can the events through which it came. And the fact that these events have been interpreted for us means that we know their *meaning*. This meaning is not found in ourselves. Nor has it been invented. It has been given by God. No such interpretation, no prophecy, "was ever produced by the will of man," Peter said. At least, no *true* prophecy ever was. The false prophets, then as now, were ever in the business of imagined and fabricated meanings. Not the true prophets. They "spoke from God as they were carried along by the Holy Spirit" (2 Pet. 1:20–21). It is a suggestive image of a boat in full sail moving swiftly before a wind.

The Holy Spirit interpreted not only the peaks in this redemptive history but everything in between as well, through Scripture. Between these mountains was terrain, sometimes deep valleys, in the movement toward Christ. The narrative shows how God was faithful to his covenant promises as well as to his own word in judgment. It contains all of his instructions for his people, his commandments, the reasons for their failures, wisdom for life, and in the Psalms the ways of the human heart in moments of deep devotion and sometimes of deep despair. When this history finally reached the time of Christ, God the Holy Spirit provided the Gospels. They recount the biography of Christ, in whom all of this redemptive history reached its culmination. The Epistles then spell out how this divinely given truth must shape how we see God, the church, ourselves, our world, and the future. In all of these different ways, God was speaking. And today, he is still speaking, indeed re-speaking the truth he has given, for "all Scripture is breathed out by God and profitable for teaching, for reproof, for correction, and for training in righteousness, that the man of God may be complete, equipped for every good work" (2 Tim. 3:16).

However, we need to think a little more about this divine speaking. Timothy Ward, in his book *Word and Supplement*, has proposed a helpful way forward. It builds on work done by some philosophers on the way language works. The basic thought is that when we speak, we are often communicating more than the bare words that we use. We can, in fact, distinguish three different aspects to this communication.

First, there are the words used in what is said. Some of these are simple, factual statements or questions. We might say, for example, "It is time to leave the house." "When will you see John again?" "Would you buy some milk?" Sometimes, though, there is more to our communication than simply making factual statements or asking factual questions.

So, second, we need to consider what the speaker wants to convey through the use of the words besides eliciting or communicating information. It may be that the speaker wants to warn, or promise, or encourage. For example, someone might say, "Westerners are in danger when they travel in radical Islamic countries." This is a simple, factual statement. But it is more. It is also an implied warning. The person is saying, "travel in these countries at your own peril!" Our language is subtle enough that we have a choice as to how we want to communicate. We can issue the blunt warning, or we can be a little more indirect and let our listener draw the conclusion for him or herself. Likewise, consider this sentence: "I'll be at the bank tomorrow at noon; count on it." Beyond the factual declaration there is also a promise.

The speaker promises not to be anywhere else at noon on the next day other than the place where the meeting will occur. With the words has come a personal commitment. The person, as it were, is bonded to the words of the promise.

Finally, in our communication there is the effect that we wish to produce by what we say. If there is an implied warning, then the desired consequence is that the warning be heeded. If there is a promise made, then the promise maker wants to be trusted to follow through.

We use speech, in fact, to effect both good and bad ends. Sometimes, for example, we say things to injure others. "Your nose is too big" might be a factually accurate statement, but saying that to a person sensitive about his facial features can only injure him. And that, sometimes, is the effect that is intended. Words can be used to hurt even as they can be used to heal.

All of this underscores the bond between the words we use and who we are. If a promise is made and deliberately not kept, then we think that the *person* has proved untrustworthy. It is not simply that the words used to make the promise turned out to be inaccurate. Words therefore are tied to a person's character, be it good or bad. There is a sense in which we engage other people through their words. Or, we might say, there is a sense in which we are present to others and they to us through words. We use our language in so many ways other than the communication of bare information.

This new line of thought does not change what people have known about the Bible as inspired, but it does help us to appreciate some nuances that we might otherwise have missed.

We start with the truth that B. B. Warfield conclusively demonstrated a long time ago, in *The Inspiration and Authority of the Bible*. It is that, in Scripture, the words used are identified as God's. What Scripture says, God says. He therefore speaks to us through the words in the Bible. They are his speech. And today, the Holy Spirit re-speaks them as we read or hear the Word of God. Thus it was, for example, that the writer of Hebrews exhorted his readers by using a quotation from Psalm 95:7–11. Hebrews ascribes the words of the psalmist to the Holy Spirit. The quotation is introduced by the words "Therefore, as the Holy Spirit says . . ." (Heb. 3:7). It is important to notice, too, that this was the present tense: "the Holy Spirit *says*." The point was that the Holy Spirit said these words through the psalmist and now is saying them again to the readers of the epistle. What God the Holy Spirit said through the psalmist was, "Today, if you hear his voice, do not harden your hearts as in the rebellion . . ." (Heb. 3:7–8). That was something the readers of Hebrews needed to heed as well. What the biblical writer had said, God said. And what the biblical writer had said, God the Holy Spirit was reiterating and continuing to say.

But now we must add these helpful nuances from recent discussions. The words of Scripture, which are simultaneously God's, are not simply conveying information. Information may be conveyed, but with the conveyance of this information, and through it, God spoke and he continues to speak. The words, in fact, arise from within his character. God speaks out of the greatness of his character. The Bible is not like an impersonal computer that is mechanically spitting out sentences. God's character is encountered in his words even as ours is in our words. We encounter his wisdom, holiness, love, mercy, kindness, and compassion when we engage with what he has said. God is present to us through his words. And he has given us these words so that there will be consequences from them in our lives.

But here we also need to go a little beyond mere human discourse. When we read Scripture, God the Holy Spirit who first inspired this Word is also by our side to enable us to receive its truth. This goes beyond what happens in person-to-person dialogue. With respect to the Holy Spirit, this is a twofold work. He must open our hearts to receive the truth and, at the same time, he must ensure that we understand enough of it to move forward in our Christian lives. The Holy Spirit knows the divine intentions that were behind the giving of these words. The "Spirit searches everything, even the depths of God," Paul said (1 Cor. 2:10). He "comprehends the thoughts of God." And this same Spirit, who knows the inner counsels of God, takes us by the hand "that we might understand the things freely given us by God" (1 Cor. 2:11–12) in Scripture. And he does so in order that the effects God intended by his speech actually happen in our lives. That, after all, is why God spoke in the first place.

In Scripture, no less than in human speech, the three aspects to communication are at work. First, there is factual information. Second, in that information we are also encountering the person who is giving it to us. We encounter God's character through the promises made, the warnings given, and assurance offered. Finally, there are the intended outcomes to that speech that he wills in the lives of all believers. He wants us to heed the warnings, trust him in his promises, receive encouragement through his assurances, and learn obedience through the truth he has given us.

It would be quite mistaken, then, for us to think of the Bible as being simply a manual, or a set of instructions, or a textbook. It is so much more than this. It is the way in which God makes himself personally present to us. Undoubtedly, there are moments when God's presence seems more real to us than at others, and there are times when we may, even though reading his Word, feel deserted. Job knew something of this loneliness, and so did the psalmists. However, we should be in no doubt that we are always engaging with, and being engaged by, God—engaging with his goodness, faithfulness, righteousness, holiness, love, and grace—when we are engaged with what he has said in his Word.

Word and Worship

It is for this reason that Scripture has had such an important role in the life of historic Protestant churches. This was early on symbolized by a raised pulpit that was visually dominant in the church. It was not declaring the authority of the preacher but, rather, the authority, sufficiency, and necessity of Scripture for the instruction and spiritual health of the church.

But the role of Scripture in the gathered church is larger than simply the preached Word, important though that is. For centuries Protestants have paid great attention to the systematic reading of God's Word in the worship service, typically by including portions from both Testaments. God gave us the whole Bible for a reason. The reason is that we need the whole Bible. We need to read it from start to finish, need to know its parts and interconnections, and need to know its teaching, because this is precisely how God has revealed himself. Nor is this all. Often, in an older kind of Protestantism, Scripture was woven through the service in other ways, too. It was used to structure the service or connect parts of it. And some of it used to be sung as well. Paul said that we are to be "addressing one another in psalms and hymns and spiritual songs" (Eph. 5:19). Almost certainly he was speaking here of the Old Testament psalms.

There have been some Protestant churches that have sung only the psalms, rejecting any hymns and spiritual songs. Indeed, some have sung the psalms without any musical instruments. But today the pendulum has swung to the other extreme. In many evangelical Protestant churches, all that remains are our (contemporary) spiritual songs. The hymns have been abandoned and, before that, the psalms. Perhaps, when Paul mentioned these hymns, he was thinking of compositions like those in Philippians 2:5–11 and 1 Timothy 3:16. But hymns of this kind, with their theological truth, do not always find a warm welcome in some churches today.

Not only have the hymns and psalms disappeared from many of the worship services being conducted within evangelical churches but so, too, have pulpits. On the face of it, this may seem like an innocent adaptation. After all, nowhere does Scripture command the use of a pulpit! Of course it is true that the Word of God can be preached anywhere . . . and it has been. It has been preached in homes and by the roadside, in fields and corporate boardrooms, in impoverished neighborhoods and in the centers of the great cities of the West. This Word has been studied, talked about, taught, and preached wherever people congregate, wherever they can meet. Pulpits are not necessary. And, indeed, pulpits are unknown in some parts of the world. The point here is not that our churches in the West, of necessity, have to have pulpits. They do not. Nevertheless we must ask ourselves, what is being communicated when pulpits are tossed out, and why do we, in the church, feel that we must do this? What is the message we are wanting to communicate?

Today, a transition has taken place, not in every church but in quite a few, from pulpit to Plexiglas stand. Then, sometimes, the Plexiglas stand has given way to a barstool. The thought was that this would better enable the preacher—or should we now say "speaker"?—to connect with the congregation. Or is it now the "audience"? However well-intentioned this may have been, there was also an unintended symbolism here. What this change pointed to is that in the church, as in a business, we have become preoccupied with the horizontal. We are focused on our clientele. We are adapting to their psychology. We have become sensitive to the fact that, in the church, we have an absolute authority which, in an age of hyper-autonomy, is likely to rub outsiders the wrong way. So our strategy has been to hide our authority. We obscure, as much as possible, the vertical dimension to Christian faith. We accentuate the horizontal.

But what this means, all too often, is that we have transitioned, not just from the pulpit but also from a serious engagement with the biblical text. We have done so because we (falsely) imagine that to be successful we must be more consumer-friendly, not just in our manner but in the substance of the faith. From biblical sermons we have therefore moved to inspirational, how-to-do-it, therapeutically driven talks. Are we then surprised that biblical illiteracy, by every measure, is skyrocketing in the evangelical church, and the knowledge of God, of his character and works, is plummeting?

Postlude

Worship is as essential to the church as breathing is to our bodies. And yet, we do not worship for our own benefit. Benefits there are, and joy in worship there is, but we worship to bring our praise to God for who he is and what he has done. What he has done in time, space, and history explains why there is a church to worship him in the first place. That there is a church means that this praise will ascend to him from those who know how deeply they need him. It is their joyous recognition of God's "worthiness."

This God-centeredness is far easier to speak about than actually to do. This is true of our worship as well as more broadly in our lives. We know ourselves to be astonishingly unfocused and, even worse, self-focused. We are a wild array of hopes, plans, daydreams, preoccupations, inward aches, confusions, and unfulfilled desires. We are prone to divided attention. We also are, in our inward world, an accumulation of bad habits, willful sinfulness, and poor appetite. Being

215

God-centered therefore goes quite against the stream of who we are and what we have become—both in our sin and in our sinfulness.

This does not mean that we should not be in church. Quite the reverse! A congregation is a fellowship of sinners, those who know their own waywardness, their own willfulness, and how much they need to be redeemed. It is precisely those who know such things who are in churches or, at least, ought to be. For it is here, in the company of others, that we learn of God's goodness and of his grace. It is here that we think together about life and its meaning. We are enriched through the gifts that God has given in the church.

And yet it is precisely the nature of the church—this company of sinners—that sometimes works against its nature as the people of *God* and, not least, the people of God in worship. It is this potential for contradiction that puts the church in a position of always needing to be reforming. The church is always in danger of following its own way, of being there for its own interests and success, of setting itself up for its own comfort, of beginning to think as the world around it does, and to think in ways that are contrary to the Word of God.

It is surely one of the great ironies of our time that the battles over the Bible's authority in the 1970s and '80s that secured for many a belief in its inerrancy did not secure a certain role for its truth in our churches subsequently. The disappearance of pulpits, perhaps insignificant in itself, points to a much greater disappearance. Serious preaching, preaching that not only engages conscientiously with the text but is also effective in bringing hearers into the presence of God, is rare. And just as rare is the preacher who can, from a biblical vantage point, bring understanding to life with depth, clarity, and wisdom.

The fact is that the meaning of life, in all of its grandeur, complexity, and tragedy should be understood nowhere more profoundly than in the church on Sunday morning. This is because it is being understood in the light of God's Word. This, however, is an uncommon experience. We are, instead, adrift in so many of our churches on a sea of triviality, amusement, and superficiality. And I dare say that none of this would be true if our knowledge of Scripture were better, if our knowledge of God were deeper, and if our desire to make him central in our worship were greater.

At the same time, where would any of us be if we could not find our way back to God after we have wandered away? And this is true of the church, too. There is a way back. We can come back to what we ought to be and to what we ought to be doing. And that is what I perceive is beginning to happen today. There is a breeze blowing. I see it in the deep discontent that is being voiced with the threadbare state of the evangelical world, with its empty worship, its market-driven superficiality, and its trivial thought. It is a breeze blowing toward better, deeper, more honest things. I suspect that it is the Holy Spirit who is blowing, that this is his breeze, and that these leaves that are shaking are the signs of better things to come within an evangelical faith that is thus being reformed. Let us all pray that it is so!

CHAPTER 9

And, Come, Let Us Serve

See the Christ-like host advancing,
High and lowly, great and small,
Linked in bonds of common service
For the common Lord of all.
Thou who prayest, thou who willest,
That thy people should be one,
Grant, O grant our hope's fruition:
Here on earth thy will be done.

SOMERSET CORRY LOWRY

A Thousand Ways

In the two previous chapters we were thinking about how our bond to Christ, and our life in the Holy Spirit, come to expression. Our sanctification and our worship are to be explained by the fact that Christ's redemptive reign has begun in our lives. It is because of God's grace, because of his holy-love, that we seek to please him and to worship him.

In this chapter, we are going to take these connections in a slightly different direction—that of our service. It is this that goes to the heart of what Christ did and which should go to the heart of who we are. "Christ became a servant" (Rom. 15:8), Paul said, to Jew and Gentile alike so that the promises made to Abraham might be fulfilled. They are being fulfilled in us today, as we have seen. For this to happen,

Christ came to "give his life as a ransom for many," and that meant coming to serve and not to be served (Mark 10:45).

It was this self-giving that established the pattern for our own discipleship. "A disciple is not above his teacher," Jesus said, "nor a servant above his master" (Matt. 10:24). He was speaking of our following him even into the hard places of life. And he was even more blunt when he said, "If anyone would come after me, let him deny himself and take up his cross and follow me" (Matt. 16:24). To follow Christ has many aspects to it but an important one is serving him.

There are a thousand different ways in which we can serve Christ in our world. Some serve him as pastors, others as elders and deacons. Some are evangelists. Others are missionaries who have left their homes and gone off to distant lands. But all of us are to serve Christ in the church through our gifts. And Christ is served in homes where parents raise their children on the truth of Scripture and model Christian virtues before them.

We also serve him in the marketplace by showing integrity and kindness—God's holy-love—because we are his. In our many different callings, we do our work, as Paul counseled slaves, "not by the way of eye-service, as people-pleasers, but as bondservants of Christ" (Eph. 6:6). That is when we become the "salt of the earth" (Matt. 5:13). Some serve Christ as artists, writers, and musicians, for now they find their natural gifts can be used to explore the meaning of life with depth and truth. Some serve him as leaders in business, in politics, and in the learned academy. We can serve in obscurity, too, by visiting a neighbor who is ill and alone, or those in prison who have been deserted by their friends. At the end of time, Christ will say, "I was hungry and you gave me food, . . . I was a stranger and you welcomed me, I was naked and you clothed me, I was sick and you visited me, I was in prison and you came to me." So unself-conscious of their virtue were these servers of Christ that they had forgotten their own acts of mercy. But Christ does not. "Truly, I say to you, as you did it to one of the least of these my brothers, you did it to me" (Matt. 25:35–36, 40).

Reformation Recovery

What I have just described is a way of seeing life that was recovered at the time of the Reformation. It is one that rests upon biblical truth, and it provides a much larger context in which to think of our service in the kingdom of God than we may be accustomed to.

Early on in the church's life, in the fourth century, Eusebius of Caesarea said that there are two paths in life. In the one, people devote themselves wholly to God. It is the higher path. This was the path priests and monks were on. Along the other path, the lower road, one is occupied only with what Eusebius called "farming, trading and other secular pursuits." Those whose spiritual desires are more tepid than those of the priests and monks, those who are less serious and whose capacities to please God are greatly reduced, walk the low road. Thus it was that the work that most people did—those who worked in the fields, or as carpenters, iron workers, cobblers, tentmakers, or merchants—was cut off from what is spiritual, for spirituality was found only in the callings in the church.

The Protestant Reformers rejected this way of thinking. It was a "pure invention," Luther thundered, that only priests and monks are called to what is spiritual while "princes, lords, artisans and farmers" have to make do with what is only secular. For Luther, all who are in Christ are called to pursue their callings—their roles and occupations in life—before the face of God. Even the hangman, Luther said, could do his work to the glory of God.

We all have a number of callings, of course. Some are called to be parents, all are called to be citizens, and most have to work at some craft, trade, or what is now described as a "profession." In all of these ways, we have received the call to live out in our world what it means to be in Christ. It is fallacious to think that church work alone is spiritual by its nature and the rest is not. No one is closer to or further from God on the grounds of their work, as the Catholic Church supposed.

At the foundation of this Protestant understanding of work was the doctrine of justification. The Reformers started with the truth that we are all equally and fatally distant from God in our sin. Some, undoubtedly, are more wicked than others, but none are closer to God in terms of salvation. On this matter, there is a fatal egalitarianism. We are equally dead in our trespasses and sins.

When we are justified, it is by grace alone, and therefore we contribute nothing to it except the sin from which we need to be redeemed.

That means there is no work—be it in or out of holy orders—that can contribute to our justification. Christian life begins with God's declaration that "there is therefore now no condemnation for those who are in Christ Jesus" (Rom. 8:1). Justification is not the verdict we hear at the end of life based on what we have done and how well we have lived or served in the church. Justification is not for the few who have withdrawn from life and insulated themselves against it in a world of asceticism. Justification is not easier for those who have wholly given themselves to the church to serve as its priests, because it is not based on what we have done. Rather, justification is for those who trust Christ and his death and who have entrusted themselves to him. And they seek to live out their standing in him in the *midst* of this life with all of its conflicts, its pain, and its evil.

Biblical Perspective

Work was there in the very beginning, when God put Adam in the garden of Eden "to work it and keep it" (Gen. 2:15). This was *before* the fall. Nature's exuberance was to be ordered and tended. This required exertion, application, effort, and diligence, as all gardens do. Here was work done before the face of God. And the fall did not change the fact that working is still part of the created order (Ps. 104:19–24; Isa. 28:23–26; 2 Thess. 3:10). God works, and that is what he intends us to do, too. What changed after the fall was only the *context* of our work.

After the fall, and because of the sin that was introduced into the world, work became toilsome (Gen. 3:17–19). Indeed, it produced great despair in Solomon. He said that all of a person's days "are full of sorrow, and his work is a vexation. Even in the night his heart does not rest" (Eccl. 2:23). I think we understand what Solomon was talking about!

In fact, studies done on the workplace in America have consistently shown that people are deeply ambivalent about their work. Some, to be sure, find it rewarding and look forward to heading out to the office each day, or sitting at their computers if they work at home. But an astounding number do not. They find their work boring, or not satisfying, or they find that they are working for no good purpose.

In the workplace we experience our own striving, straining, exhaustion, anxiety, dissatisfaction, and frustration. Here there is often pressure and stress. We also come face-to-face at times with arrogance, dishonesty, hardness, compulsive ambition, deceit, indifference to Christian faith, and sometimes outright hostility. Those who work in our cities often have to fit into bureaucracies and corporate structures with their impersonal ethos and their anonymity. It is also here in the workplace, as Dick Keyes notes, that we are face-to-face with a world saturated with "artificiality, spin, and banality." The workplace is all of these things and all of them together.

At the same time, this is also where we make human connections and where we can use and develop our natural gifts. It is where we can be productive and helpful, and can contribute to the common good. There can be great satisfaction in this. And it goes without saying that, without this workplace, without our work, we would not be able to sustain ourselves. Furthermore, for Christians the workplace is the context where many have their greatest opportunity to reflect who they are in Christ. It is, after all, the place where they spend most of their waking days during the week.

Philosophy, it has been said, never baked any bread. That is true. But it is just as true that no bread was ever baked without a philosophy. That is, everyone who works does so because, for some reason, they want to go on living. That is why they are providing for themselves. They have their own explanations as to what makes life worth living. And Christians do, too. That is what they bring to their work. Theirs is not simply a philosophy, or a reason for living; it is the knowledge of the "living God." He is the one who is dynamically present in every situation, every context, and present to every relationship. Every believer, at the end of every day, stands before the "Audience of One," as Guinness puts it. This is the audience that is ultimate. And it is this audience that gives dignity and meaning to all work that is ethical and that is done before him. This is as true of the most menial work as it is of the most lofty. In all our callings, we can and should be serving Christ.

A Different Angle

There is one aspect of our work, however, on which I want to focus in this chapter. It is our service. But rather than exploring the many avenues that are open to us to serve Christ, I want instead to think about the idea itself.

Our way into this subject, though, may be a little unexpected. It is to consider an antithesis that cuts through all of Christian life. It is the antithesis between being Christ-centered and being self-centered. Although these are stark, opposing alternatives, they are actually mirror-images of each other in how they work. In both cases, there is a center in our lives, and in both cases from this center comes an energy, a drive, to see life from the viewpoint of our center and to do certain things as a consequence. The difference lies in the two centers: Christ or self.

This truth is fundamental to Christian faith. Either we are "enslaved to sin" (Rom. 6:6) or, through Christ, we are "slaves to righteousness" (Rom. 6:19). We are either "slaves to impurity and to lawlessness" (Rom. 6:19), or, as Paul said of himself, "a servant of Christ Jesus" (Rom. 1:1). It is the one or the other. Everyone is enslaved to something. Our choice is simply to whom or to what.

This servitude of sin originally worked itself out by constricting or "contracting" the human vision. Edwards spoke about how the original greatness of the human soul became small in its sin. What had once been its large vision of God, before the fall, shrank into the smallness of a warped self. It becomes, as Edwards said, contracted "to the very small dimensions of selfishness . . . and man retired within himself." God was forsaken and fellow human beings were forsaken. What now ruled, in sin's miniature world, was self-love. And so it is today.

But exactly the reverse happens when we are in captivity to righteousness. Where in sin we were drawn into ourselves, now our vision begins to be expanded. We return to the God whom we had forsaken. We seek him with our whole heart and we reach out to fellow human beings whom we had once abandoned. In place of the narrow, constricted self-love, increasingly, is the largeness of Christ's love, of generosity, of a sensitivity to others' needs which has no payback to self-interest. And that is why it expresses itself in so many different forms of service.

We now need to explore these two patterns of life a little further. They are our pre-conversion and post-conversion lives. In doing so we must focus on this idea of captivity. For just as before we came to

Christ we were held completely captive to our own internal appetites and desires, we now experience an entirely different kind of captivity which is actually a freedom. What are the dynamics, then, in these two phases of our lives?

Upside-down World

The Old Building

The pivotal statement in understanding all of this is Paul's. Unbelievers, he said, have rejected the truth that is available to them and have "worshiped and served the creature rather than the Creator" (Rom. 1:25). The truth to which he referred is what is available through natural revelation. It is both external—the magnificence and orderliness of the creation that speaks of its Creator—and internal. Internally, it is the sense that we all have, even in sin, that we live in a moral world. The moral fabric to reality is there, of course, because of the character of God, who sustains all things. This moral reality registers in us as conscience. The Gentiles can "by nature do what the law requires" (Rom. 2:14), though not in order to please God. But when they act morally, they "show that the work of the law is written on their hearts" (Rom. 2:15) and their conscience either accuses or clears them.

However, before we came to Christ, we had refused to submit ourselves to God as life's center. For him we had substituted ourselves. We became the center of our own life. We were self-centered, and from this center, in its sin, there arose a set of life-values. These were our own choices as to what is right and wrong, and further, there arose compulsions to sin. What makes this sin seem so normal is that it receives powerful validation from the culture in which we live. We are affirmed in our way of thinking and acting by how others behave, what they assume life is about, and by what advertisers, movies, and music deliver to us.

The secular humanism that was so outspoken in the 1970s, '80s, and '90s, for example, built its own life-view upon this substitution of the creature for the Creator as life's center. It did so, though, in its own particular way. When God was displaced from the center of life, revelation was replaced by natural reason, salvation by psychology, and eschatology by social progress. However, even as this worldview

225

was becoming dominant, it also began to disintegrate. Today, it lives on quite un-chastised in pockets of our society—especially in our educational system though more openly on its learned end, in our elite newspapers, in broadcast TV, and in Hollywood—but the postmodern mind is less taken by this secularism. The rosy talk of social progress seems like a myth today given our global terror, unemployment, and the anxieties and insecurities of the workplace. The mood has changed. Reason seems more fragile and less innocent than it used to, and God seems more easily accessed within our selves than ever before.

What has lingered on is the substitution of psychology for salvation, and therefore the main thread of continuity across these decades, the thread that links the older modernist culture and our current postmodern culture, is the autonomous self. This is the self, the person in his or her inner being, who is unrestrained by the past, by any authority, or social convention, or community, or any truth as something other than his or her own private opinion. They are not restrained by any God external to themselves. This is what our culture is validating all the time. But how does this work itself out?

Before our conversion, says Paul, we were led astray. We became "slaves to various passions and pleasures" (Titus 3:3). This language of "passions" is that of deep, compelling desires. It is those appetites that drive people. These are appetites for sex, drink, power, control, success, fame, attention, or money. It is what drives people to want their own way and to be able to do their own thing.

Paul in this text also went on to speak of being enslaved to the pursuit of "pleasures." That is, people were doing whatever they had to do to find these pleasures. Presumably, he was speaking of what we might have in mind today when we talk about the affluent life. It is a life lubricated by enough money that expense is not a nagging concern. What is more important is what money can buy. It buys security. It makes want, hunger, deprivation, and risk remote. It buys what we enjoy and puts at our fingertips all the means of self-indulgence. It can also buy attention. We speak of "conspicuous consumption." It enables us to appear as successful, powerful, and cool, as having arrived, as someone who should be noticed and noted. And such success gains access to others, sometimes even to the rich and powerful. These desires come to control the values by which people live, because satisfying these desires gives them great pleasure. This kind of life shapes their worldview. They understand themselves in terms of it. It is what is meaningful to them. It is what they really want. These are powerful drives, these "desires of the flesh" (Gal. 5:16).

It would, however, be a mistake to think that this self-centeredness expresses itself in exactly the same way in every person. This clearly is not the case. What is true of all is that they have as their life's end, their greatest good, whatever it is that they want to be, or to do, or to have, or to think. And this is pursued out of relation to, and in defiance of, what God has revealed as true and right in human life. How it all unfolds, though, follows different patterns.

Sin and Culture

In recent decades, this self-orientation has been given unusually powerful validation in our postmodern culture as it has turned inward. In place of God's salvation, our therapeutic age now empowers its alternative. It is our self-preoccupation, self-promotion, and self-pursuit. This, our culture supposes, is a way to find psychological wholeness. The language of self-esteem is the new language of Zion. It assumes that the pursuit and care of the self-serving creature can actually be redemptive.

This therapeutic world, as Christina Sommers and Sally Satel observe in *One Nation Under Therapy*, is built on the belief that the American psyche is now so fragile that it is in danger of falling apart. It starts from the assumption of our desperate, wounded vulnerability. That is why we need to turn inward, to focus in on our self, to express our wounds, and to share our feelings. This inner anguish, this unfulfilled and undirected yearning, this broken self, requires a massive army of trained therapists. It has spawned sensitivity counselors and grief counselors. It employs guardians against gender, ethnic, and sexual bias, many of whom are let loose on the workplace, hired by corporations and by government, and paid to serve as our secular priests. It sponsors workshops to explore this hidden world of the self. There is now a flourishing literature of self-help techniques that enable—indeed, empower—us to make our way through life. There is such a thing as "emotional correctness." And being emotionally correct has the power, we apparently believe, to heal some of the inward tatters in which the self now lies.

This, of course, reflects our American paradox. Never have we had so much, and yet never have we had so little. Never have we had more opportunities, products, options, and access to people. But never have we been as depressed as we are now, as anxious, or as empty. This is all very real. The triumphs of modernization have filled our world with plenty, with technological triumphs, and with countless wonders. But this modernized world has also worked havoc on the human spirit, on our human relations, and on our capacity to think clearly about ourselves and about life. It has emptied us out.

This paradox shapes the way in which our sin works its way out from its center in this fallen self. It gives it its context.

Pride, for example, is towering self-sufficiency. The proud are those whose self-centered compulsions drive them, and they often ride roughshod over others. Those who stand in their way are brushed or bumped aside. Pride has no use for those who cannot be used. And if this kind of frontal force is not possible, the proud turn to manipulation, sometimes to deceit and lies, to get their way. They do so on the assumption of their own superiority and the rectitude of what they want. Because they are superior, they set themselves apart from others. Then they rationalize what they have done. And always they assume that all of the resources they need for life, for survival, are within themselves.

This is the point of connection with those in the self movement. On the surface, the appearance of these types is very different. What does the hard-driving, heartless, conceited person have in common with the wounded and self-focused, those who are spilling out each passing feeling, moment by moment, on Facebook? Underneath these two types there is, actually, much in common. Both see in the self all of the resources that are needed either for triumph, in the one case, or for self-healing, in the other. In both ways, the "creature" is being served.

What is said here about pride applies equally to many other sins as well. Envy is now embedded in our cultural psyche in America. It grows from within but it is validated externally, too.

Envy emerges from our sense of want, our sense that we have been deprived perhaps in ways we cannot understand. But it emerges in a full-blown resentment toward others for having what we want, what we do not have, and what we feel we deserve. It has been given political expression in the desire to equalize all outcomes. What others have earned, for example, is seen to be rightfully ours. And when that is slow to happen, we come to resent those who have what we want, be they of a different race or a different class, or those in a different tax-bracket or a different generation. These are the people who have robbed us of our opportunities! The Boomers, some Gen Xers have steadily grumbled, stole all the good jobs! And what others have accumulated seems to diminish those who have accumulated less. It makes them feel smaller. And this, in our therapeutic culture, strikes a grievous blow at self-esteem because in those thus afflicted, self-love has been so unrequited.

I mentioned earlier the addiction to "pleasures" of which Paul spoke. This often includes the sin of avarice. This sin is the inward satisfaction that some get from having things, possessions. Avarice, though, is not so much the pleasure in the things themselves, as Henry Fairlie has noted in *The Seven Deadly Sins Today*. It is, rather, the pleasure in possessing these things. This is what so often drives our consumption. We buy things that we do not need but, more importantly, we buy certain things because they deliver a cultural message. It is from this that we get pleasure. It is not the top-of-the-line Lexus itself, nice though that might be. It is about what *having* such a Lexus says to others about ourselves. And beneath this kind of avarice there is always an emptiness in the self. It is an emptiness we are trying to fill through our possessions. It is as if having these things gives great and deep substance to who we are. Where would our consumer culture be without these deep inward yearnings, this emptiness!

However, these sinful drives are not like the clothes that we put on and then take off. They are not passing moods. They are not even a lifestyle, if by that we mean that they can be changed at will as can any fashion. The life that they shape is not our lifestyle. It is our life. These drives are who we are. They are our own ego in motion. We are in our desires and drives. They are our point of contact with others and with the world around us. Peter spoke of those who were "slaves of corruption." Then, by way of explanation, he added that "whatever overcomes a person, to that he is enslaved" (2 Pet. 2:19). Jesus had said the same thing. "Everyone who practices sin is a slave to sin" (John 8:34). This is what these drives, ambitions, and appetites do to us. They take control of who we are and what we do. This is what Paul analyzed with such insight in Romans 7.

This chapter has sometimes been seen as Paul's pre-conversion experience. That might be so, though I am inclined to think that he was actually speaking of a Christian experience. And what we see in his analysis is the *power* of these inward compulsions toward what is wrong. In his deepest self, "my inner being" (Rom. 7:22), Paul said, he desired to serve God, but so overwhelming were these other drives that he was left paralyzed. He was left frustrated because he continued to serve "the law of sin" (Rom. 7:25). He did so against his better judgment (Rom. 7:16, 19–20). "I do not understand my own actions. For I do not do what I want, but I do the very thing I hate" (Rom. 7:15). Only Christ's power was sufficient to draw Paul out of the orbit of this sinful center.

Paul in his Christian life knew something of this lingering captivity to sin. However, this captivity is the unremitting experience of those who are not in Christ. They have only one center, and that is themselves. In them there is no civil war, no competition between the "walk" in the Spirit and the "desires of the flesh" (Gal. 5:16). At best, there are only the faint amber lights of conscience. This is a one-sided battle for them that is lost from the start. They serve only themselves as life's center, and they do so in place of serving their Creator. Their fallen nature and their ego *compel* them away from their Creator.

Under New Management

Once we are in Christ, though, our existence is changed. Now we are being compelled toward Christ, even as we were once compelled away from our Creator. We have been changed supernaturally by the Holy Spirit's powerful working. Just as God brought order out of the ancient formless void, so he has done within our own human hearts. "For God, who said, 'Let light shine out of darkness,' has shone in our hearts to give the light of the knowledge of the glory of God in the face of Jesus Christ" (2 Cor. 4:6). We have, as a result, "turned to God from idols to serve the living and true God," as did the Thessalonians (1 Thess. 1:9). Our idols were not the external ones of "images resembling mortal man and birds and animals and creeping things" (Rom. 1:23) but the internal one of the imperious self, the self which is emancipated from everything external to itself. And from our renewed self arise the impulses of righteousness, under the power of the Holy Spirit, and guided by the instruction of God's Word.

We have already considered in some detail the fact that when we came to Christ, when we were justified, we were, at the same time, sanctified. That is, in that moment, as part of our union with Christ, we were torn away from our former sinful orbit, ripped away from the dominance that the norms in the culture once had for us (Eph. 2:1–10). These had defined for us the meaning of life.

Now, we have been separated to Christ and for his service. "We know," Paul boldly declared, "that our old self was crucified with him in order that the body of sin might be brought to nothing, so that we would no longer be enslaved to sin" (Rom. 6:6). The old ego, the pre-converted person in his or her entirety, has ended. This was a decisive act, Paul said. The "old self *was* crucified." "If anyone is in Christ, he is a new creation. The old has passed away; behold, the new has come" (2 Cor. 5:17). It is true that the old impulses do linger in our new life in Christ. They are not eradicated. To suppose that we can ever become sinless and perfect in this life, as some have from time to time proposed, is entirely mistaken. What is true, however, is that a whole new existence has been begun through regeneration. This new life certainly has to be cultivated. And part of its cultivation is in its service.

We are to "put on the new self, created after the likeness of God in true righteousness and holiness" (Eph. 4:24). That is, this new regenerate self must come to dominate all that we are in exactly the same way as once our sin dominated all that we were. Once, we were "slaves" to the "weak and worthless elementary principles of the world" (Gal. 4:9). Now, we have been "called to freedom," and therefore "through love" we "serve one another" (Gal. 5:13). No longer are we slaves, says Paul; we now have the freedom of sons (Gal. 4:1–7).

What we are really thinking about, then, is the contrast between our former servitude and our current freedom. To be enslaved by Christ is not a new bondage. It is a new freedom! To unbelievers, this may seem puzzling. Why, they ask themselves, would one give up one's freedom to live as one wants? Why be subject to someone else's rules?

The answer, of course, is that the old, so-called "freedom" of the self, as we have seen, is actually the very opposite. It is a captivity to that self with all of its compulsions and appetites. The freedom we have in Christ is a freedom from the captivity to our old imperious and autonomous self. But what kind of freedom is this?

Certainly it is the freedom from the requirements of the Old Testament ceremonial law. And, certainly, we are no longer under the law's dark frown of condemnation. "If the Son sets you free," Jesus said, "you will be free indeed" (John 8:36). "For freedom Christ has set us free" (Gal. 5:1), Paul said. Now, we serve "in the new way of the Spirit" (Rom. 7:6). And with this new freedom, which is at the same time a new service to Christ, comes a growing freedom from the compulsions of sin. We have been freed *from*, in order that we might be freed *to*, and that means being freed *for*. We have been freed *from* ourselves *to* Christ and *for* his service. It is freedom from our past life and for a new life. Those who have thus been freed, therefore, are to "be careful to devote themselves to good works" (Titus 3:8). And important in this new direction is this matter of service, of serving God and others, for this is the calling of love.

Counterculture

What exactly is the nature of this service? In three brief passages from the Gospels, each of which is a paradox, we have considerable light shed on this matter.

Losing and Gaining

Once, we mistakenly saw our own captivity as freedom. Equally mistakenly, we also saw serving Christ as loss. But the truth turned out to be exactly the opposite of what we had once thought. The first paradox, then, is one that Jesus gave us: "For whoever would save his life will lose it, but whoever loses his life for my sake and the gospel's will save it. For what does it profit a man to gain the whole world and forfeit his soul?" (Mark 8:35–36).

The context is that of the disciples' vain dreams and misunderstanding. They imagined that Christ had come as a political Messiah. He would set up an earthly kingdom, and in this kingdom there would be favors and honors to be had. This saying was a sharp rebuke to those dreams.

Across time, of course, we have seen many dictators, many regimes, that would have forfeited any number of lives if, by so doing, they could have gained the whole world. People were insignificant in comparison to their cherished goals of conquest. The Marxists were that way.

But in this passage, we are not thinking of these grandiose political dreams, these proud illusions. We are thinking in more personal terms. It is *our* life that we are to think about here. In Luke's account, the unbeliever "forfeits *himself*" (Luke 9:25). So great is the value of our life, our soul, that in any trade it would be worth more than the entire world with all of its treasure. That is their relative value.

It is control over this great and precious thing, this life of ours, that we "lose" at the foot of Christ's cross. On its face, this goes against every calculation of self-interest. But these calculations are false. Here in Jesus's words, they are dismissed. This "loss" is actually "gain," even as our "freedom" to be ourselves was, in fact, our slavery to ourselves. By contrast, to be a servant of Christ is to be free for him, through the gospel, because it is to be free from ourselves. That is the gain.

Powerlessness and Privilege

In the ancient world, as in ours, power came with position. In Jesus's world, it was the ruling families among the Jews, or those in the Roman hierarchy, who had the power. In ours, it is those at the head of corporations, or in political power, or those who have money that gains them access to those who have power. With power comes influence and the ability to see one's plans carried out. That is why people devote themselves so wholeheartedly to getting into these power positions. They want to be at the top. And from the pinnacle, many of them look down on others. The "rulers of the Gentiles," Jesus said, "lord it over them" (Matt. 20:25). This attitude is so often the companion of power.

Power may be coercive. However, it can also be enabling. Whether power is good or bad depends on who is exercising it and to what ends. But one thing is certain. Power and importance are inextricably linked in our world. The unimportant have no power. The powerless live on the margins, not in the center. They are peripheral people. That is what life in a fallen world is all about.

This is upended in Christian faith. Christian faith is about transforming the way we calculate importance. It is also about how we bring a different ethic to bear on how power is used and how other people are treated. And one of these differences has to do with this thought of service.

In the second of our paradoxes, then, Jesus said, "if anyone would be first, he must be last of all and servant of all" (Mark 9:35; cf. Matt. 23:11). It follows closely what is recorded elsewhere, that "the greatest among you" should "become as the youngest, and the leader as the one who serves" (Luke 22:26). Here is the template for understanding service. If we want to know what service is all about, consider Christ, who was Lord of the universe but, in the incarnation, became a nobody. He came more or less anonymously, without fanfare, without recognition, without any of the trappings of regal power. He came as a humble servant.

In the kingdom of God, greatness is the exact opposite of what it is in the world. In God's kingdom, greatness is all about giving ourselves away, even as Christ did. It is what inverts the pyramid. Those on the bottom of life's hierarchy, those on the margins of life, its peripheral people, those who simply do not count, the powerless, are those who, if they are true servants of Christ, are great. They are, as it were, at the top of his pyramid. Those on the bottom are those solely devoted to themselves no matter how powerful and connected they may also be.

Paul contemplated the possibility that some people might give away all they possessed and even give up their body "to be burned" (1 Cor. 13:3). There have been acts of extraordinary heroism and generosity like this. But no one can sustain consistent self-giving, freely and joyfully, over a lifetime, unless they are hearing the music of another "age." It is a sign of God having invaded our lives with his grace. "We know that we have passed out of death into life, because we love the brothers" (1 John 3:14). And love always expresses itself in service and with humility. That, as we have seen, is what love is all about, because this is what God's love is like.

Hostility and Joy

Our world is at times indifferent to Christian faith, but it can also be hostile to it. Indeed, today the incidence of persecution, and sometimes of martyrdom, is greater than it ever has been. This is carried out not only by individuals but also by governments, especially some of those whose commitments are to Islam. They are using their power to try to damage or eliminate Christian faith. And before this new strain of militancy had captured significant segments of Islam, the Marxists and Maoists tried to do the same thing.

In the third of our paradoxes, Jesus said that those who are "persecuted for righteousness' sake" are "blessed." So, too, "when others revile you and persecute you and utter all kinds of evil against you falsely on my account" we are to consider ourselves "blessed" (Matt. 5:10–11). Perhaps Jesus was not thinking of persecution in the wide perspective with which I began but, rather, more narrowly. It was persecution "for righteousness' sake." He had in view those who are mocked for their integrity, laughed at for being principled in some matter, pushed around, discriminated against, or pushed aside because they raise principled objections to doing what is wrong.

And yet, there can be no doubt that this bullying, hostile attitude to the practice of Christian "righteousness" will respond in the same way to the faith that produces that righteousness in the first place. It is, therefore, not a big step to take to see that what might begin as hostility to an upright life can blossom into attacks on the people who hold such faith. And where this hostility is also motivated by religious zeal, it can lead to jail, torture, and death for Christians. And so it has. Yet all of those who are thus persecuted are to count it all joy!

It is an extraordinary contradiction. No hardship, suffering, deprivation, insult, or harsh treatment is ever welcome to us (cf. Heb. 12:11). We all shrink from suffering. No one likes being treated maliciously or disrespectfully. The "blessed" experience of which Jesus spoke, therefore, must be understood in light of the great reversal that is yet to come. It is not a natural response. In that reversal, all sin will be judged and destroyed, as will those who carried it out. Today, those who live for themselves are satisfied. Then, they will be gnashing their teeth. And, in a sense, this great reversal is already penetrating Christian lives today. It rearranges how we see things. It brings into the lives of Christians, even in those dark moments of rejection, the music from this other world. In fact, along with that music comes the Lord of that music.

In these three brief sayings, Jesus captured the essentially counter-cultural character of Christian service. It runs counter to all of the calculations of self-interest that rule in our society and that define how people live. It inverts the way people count importance, or greatness, in this fallen world. Those who have no shot at ever being anybody, of ever counting at all in our society, can, indeed, be among those who count in God's kingdom! These passages anticipate the renewal that is coming when Christ ushers in with finality his rule over the whole of reality. Already this renewal, this new order, this otherworldliness, is penetrating life, and in so doing it points beyond itself to what is yet to come.

Holy-love

We are now in a position to think of what is happening when men and women of faith serve Christ in this world as an act of faithfulness to him. In his incarnation, life, and death, Christ was the ultimate model for what serving should look like. In this, we are to do as he did. Whoever "says he abides in him," John wrote, "ought to walk in the same way in which he walked" (1 John 2:6). In Christ, we see God's holy-love at its deepest level of self-disclosure. And, as we have seen, it is this holy-love that explains how we are justified in Christ's death. This holy-love defines and impels our sanctification. It should be at the heart of our worship. And it explains how our service for Christ unfolds.

Love

Those who serve Christ in whatever venue often have to defy their own self-interest. Sometimes they do so in small ways, but at other times the ways are large.

Why would anyone give of their time to help others and do so consistently? Why would anyone give up a promising career to head overseas and help raise orphans? Why have some of the brightest and best turned their backs on worldly recognition and reward to work among the abandoned in our cities, the lonely, those without access to power? Why would anyone be consistently generous with their resources when those same resources could be used to fund the "good life" for themselves? Why have talented linguists left the comfort of their homes to go to remote places on the earth, to insignificant tribes, in order to translate the Scriptures for them? Why do others heed the call to serve as pastors in churches despite the fact that they know the work is difficult and the pay is sometimes meager? Why do others go and work among prisoners, those encumbered by multiple troubles and whose lives have been wrecked? Why give one's time in such a seemingly hopeless pursuit? Why do others work behind the scenes, perhaps in an old-people's home, in order to help the needy? They know that they will never be noticed and will never receive the credit. Why do people do things like this?

In 2010, the Third Lausanne Congress on World Evangelization was held in Cape Town. Four thousand delegates attended from 198 countries. Among them was a young woman, Gyeong Ju. She was born in Pyongyang, North Korea. Her father had worked within the inner circle of Kim Jong Il, the country's former, iron-fisted leader. However, there was a falling out in his *entourage* and her father had to flee. The family started over again in China. It was there that, for the first time, they heard the gospel and came to believe in Christ. Not long after this, her father felt Christ's call to return as a missionary to North Korea. He did. In 2006, after he had returned, he was unfortunately discovered. He was arrested and, it appears, executed. But now his young daughter is resolved to return to North Korea as a missionary herself as soon as she is able. Why? With her father's death still fresh on her mind, why would she do this? How could she even contemplate doing it? One can only say that it is because the love of Christ constrains her and because the Lord of the harvest has called her to go. And she is willing to serve.

It is because of God's holy-*love* that people do these kinds of things. It is this love that "has been poured into our hearts through the Holy

Spirit who has been given to us" (Rom. 5:5). This explains why there is this kind of selfless serving. This love is what enables people to see beyond the suffering, inconveniences, even ill-treatment that they may experience, to the people who need to hear the gospel and who need the Word of God. They are doing for others what Christ first did for them. This is what impels people to serve Christ even in the hard places of life.

Love makes no self-calculations. It does not ask to be noticed. It does not stand on ceremony. It lives by a different set of rules. At its heart, it is self-abnegating and self-giving. It is intent on promoting the good of others. It does not keep tally of what it gives up or of what anyone owes it. Its nature is always to give, always to give itself away. This explains why people serve Christ as they do. It explains what impels them.

Holiness

In Cape Town, at this same Lausanne Congress, one of the speakers was Archbishop Ben Kwashi from Jos, Nigeria. He told of an experience he had before he moved to Nigeria. He was, at that time, in Zaire. It was 1987. That was the time when a hundred churches were burned down there and three hundred Christian homes destroyed. It was a time of great civil strife and deep suffering. But he circulated a letter to the churches urging them to do nothing by way of retaliation. They did not.

Twenty-three years later, to the day, he was in Jos. Muslims attacked Christians in three villages outside the town, killing many of them and leaving a number of their children as orphans. Again, the Archbishop begged the Christians not to respond, not to retaliate, not to try to get even. They did not. Rather, he said, they wept until they had no more tears. How could these poor people who had been brutally attacked do nothing? Why would they act in a way so contrary to the way people normally act when attacked—to the way conflicts normally play themselves out?

The answer is that they so acted because of Christ, to whom they belonged, and because of the cause of his gospel that they served. That is what compelled them. They served Christ by their righteous restraint, and they commended the gospel by so doing.

Why would the CEO of a large American corporation, known for his Christian faith, insist that no corners be cut, that standards of integrity in business be upheld even if it cut into profits? Because serving Christ also means doing what is *right*.

Why have some Christian people gone into the murky places in our world, where life is seamy and broken, and taken the gospel and the love of Christ there? Why do they work with such people? It is not only that they have been constrained by Christ's love, though in fact they have been. It is also because those to whom they go—sometimes prostitutes, pimps, drug dealers and users—are involved in something terribly wrong, and so these Christians have gone—because they care about what is right.

It is, of course, quite true that Christians have sometimes also been painfully slow in opposing what is painfully wrong in societies. And sometimes unbelievers have acted with far more sensitivity and compassion than Christians have. I have seen this myself.

Oppressors typically use lies to conceal what they are doing, and it is frequently dangerous for those who care about what is right to intervene. I can recall, as if it happened yesterday, demonstrating outside the South African parliament against *apartheid*. This was fifty years ago, long before it became fashionable, even chic, to be opposed to this system of racial segregation. Cape Town University was being closed to blacks. So, we did what we could. We demonstrated to call attention to this act of injustice.

Not long after the demonstration had started, a tank rumbled up the street and moved, menacingly, toward us. A soldier, manning an automatic weapon, was at the ready. However, before there was any confrontation, the demonstrators decided to disperse. The interesting thing about this demonstration, though, was that the demonstrators who were there were more of the radical, political kind than of the serious Christian kind. Many Christians, it seems, had believed the justifications for the long-standing *apartheid* policies.

But it should not be so. And, indeed, there is a rich history of Christian practice that has proved to be completely exemplary. Men and women have gone off to serve, or they have found ways to serve nearby, to bring into the world the saving knowledge of God as well as a myriad of gracious actions. They have been reminders to those around them that they serve a God of utmost holiness. They also have been impelled to act by his grace. They go because they know of his goodness, his righteousness, and his justice. They go because they themselves have seen the glories of his love.

In defending himself to the skeptical Corinthians, Paul appealed to his own biography but in so doing gave us a remarkable model of what "servants of God" look like. Of the cost that is entailed we should not be in doubt. In his own life, Paul had experienced outwardly difficult circumstances: "afflictions, hardships, calamities . . . sleepless nights, hunger" (v. 5). He had also been on the receiving end of harsh treatment meted out by his opponents: "beatings, imprisonments, riots" (v. 5). But in all of this, he was acting on God's holy-love. He had sought to demonstrate "purity, knowledge, patience, kindness . . . genuine love, by truthful speech." He had depended solely on "the Holy Spirit . . . the power of God" (vv. 6–7). In all of this, he had the "weapons of righteousness," which are the prerequisite of a servant of God. The Corinthians were questioning his authenticity. Paul answered their questions by pointing to the genuineness of his service for Christ.

Seeing Tomorrow

Today, American culture validates, even celebrates, its own self-centeredness. This self-focused, self-preoccupied, self-promoting, self-seeking, and self-serving ethos pervades our workplace, TV, blog sites, the social media, and movies. It has become a part of the air that we all breathe. It is so much a part of how life is that it almost passes unnoticed. This culture, this psychologized world, is the bad turn that we took in the road. Sooner or later, we are all going to find that it has brought us to a sorry end. No culture can survive such a steady, unrelenting onslaught as this.

Today, our culture and the truths of the gospel are ever more sharply contrasted. In the one, we are validated for serving ourselves, and in the other we surrender all of this to serve Christ. In the one, there are no moral absolutes, but in the other there are. In the one we are at the center of life, but in the other our triune God is. In the one, all that we have to think about is getting our stuff now, filling our pockets, buying our toys, going to exotic places, and doing our own thing. In the other, we see beyond this life to a different world, one where what is right and true has triumphed and where there are no longer any tears. Rarely have these two visions of life been more starkly contrasted than they are today.

This is a great time for Christian faith! However, the church does need to remind itself that it is living in an age of spin, hype, propaganda, and marketing. The Christian gospel is so often seen as just another scam, another piece of self-promotion by those seeking to profit from it, for, after all, this is what now fills our society. Indeed, among twenty-somethings, the dominant view of the born-again is that they are all hypocrites. This may seem harsh, but it is inevitable when born-againers apparently live no differently from the way that outright secularists do. How, then, is the gospel going to be commended if our words are discounted the moment they are uttered?

It is Christian service—in all of its many varieties—that provides the context that lends a human authenticity to the word of the gospel. It was so with Paul in Corinth, and it is so with us today. We are the context within which others hear the gospel. It is in the context of what Christians do, and who they are in themselves, that the gospel is read by unbelievers. And in this age of self-promotion and lying, nothing disarms the suspicion toward believers more easily than the authenticity that Christian practice brings to Christian believing.

The reason, quite simply, is that authentic Christian practice signals the presence of another world, a different world, one that is making itself known in our own. This other world, though, does not intrude loudly. It does not raise its voice. It is as gentle as an evening breeze. This is the remarkable thing about God. Though he holds all things together, though he is the very center of reality, though he is the very measure of all that is true and right, and though he sovereignly rules over all of life, he nevertheless stoops and makes himself known through others. He made himself known through the prophets and apostles and through the biblical writers. Now, he is making himself known through those who preach that biblical truth, but that truth may ring hollow in our world outside of the context of its practice.

Truth that is practiced is the way in which Christ is often glimpsed for the first time. It is in his people. It is here that he takes to himself hands and voices, hearts and feet in the cities of our world, in its corporations, its industry, its hospitals, and its places of suffering. It is in those who serve, who serve in a thousand different ways, that glimmers of the holy-love of God are often seen for the first time by our skeptical world.

Authentic Christian practice is not itself the gospel. But this practice would be impossible without the gospel. It would be inexplicable had God not unveiled his character and purposes to us and had these not been seen in the life of Christ. More than that, it would be impossible had that disclosure not run its course to the cross, to the place where his eternal counsels reached their completion in the death of the Son. But God has done even more. The Holy Spirit was sent to point men and women to Christ and to regenerate them, thus bringing them into the knowledge of God. God has made us knowers of himself, and as he has done so, we have experienced his holy-love. All of this is what lies behind that kind of Christian practice that is authentic and, in consequence, countercultural.

Today, though, we need a fresh vision of God and his character of holy-love. Our understanding of his greatness gets worn down, sometimes worn out, by the constant rubbing against our highly modernized life. It is this vision, though, this knowing of God, that puts steel into spines and fire into Christian hearts. When we are God-centered in our thoughts, God-fearing in our hearts, when we see with clarity what his character of holy-love is like, he begins to have weight in our lives. When that happens we become, not just occasional visitors to the eternal, but its permanent residents, its citizens. And that is when the church becomes more than just another organization but, in fact, the outpost of eternity in this wounded world. May the church indeed be all that it is in Christ, so that through its life the glory of God will be seen anew in all its splendor!

Selected Bibliography

Allison, Gregg R. *Sojourners and Strangers: The Doctrine of the Church.* Wheaton, IL: Crossway, 2012.

Baumann, Zygmunt, *Globalization: The Human Consequences.* New York: Columbia University Press, 1998.

Beale, G. K. *A New Testament Biblical Theology: The Unfolding of the Old Testament in the New.* Grand Rapids, MI: Baker Academic, 2011.

Beeke, Joel. *Puritan Reformed Spirituality.* Grand Rapids, MI: Reformation Heritage, 2004.

Begbie, Jeremy. *Theology, Music, and Time.* Cambridge: Cambridge University Press, 2000.

Bell, Rob. *Love Wins: A Book about Heaven, Hell, and the Fate of Every Person Who Ever Lived.* New York: Harper One, 2011.

Berger, Peter L., and Richard John Neuhaus, eds. *Against the World For the World: The Hartford Appeal and the Future of American Religion.* New York: Seabury, 1976.

Berman, Morris. *The Twilight of American Culture.* New York: Norton, 2000.

Bock, Darrell L., and Mitch Glasser. *The Gospel according to Isaiah 53: Encountering the Suffering Servant in Jewish and Christian Theology.* Grand Rapids, MI: Kregel Academic, 2012.

Boers, Arthur. *Living into Focus: Choosing What Matters in an Age of Distractions.* Grand Rapids, MI: Brazos, 2012.

Boyer, Steven D., and Christopher A. Hall. *The Mystery of God: Theology for Knowing the Unknowable.* Grand Rapids, MI: Baker Academic, 2012.

Bray, Gerald. *God Is Love: A Biblical and Systematic Theology.* Wheaton, IL: Crossway, 2012.

Brunner, Emil. *The Mediator: A Study of the Central Doctrine of the Christian Faith.* Translated by Olive Wyon. London: Lutterworth, 1952.

Carroll, Jackson W. *God's Potters: Pastoral Leadership and the Shaping of Congregations.* Grand Rapids, MI: Eerdmans, 2006.

Carson, D. A., ed. *Right with God: Justification in the Bible and in the World.* Grand Rapids, MI: Baker, 1992.

———. *The Difficult Doctrine of the Love of God.* Wheaton, IL: Crossway, 2000.

Carson, D. A., and Timothy Keller, eds. *The Gospel as Center: Renewing Our Faith and Reforming Our Ministry Practices.* Wheaton, IL: Crossway, 2012.

Charnock, Stephen. *The Existence and Attributes of God*. Grand Rapids, MI: Baker, 1996.

Clapp, Rodney. *Border Crossings: Christian Trespasses on Popular Culture and Public Affairs*. Grand Rapids, MI: Brazos, 2000.

Clowney, Edmund P. *Preaching Christ in All of Scripture*. Wheaton, IL: Crossway, 2003.

———. *The Unfolding Mystery: Discovering Christ in the Old Testament*. Phillipsburg, NJ: P&R, 1988.

Colijn, Brenda B. *Images of Salvation in the New Testament*. Downers Grove, IL: InterVarsity Press, 2010.

Copan, Paul, and William Lane Craig, eds. *Contending with Christianity's Critics: Answering New Atheists and Other Objectors*. Nashville: B&H, 2009.

Coppedge, Allan. *Portraits of God: A Biblical Theology of Holiness*. Downers Grove, IL: InterVarsity Press, 2001.

Cullmann, Oscar. *Early Christian Worship*. Translated by A. Stewart Todd and James B. Torrance. London: SCM, 1953.

Davis, John Jefferson. *Meditation and Communion: Contemplating Scripture in an Age of Distraction*. Downers Grove, IL: IVP Academic, 2012.

Dawn, Marva. *Reaching Out without Dumbing Down: A Theology of Worship for the Turn-of-the-century Culture*. Grand Rapids, MI: Eerdmans, 1995.

Delbanco, Andrew. *The Real American Dream: A Meditation on Hope*. Cambridge, MA: Harvard University Press, 1999.

Denney, James. *The Death of Christ: Its Place and Interpretation in the New Testament*. New York: American Tract Society, 1903.

Detweiler, Craig, and Barry Taylor. *A Matrix of Meanings: Finding God in Pop Culture*. Grand Rapids, MI: Baker Academic, 2003.

Dever, Mark, J. Ligon Duncan, R. Albert Mohler, and C. J. Mahaney. *Preaching the Cross*. Wheaton, IL: Crossway, 2007.

Dever, Mark, and Michael Lawrence. *It Is Well: Expositions on Substitutionary Atonement*. Wheaton, Crossway, 2010.

DeYoung, Kevin. *The Hole in Our Holiness: Filling the Gap between Gospel Passion and the Pursuit of Godliness*. Wheaton, IL: Crossway, 2012.

Douthat, Ross. *Bad Religion: How We Became a Nation of Heretics*. New York: Free Press, 2012.

Duin, Julia. *Quitting Church: Why the Faithful Are Fleeing and What to Do About It*. Grand Rapids, MI: Baker, 2007.

Eck, Diana L. *A New Religious America: How a "Christian Country" Has Become the World's Most Religiously Diverse Nation*. San Francisco: Harper, 2001.

Estelle, Bryan D., J. V. Fesko, and David VanDrunen, eds. *The Law Is Not of Faith: Essays on Works and Grace in the Mosaic Covenant*. Phillipsburg, NJ: P&R, 2009.

Fischer, Claude S. *Made in America: A Social History of American Culture and Character*. Chicago: University of Chicago Press, 2010.

Fitch, David E. *The Great Giveaway: Reclaiming the Mission of the Church from Big Business, Parachurch Organizations, Psychotherapy, Consumer Capitalism, and Other Modern Maladies.* Grand Rapids, MI: Baker, 2005.

Froese, Paul, and Christopher Bader. *America's Four Gods: What We Say about God—and What That Says about Us.* New York: Oxford University Press, 2010.

Gallagher, Winifred. *New: Understanding Our Need for Novelty and Change.* New York: Penguin, 2012.

Gibb, Richard, and Bruce Milne. *Grace and Global Justice: The Socio-political Mission of the Church in an Age of Globalization.* Carlisle, UK: Paternoster, 2006.

Gilmore, James H., and Joseph Pine. *Authenticity: What Consumers Really Want.* Cambridge, MA: Harvard Business School Press, 2007.

Goldsworthy, Graeme. *According to Plan: The Unfolding Revelation of God in the Bible.* Downers Grove, IL: InterVarsity Press, 1991.

Guinness, Os. *A Free People's Suicide: Sustainable Freedom and the American Future.* Downers Grove, IL: InterVarsity Press, 2012.

Gunton, Colin E. *Act and Being: Towards a Theology of the Divine Attributes.* Grand Rapids, MI: Eerdmans, 2002.

Hall, Christopher A. *Worshiping with the Church Fathers.* Downers Grove, IL: IVP Academic, 2009.

Hamilton, James. *God's Glory in Salvation through Judgment: A Biblical Theology.* Wheaton, IL: Crossway, 2010.

Hannigan, John. *Fantasy City: Pleasure and Profit in the Postmodern Metropolis.* New York: Routledge, 1998.

Hansen, Collin. *Young, Restless, Reformed: A Journalist's Journey with the New Calvinists.* Wheaton, IL: Crossway, 2008.

Heim, S. Mark. *Saved from Sacrifice: A Theology of the Cross.* Grand Rapids, MI: Eerdmans, 2006.

Horton, Michael. *A Better Way: Rediscovering the Drama of God-centered Worship.* Grand Rapids, MI: Baker, 2002.

———. *The Christian Faith: A Systematic Theology for Pilgrims on the Way.* Grand Rapids, MI: Zondervan, 2011.

Hunter, James Davison. *To Change the World: The Irony, Tragedy, and Possibility of Christianity in the Late Modern World.* New York: Oxford University Press, 2010.

Husbands, Mark, and Daniel J. Treier. *Justification: What's at Stake in the Current Debates.* Downers Grove, IL: InterVarsity Press, 2004.

Jackson, Maggie. *Distracted: The Erosion of Attention and the Coming Dark Age.* New York: Prometheus, 2008.

Jeffery, Steve, Mike Ovey, and Andrew Sach. *Pierced for Our Transgressions: Rediscovering the Glory of Penal Substitution.* Nottingham, UK: Inter-Varsity Press, 2007.

Jenkins, Henry. *The WOW Climax: Tracing the Emotional Impact of Popular Culture.* New York: New York University Press, 2007.

Jenkins, Philip. *The New Faces of Christianity: Believing the Bible in the Global South.* New York: Oxford University Press, 2006.

Johnson, Dennis E. *Him We Proclaim: Preaching Christ from All the Scriptures.* Phillipsburg, NJ: P&R, 2000.

Keck, Leander. *The Church Confident: Christianity Can Repent, but It Must Not Whimper.* Nashville: Abingdon, 1993.

Keller, Timothy. *Generous Justice: How God's Grace Makes Us Just.* New York: Dutton, 2010.

Kelly, Stewart E. *Truth Considered and Applied: Examining Postmodernism, History, and Christian Faith.* Nashville: B&H Academic, 2012.

Kevan, Ernest F. *The Grace of Law: A Study in Puritan Theology.* London: Carey Kingsgate, 1964.

Keyes, Dick. *Seeing through Cynicism: A Reconsideration of the Power of Suspicion.* Downers Grove, IL: InterVarsity Press, 2006.

Kidd, Reggie M. *With One Voice: Discovering Christ's Song in Our Worship.* Grand Rapids, MI: Baker, 2005.

Levering, Matthew. *Predestination: Biblical and Theological Paths.* New York: Oxford University Press, 2011.

Livingston, James. *The World Turned Inside Out: American Thought and Culture at the End of the 20th Century.* New York: Rowman & Littlefield, 2010.

Lofton, Kathryn. *Oprah: The Gospel of an Icon.* Berkeley: University of California Press, 2011.

Mahady, William, and Janet Bernardi. *A Generation Alone: Xers Making a Place in the World.* Downers Grove, IL: InterVarsity Press, 1994.

Máté, Ferenc. *A Reasonable Life: Toward a Simpler, Secure, More Humane Existence.* New York: Albatross, 1997.

McCall, Thomas H. *Forsaken: The Trinity and the Cross, and Why It Matters.* Downers Grove, IL: InterVarsity Press, 2012.

McCormack, Bruce L., ed. *Engaging the Doctrine of God: Contemporary Protestant Perspectives.* Grand Rapids, MI: Baker, 2008.

McCracken, Brett. *Hipster Christianity: When Church and Cool Collide.* Grand Rapids, MI: Baker, 2010.

Mohler, R. Albert. *Culture Shift: Engaging Current Issues with Timeless Truth.* Colorado Springs: Multnomah, 2008.

Moltmann, Jürgen. *The Crucified God: The Cross of Christ as the Foundation and Criticism of Christian Theology.* New York: Harper & Row, 1973.

Moody, Josh. *The God-centered Life: Insights from Jonathan Edwards for Today.* Vancouver: Regent College Publishing, 2006.

Morgan, Christopher, and Robert A. Peterson, eds. *The Kingdom of God.* Wheaton, IL: Crossway, 2012.

Morris, Leon. *The Biblical Doctrine of Judgment.* Grand Rapids, MI: Eerdmans, 1960.

———. *Testaments of Love: A Study of Love in the Bible.* Grand Rapids, MI: Eerdmans, 1981.

Mouw, Richard J., and Mark A. Noll, eds. *Wonderful Words of Life: Hymns in American Protestant History and Theology*. Grand Rapids, MI: Eerdmans, 2004.

Myers, David G. *The American Paradox: Spiritual Hunger in an Age of Plenty*. New Haven, CT: Yale University Press, 2000.

Nisbet, Robert. *The Twilight of Authority*. New York: Oxford University Press, 1975.

Nygren, Anders. *Agape and Eros*. Translated by Phillip Watson. London: S.P.C.K., 1953.

Oliphint, Scott K. *God with Us: Divine Condescension and the Attributes of God*. Wheaton, IL: Crossway, 2012.

Oppenheimer, Mark. *Knocking on Heaven's Door: American Religion in the Age of Counterculture*. New Haven, CT: Yale University Press, 2003.

Owen, John. *Overcoming Sin and Temptation*. Edited by Kelly M. Kapic and Justin Taylor. Wheaton, IL: Crossway, 2006.

Packer, J. I. *A Quest for Godliness: The Puritan Vision of the Christian Life*. Wheaton, IL: Crossway, 1990.

Pearse, Meic. *Why the Rest Hates the West: Understanding the Roots of Global Rage*. Downers Grove, IL: InterVarsity Press, 2004.

Peterson, David. *Possessed by God: A New Testament Theology of Sanctification*. Downers Grove, IL: InterVarsity Press, 1995.

Piper, John. *Counted Righteous in Christ: Should We Abandon the Imputation of Christ's Righteousness?* Wheaton, IL: Crossway, 2002.

———. *God Is the Gospel: Meditations on God's Love as the Gift of Himself*. Wheaton, IL: Crossway, 2005.

———. *The Future of Justification: A Response to N. T. Wright*. Wheaton, IL: Crossway, 2007.

Plummer, Robert L., ed. *Journeys of Faith: Evangelicalism, Eastern Orthodoxy, Catholicism, and Anglicanism*. Grand Rapids, MI: Zondervan, 2013.

Prothero, Stephen. *American Jesus: How the Son of God Became a National Icon*. New York: Farrar, Straus, & Giroux, 2003.

Putnam, Robert D., and David E. Campbell. *American Grace: How Religion Divides and Unites Us*. New York: Simon & Schuster, 2010.

Roof, Wade Clark. *A Generation of Seekers: The Spiritual Journeys of the Baby Boom Generation*. San Francisco: Harper, 1997.

———. *Spiritual Marketplace: Baby Boomers and the Remaking of American Religion*. Princeton, NJ: Princeton University Press, 1999.

Schreiner, Thomas R. *New Testament Theology: Magnifying God in Christ*. Grand Rapids, MI: Baker Academic, 2008.

Smith, Christian, and Melinda Lundquist Denton. *Soul Searching: The Religious and Spiritual Lives of American Teenagers*. New York: Oxford University Press, 2005.

Smith, Christian, and Patricia Snell. *Souls in Transition: The Religious and Spiritual Lives of Emerging Adults*. Oxford: Oxford University Press, 2009.

Sommers, Christina Hoff, and Sally Satel. *One Nation Under Therapy: How the Helping Culture Is Eroding Self-reliance.* New York: St. Martin's Press, 2005.

Stott, John R. W. *The Cross of Christ.* Downers Grove, IL: InterVarsity Press, 1986.

Thielman, Frank. *Theology of the New Testament: A Canonical and Synthetic Approach.* Grand Rapids, MI: Zondervan, 2005.

Thompson, William Irwin. *The American Replacement of Nature: The Everyday Acts and Outrageous Evolution of Economic Life.* New York: Doubleday, 1991.

Torrance, Thomas F. *Atonement: The Person and Work of Christ.* Downers Grove, IL: InterVarsity Press, 2009.

———. *Incarnation: The Person and Life of Christ.* Downers Grove, IL: InterVarsity Press, 2008.

Trueman, Carl R. *The Wages of Spin: Critical Writings on Historic and Contemporary Evangelicalism.* Ross-shire: Christian Focus, 2004.

Twitchell, James B. *Shopping for God: How Christianity Went from In Your Heart to In Your Face.* New York: Simon & Schuster, 2007.

Van Neste, Ray, and C. Richard Wells, eds. *Forgotten Songs: Reclaiming the Psalms for Christian Worship.* Nashville: B&H, 2012.

Vanhoozer, Kevin J. *First Theology: God, Scripture, and Hermeneutics.* Downers Grove, IL: InterVarsity Press, 2002.

Velasquez, Eduardo. *A Consumer's Guide to the Apocalypse: Why There Is No Cultural War in America and Why We Will Perish Nonetheless.* Wilmington, DE: ISI Books, 2007.

Vickers, Brian. *Jesus' Blood and Righteousness: Paul's Theology of Imputation.* Wheaton, IL: Crossway, 2006.

Volf, Miroslav. *Against the Tide: Love in a Time of Petty Dreams and Persisting Enmities.* Grand Rapids, MI: Eerdmans, 2010.

Vos, Geerhardus. *Biblical Theology: Old and New Testaments.* Grand Rapids, MI: Eerdmans, 1948.

Ward, Timothy. *Word and Supplement: Speech Acts, Biblical Texts, and the Sufficiency of Scripture.* New York: Oxford University Press, 2002.

———. *Words of Life: Scripture as the Living and Active Word of God.* Downers Grove, IL: IVP Academic, 2009.

Wolfe, Alan. *The Future of Liberalism.* New York: Alfred A. Knopf, 2009.

———. *The Transformation of American Religion: How We Actually Live Our Faith.* New York: Free Press, 2003.

Wolterstorff, Nicholas. *Justice in Love.* Grand Rapids, MI: Eerdmans, 2011.

———. *Captive to the Word of God: Engaging the Scriptures for Contemporary Theological Reflection.* Grand Rapids, MI: Eerdmans, 2010.

Wuthnow, Robert. *The Struggle for America's Soul: Evangelicals, Liberals, and Secularism.* Grand Rapids, MI: Eerdmans, 1989.

Zengotita, Thomas de. *Mediated: How the Media Shapes Your World and the Way You Live in It.* New York: Bloomsbury, 2005.

General Index

Abraham, 39, 42, 43, 57–58, 62, 63, 75, 91, 136, 208–209; covenant of with God, 46–47, 48, 120; and faith, 49–51, 96; God's promise to, 55–56, 143, 207–208; and grace, 44–46, 49; justification of, 45, 46–47, 52–53, 54, 56, 141–142
Absalom, 124
Adam, 42, 143, 144, 222; as born sinless, 61; connections between Adam and Christ, 60–64, 71; as representative of the human race, 62–63; temptation of, 61
Africa: "miracle centers" in, 24; spread of the "health and wealth" gospel to, 24
agape, 82, 179
Agape and Eros (Nygren), 82
"American Paradox," 22–23; and our understanding of God, 24–25
America's Four Gods: What We Say about God––and What That Says about Us (Froese and Bader), 19
Amusing Ourselves to Death (Postman), 28
anger, 121
animal rights, 30
Anna, 68
antinomianism, 159, 175
apostles, the, 43, 143, 203–204, 205
Aquila, 193
Asia, 22, 69
atheism, 19, 97
atonement, 62–63, 65–66, 151, 152
Augustine, 137

Bad Religion (Douthat), 21
Bader, Christopher, 19
Barna, George, 35, 77, 158
Berman, Morris, 29
Bible, the: debates over the authority of, 216; as the inspired word of God, 211–213
Bonfire of the Vanities, The (Wolfe), 26
Boomer Generation, 27
Bridges, Matthew, 129
Bunyan, John, 37

Cain, Susan, 35
Calvin, John, 127
Charnock, Stephen, 16
Christ-centeredness, 42, 224
Christian practice, 241–242
Christianity, 23, 24, 32, 34, 86
Christians/believers, 129; as God's children, 18; persecution of, 235, 238
church, the: as Christ's body, 194; Christ's love for, 193–194; as an extension of the Old Testament people of God, 194; as the household/people of God, 194–195, 216; and human diversity, 200; truths upon which the church is built, 195–196; unity of, 192–193; worship in the early church, 203–205. *See also* fellowship
circumcision, 45, 46
"conspicuous consumption," 226–227
creation, 63; disordered nature of, 64; sovereignty over, 63–64
cultural mandate, the, 63, 65

James, 43, 141, 143, 196; on obedience, 142
Jeremiah, 67, 68; vision of, 104
Jeroboam, 202
Jerome, 36–37
Jesus Christ, 15, 43–44, 56, 88,
112, 116, 124, 141, 149, 155, 207,
242; acceptance of the cross
by, 179–180; as "anonymously"
present in other religions, 58;
attributes of God in, 93; on
becoming a servant, 234; as
"beloved" Son of God, 91–92;
connections between Adam and
Christ, 60–63; crucifixion of,
129–131, 209; eternal purpose
of, 131–132; glory of, 64–65, 93;
as the good shepherd, 195; High
Priestly Prayer of, 92; as the
image of God, 170; incarnation
of, 45, 53, 59, 91, 92–93, 94, 98,
134, 151, 153, 234; kindness of,
94–95; kingdom of, 71; love of,
93–94, 94–95, 224; on love for
God and neighbor, 171; obedience
of, 143–144; prayer of for his
disciples, 192; righteousness of,
118–119, 143, 144–145; on rulers,
233–234; as sent by God, 94;
"substitutionary" death of, 56,
57–58, 65, 131, 137–140, 148; as
the true Israel, 68; uniqueness of
Christ as our means of access to
the Father, 51–54; work of, 48,
54, 166. *See also* Christ-centeredness; Trinity, the
Jesus' Blood and Righteousness (Vickers), 143
Jews, 68, 96, 194, 233; and legalism, 45, 46; national identity of,
46, 47
Job, 213
John the Apostle, 149, 196; on the
concept of holy-love, 172–173
John the Baptist, 141
Ju, Gyeong, 237
Judas, 119, 131–133
justice, 171–172

justification, 43–44, 56, 119, 140,
149, 158, 160, 221–222; Catholic interpretation of, 168, 221;
comparison of from the Old
Testament to the New Testament, 57–58; different meanings
(primary and secondary) in the
language of the New Testament, 140–142; of Gentiles, 49;
mistake in making justification
part of sanctification, 167–170;
New Testament view of, 48–49;
Reformation views of, 47–49; as
righteousness declared, 142; and
sanctification, 161–162

Kazantzakis, Nikos, 152
Keyes, Dick, 223
Khayyam, Omar, 178
kingdom of God, 32, 71, 164–165;
greatness in, 234
Kingdom of God, The (Niebuhr), 175
Koyama, Kosuke, 69
Kuhn, Thomas, 29
Kwashi, Ben, 238

language/speech, and communication, 210–211; three primary
aspects of communication,
212–213
Last Temptation of Christ, The (1988),
152
laws: criminal and civil laws,
28–29; Old Testament ceremonial law, 232
legalism, 152, 175; Jewish legalism,
45, 46
Lewis, C. S., 16
liberation theology, 69
Livingstone, James, 29
Lord's Supper, the, 66, 196, 197, 205
*Losing Our Virtue: Why the Church
Must Recover Its Moral Vision*
(Wells), 25–26
love, 171–173, 236–238; connection of with holiness, 175–176;
difference of from holiness,

Shenk, David, 184
sin, 64, 65, 88, 114, 123, 124, 164, 236; action of God's love on our sin, 99–100; captivity to sin, 148–150, 230; Christ's death as atonement for, 138–140; and culture, 227–230; forgiveness of, 98; indifference to, 175–176; liberation from and victory over sin through Christ, 68, 139, 150–151; servitude of, 224
Smith, Christian, 21; on "Moralistic Therapeutic Deism," 21
Solomon, 89, 116, 202
Sommers, Christina, 227
Soul Searching (Smith), 21
soul/body distinction, 30
spirituality, in the West, 109–110
Stephen, 208; death of, 97–98
Stone, Oliver, 26
suffering, 235–236

technology, 35–36, 183–185; dangers of, 184
Tennent, Julie, 57
Third Lausanne Congress on World Evangelization (2010), 237, 238
Tocqueville, Alexis de, 22
Tozer, A. W., 15
transcendence, 31
Trinity, the, 90–91, 94; generosity of God's love as shown in, 95–96
Twilight of Authority (Nisbet), 28
Tyranny of E-mail, The (Freeman), 35

Uzziah, 105

Vickers, Brian, 143

Wall Street (1987), 26
Ward, Timothy, 210
Warfield, B. B., 211
Water Buffalo Theology (Koyama), 69
Wesley, Charles, 77, 100
Winfrey, Oprah, 27–28
Wolfe, Tom, 26
Word and Supplement (Ward), 210
work: biblical perspective on, 222–223; Protestant understanding of, 221. *See also* service
worship, 113–114, 187–188, 215–217; central element of, 113; contemporary worship forms, 189; content of, 188–189, 190, 197; in the early church, 204; in evangelical churches, 198–199; form of, 188, 190; God's first coming to us as the reason for our worship, 202–203; making God central to worship, 201; as a means to bring ourselves before God, 206; and music, 189–190; needs-shaped worship, 190; purposes of, 191–191, 200; and the role of Scripture in, 213–215; theological themes of, 190–191; "worship wars," 188–191, 199–200

Scripture Index

110:1	108	52:3–12	68
111:7	123	52:13–53:12	53, 70
113:4	107	53:4	70
119:11	186	53:4–5	70
119:15, 23, 99	186	53:6	70, 138, 195
119:16, 47, 97,	169	53:9	138
129		53:10	138
119:105	112	53:11–12	70
132:11	208	57:15	108
135:8–12	208	63:9	90
136:1	116		
139:4	80	*Jeremiah*	
139:6	80	1:4–10	104
145:8	89, 97	2:32	67
145:9	116	3:21	67
145:21	125	13:25	67
146:8	89	15:15–18	97
148:13	109	17:12	108
		23:5	70
Ecclesiastes		23:7–8	68
2:23	222	23:27	67
		33:25–26	120
Isaiah		50:6	67
1:4	104		
2:21	124	*Ezekiel*	
5:1–4	105	1:28	104
5:19	104	19:4	68
6:1	105	20:34–36	68
6:3	106, 113	20:41	114
6:5	113	28:22	114
6:6–7	113	36:23	114
6:9–13	106	38:16	114
6:10	107	39:7	103
6:11	106		
9:6	70	*Daniel*	
9:6–7	70	1:1–6	104
10:20	104	4:17	107
11:6–9	64	4:25, 32	107
28:23–26	222	7:9–14	104
40:25	80	7:21–22	107
40:27	97		
42:1–3	91	*Hosea*	
42:6	120	2:14–23	68
43:3	104	2:19	123
45:21	120	3:1	90
49:23	136	4:10	123
51:5–6	120	7:16	68

2:8	63, 64	4:12	140
2:9	64, 65, 137	4:14	79
2:10	62		
2:16	43, 62	*1 Peter*	
2:17	148	1:3–8	180
3:3	68	1:11	73
3:6	194	1:12	187
3:7	211	1:19	119
3:7–8	212	1:20	54
4:9	194	1:20–21	134
4:15	62, 73	2:10	194
5:8–9	62	2:11	181
6:13	43	2:21	137
6:20	137	2:22–25	70
7:1–10	43	2:23	124
7:24	137	2:25	195
8:1	108	3:18	137
9:9	54	4:5	125
10:1, 11	54	4:17	194
10:4	54	5:4	195
10:12	54, 138		
10:12, 18	204	*2 Peter*	
11:8	50, 209	1:5–7	165
11:11	50, 51	1:17	91
11:17	43	1:20–21	209
11:17–19	49	2:19	230
11:39	60	3:8–10	98
12:2	180	3:10	125
12:3	93	3:12	125
12:11	235	3:13	125
12:16	138		
12:23	194	*1 John*	
12:29	85, 115	1:5	85, 114, 173
13:20	195	2:1	119
13:24	163	2:2	138, 148
		2:3	173
James		2:5	173
1:13	114	2:6	153, 173, 236
1:17	42, 116	2:7	173
2:8	172	2:8	174
2:14	160	2:13	15
2:18–26	141	2:27	95
2:21	141	2:29	118
2:21–23	43	3:3	165
2:26	160	3:8	149
3:9–10	172	3:10	173
3:17	109	3:14	235